coming up with *the goods*

Michael Pearson was born in Paisley, Renfrewshire in 1952 and emigrated to England on the *Queen of Scots* two years later. Educated in Leicestershire, Yorkshire and Lancashire, he has worked in printing, publicity and publishing. He is married with two children. If he had any spare time he would take up bee-keeping, learn to play the accordion and go to Poland.

On course to triple its business within ten years, EWS has increased traffic volumes, won new customers to rail and invested over £600m in new equipment and technology, including 280 locomotives and 2,500 wagons.
It moves more than 100m tonnes of freight by rail each year in markets as diverse as coal, timber, cars and steel.

Cover photographs: The Safeway train at Mossend near Glasgow; and sunset over Arran on the Killoch Branch, Ayr.

coming up with *the goods*

journeys through britain by freight train

michael pearson

WAY**Z**GOOSE

Published by Wayzgoose 1999

Copyright Michael Pearson

Wayzgoose is an imprint of:
J.M.Pearson & Son (Publishers) Ltd
Tatenhill Common
Staffordshire
England
DE13 9RS
Tel: 01283 713674
www.jmpearson.co.uk

ISBN 0 907864 81 3

A CIP catalogue entry for this book is available
from the British Library

Printed and bound in Italy
by STIGE of Turin

contents

Res Class 47 departs March with an Enterprise service for Ely

Kingmoor, Carlisle

foreword

EWS has come a long way since it was formed in 1996. Growth of freight on rail has become a reality, fuelled by Government policy and concerns about road congestion and environmental pollution and propelled by EWS purchasing new equipment and offering a range of services to attract individual truckloads and full trainloads.

By the close of 1999 EWS was running over 7,000 trains a week and moving over 100 million tonnes a year. Massive investment was beginning to bear fruit in terms of new Class 66 and Class 67 locomotives, new wagons of every shape (but all in *big* sizes), new buildings and terminals and sophisticated computer control systems.

All these things are required to run a successful freight service, but there is another vital, irreplaceable ingredient that forms a thread throughout this book. People. Railwaymen, and increasingly women, who have an innate and almost instinctive feel for their industry, the trains and the customers they serve. People with a sense of history, pride and dedication unmatched anywhere else in UK industry. For me this shines through the pages of this book, giving readers a novel and practical insight into the way EWS operates.

Ian Braybrook
Managing Director
EWS

Saltley, Birmingham

Binliners, Hatfield Main

introduction

Imagine me in the Highlands, a late, midge-free August afternoon in Glen Truim. I've come to photograph the Inverness-Mossend (Glasgow) 'Enterprise' freight train and, as always - because my mother brought me up to be early for everything - there is time to kill. Half an hour passes before the train comes into view, and in that half an hour I idly begin to count the lorries on the neighbouring A9. Maths are not my strong point, but I come to the conclusion that well over a thousand lorries a day are using this vital road link with the north of Scotland. When the train comes closer - the *only* southbound goods train of the day - I see that it consists of seventeen wagons.

It is a parable the Disciples would not pester Jesus to explain. Evidently, only the tiniest proportion of freight reaches the Highlands by rail. The national average is a measly six or seven per cent; though I suspect this figure to be misleadingly inflated by heavy flows like coal, steel, petroleum and aggregates. Clearly such statistics are an environmental disaster and a national disgrace. Even in a country as obsessed with road transport as America, a majority of freight goes by rail. Similarly, throughout mainland Europe - now rail linked to Britain, of course, by the Channel Tunnel - rail freight continues to carry a much higher average.

How has this dispiriting state of affairs come about? What can be done, other than the payment of political lip service, to transfer traffic from Britain's grid-locked roads and road ravaged town centres to a segregated, safer and environmentally more harmonious method of carrying goods? These are questions which I hoped to find answers to on my journeys through Britain by freight train. But, in truth, I don't suppose I discovered anything that I didn't already know. Even post privatisation, rail freight has to compete on a playing field more steeply graded in favour of road than Yeovil's folklore football ground. My travels have illustrated how difficult rail finds it to compete. Firm quotes are hard to come by, but I guessed that English Welsh & Scottish Railway, whose trains I travelled on exclusively, make significant payment to Railtrack per mile for access to the network whereas, I am sure I don't need to tell you, no such charge exists for road users.

So how does rail compete at all? It can, and it does, give road transport a proverbial run for its money by being inherently more efficient. As I saw on my trip on the Mendip Rail stone train from Westbury, a single engine driver can be responsible for as much as three thousand tonnes of freight, a total it would take over seventy-five lorry drivers to move. The problem comes when you want to move smaller tonnages. Forty tonnes represents a significant load for a lorry, but barely a full wagon on the railway. Moreover, years of rationalisation of the railway network, accompanied by a concomitant growth in greenfield site industrial development, has isolated the bulk of the business community from direct contact by rail. Transhipment, then, becomes necessary, nine times out of ten, if rail is to be utilised. Fortunately this need not be so problematical and time-consuming as was once the case. The technology exists, only its use needs to be encouraged. My journey through the Highlands with a container train for Safeway is a perfect example of what can be achieved, and it seemed to me, as an admittedly non-expert eyewitness, that only 'finance' stands in the way of a much wider use of this system of working. If I had the political will and influence of, say, John Prescott, I would be underwriting a nationwide network of swap-body and piggyback services for road hauliers to use. I would be inclined to make these access free, to encourage their widest possible use, a bit like the road system itself!

A pipe dream? Not necessarily. Were we starting from scratch, I am sure that this would be the game plan. Only we are saddled with history and imbalance and prejudice, all of which amount to inertia: vested interests enervate initiative. Only the reality of gridlock is likely to induce road haulage companies to consider rail as an option. Only price cutting can convince logistic managers to think rail. Only a sea change in Railtrack's approach to track capacity can provide enough 'paths' for freight to blossom, and their shareholders will only sanction such investment if there is a corresponding hike in revenue. "Rail freight doesn't pay," Railtrack's chief executive, Gerald Corbett, went on record as saying in the midst of my journeying. He might have being addressing me personally. I certainly took umbrage, *personally,* until I realised that he was probably only putting a political spin on a quasi truth. What Corbett is after, and who can blame him, is more input from the Government. The passenger franchises are publicly supported, so why not freight? To tip the balance in favour of rail, it needs to be made demonstrably *cheaper* as well as reliable. "Freight growth on rail is not an optional extra, it's a 'must have'," says Julia Clarke, Freight Director of the Strategic Rail Authority

And change won't happen overnight. I would like to see a five year trial service of intermodal operations provided between designated, strategic centres as an alternative to the motorway network. A turn up and go system on which, for example, you could place a lorry trailer in Birmingham on a flat wagon at noon and have it delivered to Glasgow by teatime. We have the technology; Railtrack could be financially induced to provide the capacity; EWS and others have the acumen and expertise to deliver: the general public want an uncoagulated road network back; it's a vote winner, a home banker, but only the Government is in a position to come up with the goods!

*   *   *

I've a feeling it was Huw Philips of EWS at St Blazey who pointed out how lucky I was to be making these journeys. "A lot of guys would give almost anything to do what you're doing," he had confided. And of course he was right as far as train buffs went; though, conversely, many a glazed expression followed my cagey reply to an innocently asked "What are you working on now, Michael?" Goods trains are only romantic in the eyes of a certain, esoterically ridiculed strand of British society. They carry coal and coke and cars, but they do not carry kudos; they are not perceived mythically and cinematically as in the U.S.A. But I was determined to kick such indifference into touch. I wanted people to wake up to both the environmentally beneficial potential of rail freight and its *beauty.* I wanted the red and gold colours of English Welsh & Scottish Railway to become as immediately recognisable as Eddie Stobart's green and white. I wanted fast food chains to be giving away a new generation of EWS inspired *Thomas the Tank Engine* toys, and I hoped that my book would at least kick start consideration of these aims.

But it goes without saying that I enjoyed myself. Not since my journeys on cargo-carrying barges in

Tyne Yard

Longannet, Fife

the Seventies had I met a more interesting bunch of people, nor travelled between such disparate places. With few exceptions, I encountered a vocational zeal at every level. Nothing less would suffice in the cup tie atmosphere of rail's unequal contest against road. Donning my high-visibility vest, I felt like Clark Kent emerging from a telephone box transformed into Superman. Above all else I relished being part of a team. No one is as isolated as a writer, and the camaraderie was infectious. In their well-defined sense of discipline and adherence to the strictures of a formal hierarchy, railwaymen remind me of the police and the armed forces, and it seems no coincidence that they don't have holidays so much as 'go on leave'.

In a sense this book wrote itself; all I had to do was watch and listen. Illustrating it was harder. Quixotic weather, early running, late running, diversions, customer cancellations, all conspired, at one time or another, to leave me stranded by the lineside. "I don't know what you're worried about," laughed Andy Lickfold, my contact in the press office at English Welsh & Scottish Railway headquarters in Islington: "I wouldn't mind sitting on a hillside for three hours with a camera, sandwiches and a beer or two." Only it wasn't always like that Andy: there were clouds bubbling over the sun just as the train appeared; there were locations which looked fine on the map that turned out to be compromised by intrusive power lines or excessive vegetation; there were wagons marshalled at the wrong end of the train; and Andy, I did my best to get you pictures of 'red' engines, it's just that sometimes the odds seemed stacked against me! Frustrating? Definitely!

But rewarding too! I found myself on the banks of some of Britain's most beautiful rivers - the Findhorn, the Ayr, the Tiddy, the Kennet. I sat high on ridges in the Pennines and the Welsh Marches. I lay beside estuaries and crouched on factory roofs, knocked on strangers' doors and asked to borrow their view. The project took me to places only railwaymen have ever heard of: Hither Green, Thornaby, Mossend, Washwood Heath, Roxby Gullet, Dee Marsh. Moreover I only scratched the surface. I should have made more of intermodal, I didn't sample the massive growth in timber, I barely touched the West Coast Main Line, Merseyside or the West Highlands; sadly there just wasn't time.

Beyond the bare bones of my acknowledgements, at the back of this book, I owe a duty of thanks to English Welsh & Scottish Railway for allowing me backstage. It took a giant leap of faith to invite an unknown outsider into the midst of a three-year-old company. I hope I haven't let them down.

Finally, an occupational hazard. In my guidebook writing days, even when miles away from the areas of my research, I could never prevent myself from making mental notes of post offices, telephone boxes, launderettes and fish & chip shops. Now I have a new obsession: watching lorries - seeing where they come from, wondering what they are carrying, calculating how easily their contents might be transferred to rail ...

Michael Pearson

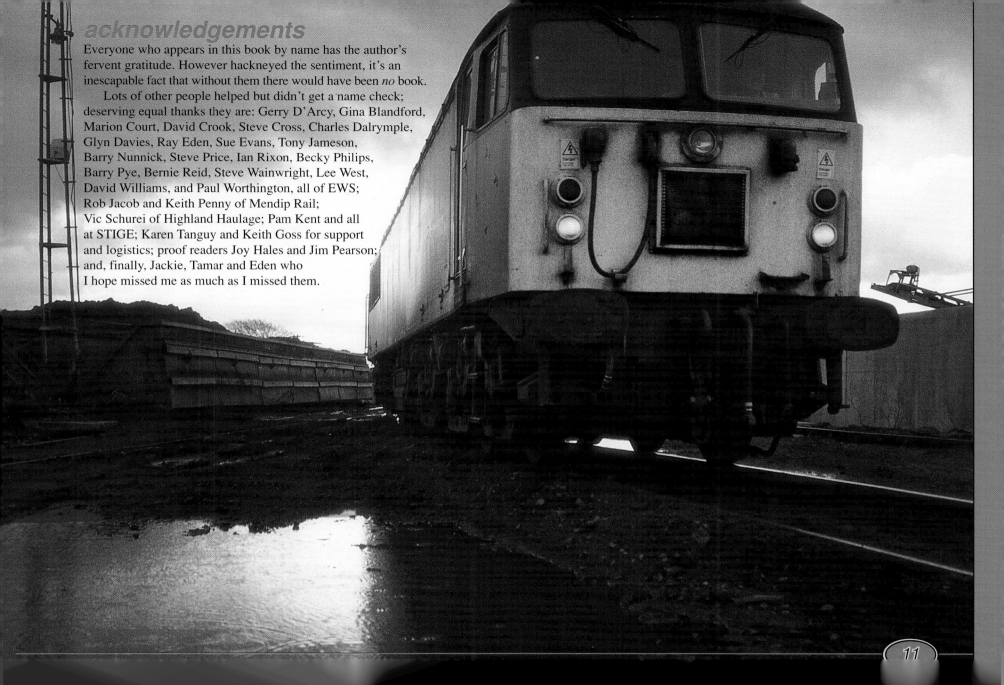

acknowledgements

Everyone who appears in this book by name has the author's fervent gratitude. However hackneyed the sentiment, it's an inescapable fact that without them there would have been *no* book.

Lots of other people helped but didn't get a name check; deserving equal thanks they are: Gerry D'Arcy, Gina Blandford, Marion Court, David Crook, Steve Cross, Charles Dalrymple, Glyn Davies, Ray Eden, Sue Evans, Tony Jameson, Barry Nunnick, Steve Price, Ian Rixon, Becky Philips, Barry Pye, Bernie Reid, Steve Wainwright, Lee West, David Williams, and Paul Worthington, all of EWS; Rob Jacob and Keith Penny of Mendip Rail; Vic Schurei of Highland Haulage; Pam Kent and all at STIGE; Karen Tanguy and Keith Goss for support and logistics; proof readers Joy Hales and Jim Pearson; and, finally, Jackie, Tamar and Eden who I hope missed me as much as I missed them.

coast to coast chemicals

Nightscene, Tees Dock

> "I would be travelling through the watches of the night - somewhat less mysteriously, but no less profoundly - to Workington in far-flung Cumbria."

IT began, like Graham Greene's *Stamboul Train*, in a dockland setting. There was the same "wilderness of rails and points"; "lamps glowing like chains of blue beads"; "the pervading sounds of water;" and "giant cranes sweeping and descending." And, being my first journey for this book, I shared something of his characters' "melancholy of departure and fear of strangeness." In fact I felt - not to put too fine a point on it - like a character in search of a plot. But in place of Ostend this was Teesport, Middlesbrough; and instead of a three day journey to Constantinople, I would be travelling through the watches of the night - somewhat less mysteriously, but no less profoundly - to Workington in far-flung Cumbria. Nor for me the comfort, however transient, however illusory, of a Wagon Lit, I was to be cakewalking it on the footplate of a diesel, hauling a trainload of chemical containers from coast to coast.

EWS, under contract to the Hamburg container operator, Hoyer, carries purified teraphthalic acid (PTA) to Eastman Chemicals at Workington where it is converted into polyethteraphthate (PTE) for use in the manufacture of plastic bottles. A certain amount of the PET is returned by container to Rotterdam. It's apparently more cost effective for the containers which contain this non-hazardous chemical to be transhipped in Teesport than sailed round Land's End. The service operates six nights a week out of Teesport, via Enterprise, and it pleased Chris Harvey, General Manager of EWS Petroleum & Chemicals at the time of my journey, because it illustrated how rail could be competitive on distances of around a hundred miles when most logistical preconceptions suggest otherwise.

Ann Buckley, my EWS contact from Crewe, had organised a cloak and dagger assignation for me at "the shunter's cabin, Teesport". Even the taxi driver was dubious - "the docks do you mean?" I'd flagged him down outside Middlesbrough's lugubriously Gothic station, designed by William Peachy for the North Eastern Railway in 1877. Railtrack was hacking it about a bit, trying to exorcise the smell of tom cats from the vitreous-tiled subway. The effect was seedy. Here and there, however, were fragments of a former nobility: a lofty, echoing, church-like hammer-beam roof above the booking-hall; some delicately elegant ironwork; an attractive and authentic tiled map of the old North Eastern's incredibly dense network of lines. No wonder it could afford to build grandiose stations given the profitability of the steel and coal industries on its doorstep.

Any travel writer will vouch for taxi drivers as a source of local colour. Mine waxed pessimistically lyrical on Teesside's decline. Jobs haemorrhaged from ICI and British Steel. The police were indifferent to, or impotent in the face of, prostitution and drugs. Gangsters used the area's taxis like a courtesy fleet, there being no question of payment at the end of the ride unless you fancied a long walk off Saltburn's short pier. Christmas was a week away but Middlesbrough, he said, wasn't shopping and wasn't clubbing. Personally, he was eking out a living carrying drug barons and journalists. Unfortunately, he rightly divined that I represented the latter, and charged me a tenner for the ride and the philosophy.

It was a *Marie Celeste* of a shunters' cabin. I invited myself in to keep warm. Its portacabin walls were decorated with arcane notices of procedural advice and working methods interspersed with photographs of football teams and steam locomotives. Intermittently the telephone rang and I engaged in oblique, Pinteresque conversations. One caller evinced surprise that I was in the shunters' cabin at all. "They're expecting you down at Thornaby, mate," he chuckled before vanishing into the ether. But before panic set in, the phone rang again and it was Jim Smith, my contact, calmly indifferent to the mix up and telling me to sit tight while he came round to pick me up by road.

In the interim the door burst open and the shunter breezed in, not batting an eyelid at the stranger in his midst, as if he'd grown used, on the railway, to expecting the unexpected. He took one look at a computer which had been happily humming away to itself and groaned: "Making up the trains is one thing," he sighed: "but then having to come back here and tap it all into that thing ..." He left his sentence unfinished with the air of a school teacher bogged down by a massive class yet expected to deal with the manifold demands of the National Curriculum as well. "We need two blokes here," he warmed to his theme: "One to deal with the real world out there and one to work this monstrosity." It went without saying which of the two jobs he'd prefer.

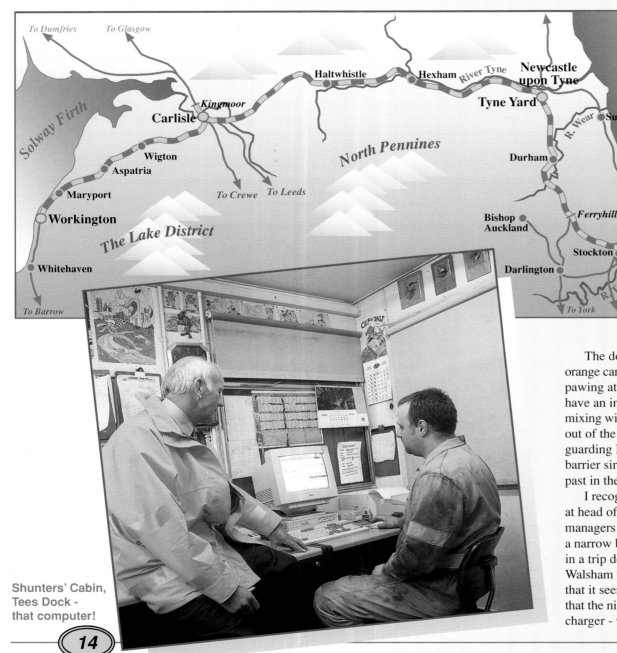

"Railwaymen have an innate sense of sociability honed by generations of spontaneous mixing with men at distant depots."

Shunters' Cabin, Tees Dock - that computer!

The door opened again and two men dressed more or less totally in orange came into the cabin. Outside they'd left a behemoth of a locomotive pawing at the track. They nodded affably in my direction. Railwaymen have an innate sense of sociability honed by generations of spontaneous mixing with men at distant depots. They'd come to get authority to proceed out of the docks and to get the shunter to operate the crossing barriers guarding Kinkerdale Road. The three men rushed out into the night, the barrier sirens wailed, and *my train* of shiny chemical containers roared past in the direction of Thornaby!

I recognised the containers from pictures Chris Harvey had shown me at head office in Islington. Chris had been the most enthusiastic of EWS' managers about my nascent book. We had canals in common: he lived on a narrow boat; I'd spent twenty years writing about them. I had pencilled in a trip down East Anglia's salty coast with condensates from North Walsham to Harwich, but Chris was so enthusiastic about the Hoyer traffic that it seemed churlish to resist. Now, though, I was beginning to think that the night was going terribly wrong. But then Jim drew up on his white charger - well in a white van actually. The fact that our train's tail lamp was flashing round the corner appeared to be of no consequence to him. If it had been necessary to abseil on to the moving train from a hovering helicopter, I don't think he'd have batted a railway eyelid. Calmly he explained that the returning empties from Workington had met with delay, and that instead of a Carlisle driver throughout, a Thornaby man would fill in as far as Tyne Yard. Consequently were going up to Thornaby as a 'trip working' and there, with a fresh locomotive, we would start our journey for real.

Over the next few hours I got the distinct impression that it would take a good deal to force the mask of imperturbability to slip from Jim Smith's visage, and I was not surprised to learn that he was regularly assigned to the Royal Train where they work to schedule tolerances of fifteen seconds either way - just as well, then, that they ask EWS to provide their motive power!

As we drove over to Thornaby in the van - somehow a much shorter journey than it had seemed by taxi - Jim succinctly outlined the salient points - no pun intended - of Middlesbrough's railway network while I gazed out of the window watching the Riverside Stadium glide by and catching a glimpse of the Tees transporter bridge bathed a subdued, floodlit blue.

Jim Smith had started on the railway in 1961 and come through the ranks from engine cleaner to the responsible position of Standards Inspector. As well as dealing with the Queen and me, one of the most interesting facets of his work is accompanying

Jim Smith does a spot of window cleaning - the old way

EWS crews on steam charters. In the last sombre days of 'real' steam he had worked out of Hartlepool shed firing J27s and Q6s; throwbacks to an Edwardian England, puffing their diminishing trails of sulphur across the County Durham coalfield. In many respects, Jim told me, he regretted not having been promoted in time to drive steam himself. So he'd been delighted to get a second chance. A few weeks before he'd accompanied *Green Arrow* on a charter from Preston to York via Carlisle and Newcastle and had loved every nostalgic minute of it, apart from being consigned to the slow line south of Darlington when everyone on the footplate had wanted to "clear the engine's throat a bit" on the traditional racing track to York.

So we did a whistle-stop tour of Middlesbrough's railway infrastructure: I saw where the thriving potash and rock salt traffics discharge for worldwide shipping and onward consignment by road respectively; heard about the Port of Teesside's own dock shunting locomotives; learnt how the steel industry - notably Lackenby plant - still made considerable demands on the resources of EWS and Railtrack; and discovered that Jim and I shared a common interest in long-distance running, albeit he'd done the New York and Athens marathons in times that I could only speculate about in my dreams.

Thornaby is little more than a slip road on the A19 to most people but, as so often is the case, in railway circles the name takes on far more significance. The motive power depot dates from 1958, being an amalgamation of the old steam sheds at Middlesbrough and Newport. Even back then it cost a cool one and a quarter million, and occupied a seventy acre site on the south bank of the River Tees. Initially it dealt almost entirely with steam locomotives, but had been designed in such a way as to make the transition to diesels a formality. Over the ensuing forty years it had been a key depot for British Rail. Following privatisation it had become the property of the shadow franchise Loadhaul. Now it belongs to EWS and is used for the inspection, light maintenance and fuelling of locomotives.

Steam Age men would still be at home in Thornaby shed. They'd know where to look to find their links, their rosters and their 'must read notices'; though they might be bemused by the shed foreman's apparent devotion to television. We know, of

Thornaby twins - two former Loadhaul Class 56s undergo maintenance

course, that it's a computer terminal that he's glued to, sourcing locomotives for diagrams far and wide. For Thornaby is a 'hub' depot with 'spokes' at York and Tyne Yard, a dramatic reversal in status; York once being coded '50A', the head depot of the North Eastern Region, and Thornaby an insignificant '51L'.

Jim told me that Thornaby has around ninety drivers now. They are still organised by EWS in links but these are defined by route knowledge and hours worked rather than seniority. In the old days the engine driver's life, coveted by every right-minded boy, began - like a lowly football apprentice scraping mud off the first team's boots - with the drudgery of engine cleaning and ash dropping. Twenty years might well elapse before you were elevated to the giddy heights of engine driver. These days EWS reckons it can take a man (or woman for that matter) 'off the street' and have them driving in twenty-one weeks. Time, tide and technology wait for no man.

Generally speaking, rail privatisation has resulted in longer working hours for drivers but more rest days. EWS operates a policy of twelve-hour shift patterns, followed by twelve-hour breaks, but of course the demands of the working timetable can echo Robbie Burns's thoughts concerning 'mice and men' and 'best laid plans'. Currently, Thornaby men work as far north as Northumberland and as far south as Northamptonshire, Jim told me as we picked our way past locomotives being made ready for their next duty. Though I wasn't exactly wearing an anorak, I 'spotted' a couple of celebrity engines: 37350 (a.k.a. D6700) which has been restored more or less to its original 1960 condition by some of Thornaby's devoted maintenance men, pending an assured future at the National Railway Museum; and 60006 in the light blue house-colours of British Steel, a gesture of fraternity by EWS to a historical ally and significant present-day customer.

Thornaby has a sideline in wagon maintenance - all the business under one roof for a lean outfit like EWS. Rolling Stock Technicians (artists formerly known as wagon examiners - and probably wheel-tappers once) scurry about to ensure that every

Andy Hogan in the
shunters' cabin
at Thornaby

wagon capable of turning a wheel is available for every potential payload. Beyond the purlieus of the locomotive depot lies Tees Yard, one of three massive marshalling yards created by the North Eastern Region of British Railways in the early Sixties. White elephants almost overnight, they were victims of Beeching's bulk trains and fixed flows formulae. Shunting became anathema. A policy honed to the point of imbecility by British Rail in the Eighties, when loyal customers were turned away if their logistic requirements didn't match the game plan. Jim led me into another shunters' cabin. I was beginning to feel at home in them. A young man, dressed as if he'd just been Tangoed, was peering intently at the computer screen. He turned to Jim with a wry smile: "The prossies are back - entertaining their clients at the back of the old shed. I swear I'm gonna rig up some nails on the road so's the punters all get more than they bargained for!" The orange man turned his attention from moral matters to Tops 2000, EWS's computerised traffic control system, and explained the colour codings for my benefit. "Blue for wagons in use - with a red border if they're loaded. Green for cripples; yellow for maintenance jobs, pink for condemned; brown if they're in store."

"So the screen depicts graphically what's out there in the yard at any given time," I hazarded.

"Not exactly, no!"

Jim reckoned it was time to go and find our train. A grey, growling shape loomed up under the baleful glare of the floodlights - 'Boro' wouldn't get far in this kind of light at the Riverside - and ran down past the silvery Hoyer containers which formed our train. It was a Class 37 called *Caithness*, which seemed to suggest that it had operated in Scotland at one time or another. If you're not familiar with the looks of a 37 it's best described as having

descended from those classic American diesels with big noses that featured in so many Hollywood films of the Fifties. Over three hundred of them were built by English Electric of Newton-le-Willows in Lancashire for British Railways in the early to mid-Sixties, and under licence by Robert Stephenson in Darlington, and they have been pretty much a fixture in the North-east ever since. As locomotive designs go they have been very successful, wide-ranging in their use as a mixed traffic engine, equally at home on semi-fast passenger trains and all manner of goods. A couple of hundred of them survive, mostly owned by EWS, and perhaps half of these, extensively refurbished a few years back, will be working goods trains well into the next millennium. Forty have recently been leased to SNCF for infrastructure duties in France. Paradoxically, some have already been preserved by enthusiasts for whom they are every bit as significant and attractive as the steam engines they replaced.

Caithness trundled up to the west end of the yard before reversing on to our train. A shunter called Jeff, crunching the ballast in heavy duty boots, went down the train to check that the disc breaks had come off on all the eight flat-bed FGA bogie wagons which made up our 'consist'. American railroading terms are creeping into our terminology, but perhaps this is no surprise given the Wisconsin based background to EWS's parent firm.

Jim hoisted himself adroitly up into the forward facing of *Caithness's* two cabs. It seemed mountain high to me, more used to boarding trains with the benefit of a platform, and I clambered up inexpertly in his wake. Jim introduced me to the driver, Gary Fenwick, who was substituting for the delayed Carlisle man as far as Tyne Yard on the outskirts of Newcastle. Gary was on the 'fill in' turn; potentially a mystery trip scenario. Tyne Yard seemed to suit him as well as anywhere and he reacted calmly to the brush with fame that my article will give him. In fact he was too busy watching for the ground signal to give us clearance into the yard throat to pay too much attention as Jim and I attempted to make ourselves comfortable.

Beyond the ground signal, a cab-high colour light controlled access on to Railtrack metals. All this Balkanisation of the railway must be perplexing to men reared on the certainties and integrities of British Rail. Many of them, you sense, are still reeling from a succession of reorganisations. First they were sectorised, then broken up into shadow franchises then, as far as freight is concerned, predominently regrouped into English Welsh & Scottish. But it must still seem strange to be travelling on someone else's track, and the railway press is full of antagonisms and anomalies at the interface of the train operating companies and Railtrack. Though, as I would see later in this journey, there have been plenty of sensible collaborations too.

The shunting signal tweaked to go and we got a green light from Railtrack. One of my earliest railway memories is of seeing coal trains start with an immense juddering and knashing of buffers, and I was astonished how smoothly Gary got our sixteen bogies under way. Of course I'm recalling loose-fitted trains whereas these days nearly everything is air-braked, and no longer is there any need for a quaint guard's van. Just as well really, with EWS around we would be calling them cabooses.

Effortlessly, we crawled past Thornaby's bus-sheltered platform and crossed the Tees, Chris Rea's *Steel River,* where returning salmon are of no consolation to men who've lost jobs in steel and shipping. Stainsby's also nearby, and I only hope the feisty eponymous girls of another of his songs haven't evolved into the ladies at the back of the shed. Come to think of it, Chris did a song called *Deltics* as well - the celebrated East Coast 'racehorses' also built by English Electric - so I am sure he would envy me this footplate ride and be inspired to provide some funky slide guitar to accompany it.

Beyond Stockton, Gary throttled down to take the curve at Norton South Junction at a steady 25mph. Briefly, we came under the time-honoured control of semaphore signalling. Still lit by oil, the spectacles on the inner end of each arm were showing green for us and we passed beneath arms raised obliquely at a forty-five degree salute. The line from Stockton to Ferryhill has been goods-only for many years, part of it was once notably used for early experiments in electrification by the North Eastern Railway. Jim pointed out the earthworks of old colliery branches and a stretch where the track was once quadruple. One or two of the overbridges required a reduction in speed. At 8ft 6ins wide the Hoyer containers are within a whisker of loading gauge tolerances. Another Class 37 went by on the opposite track, the driver switching his cab light on and off by way of a friendly gesture. Gary and Jim identified it as a train of empty steel wagons returning from Workington to Lackenby, Middlesbrough. I'd become accustomed to the rhythms of the footplate, a throwback in terminology to steam days. Jim and I preferred to stand, though there was a second seat. But I enjoyed the view through the central, and highest, of the cab's three forward-looking windows. I had expected it to be draughty and cold, and accordingly my wife had wrapped me up in five layers of clothing, but I was beginning to shed these, one by one. Gary even had the old locomotive's stove on to add extra heat.

Peculiarly it's located on the floor and so apparently it was always easy to spot a secondman, in the days when they had them, by his melted boots. Outside the night was clear with a sky of low scudding clouds. The lights of remote farms peppered the Durham countryside.

Caithness ran swiftly down into Ferryhill and joined the East Coast Main Line. Jim and Gary simultaneously pointed out a southbound coal train working with one of the new Class 66 diesels at its head. It was one of an initial order for two hundred and fifty machines being supplied by General Motors from its plant in London, Ontario. At the time of my trip, Thornaby had one of them for crew training but, by all accounts, the guys hadn't been won over yet. "They're not up to a 'Sixty' - not as powerful, noisier and rougher-riding," was the initial feeling, though railwaymen are traditionally cautious when it comes to new motive power. Thirty-five years ago Thornaby lads were probably shaking their heads over their new fangled 37s and swearing that they'd never do the work of a B1 steamer!

It was now about ten-thirty. The Great North Eastern Railway electrics had just about turned in for the night, leaving the smooth main line and its welded rails to goods trains like us. We bowled along at a mile a minute, sixty being the maximum permitted speed for a train such as ours. This part of the East Coast Main Line is bi-directionally signalled so there were colour light signals ahead controlling each of the two tracks. As we roared round a curve a green light ahead lit up our faces and the Advanced Warning System bell sounded clear in the cab. Jim regaled us with the tale of a troop train which smashed into the wreckage of a derailed goods train hereabouts with considerable loss of life. We crossed Durham Viaduct and had our minds taken off tragedy by the beguiling view of the castle and cathedral floodlit against the inky night sky. Talking of landmarks, Gary and Jim were keen to point out Anthony Gormley's *Angel of the North* on its elevated site above Gateshead. It's not floodlit, but they thought we should be able to see it silhouetted against the night glow of Newcastle. At first I couldn't make it out above the criss-crossing wires of the electric catenary and, having learnt the moral of the story of the *Emperor's New Clothes* at an early age, I wasn't going to say I could see it if I couldn't. Then just as we turned off the main line into Tyne Yard I did catch a glimpse of it, massively dominating the skyline even in the black of night - half a million well spent I'd say!

Tyne Yard lies four miles south of Newcastle. It's another of the big yards built by the North Eastern Region of British Railways during the modernisation frenzy of the early Sixties when it seemed that all we had to do was *modernise* and the future would, by definition, take care of itself. At its zenith it occupied 135 acres of land and was designed to cope with four thousand wagons passing through each day. Jim said that Harold Wilson had opened it, but being a diligent researcher I found *Modern Railways'* September 1963 issue crediting the ceremonial stuff to Viscount Hailsham; perhaps he'd got a Gannex mac just like Harold's. But all this history is bunk, so to speak, and, though much rationalised, Tyne Yard has regained some self respect in the rejuvenated role it now plays for EWS.

Jim and Gary disappeared into the night, scurrying across the tracks to get aboard the returning empties. Like underground resistance couriers they handed me over with the minimum of fuss to a new driver, Steve Teenan of Carlisle, and a new Standards Inspector, Peter Armstrong, of Tyne Yard. Normally our train wouldn't linger here and in any case we had one eye on the clock due to the signalling curfew on the Newcastle-Carlisle line. "Don't they wait up for you?" I asked Peter, and he replied with a rueful grin: "Not them, if we haven't left here by eleven they'll shut up the shop and we'll be left kicking our heels here until the morning shift comes on!"

So we didn't hang about. We growled off round the Low Fell loop with its nocturnally busy Royal Mail terminal, went down through Dunston and past the Metro Centre, as paradoxically silent without its shopping hordes as a nightclub in daytime. The Tyne came close, streetlights twinkling in its waters, and we went through Blaydon and Wylam (paying silent homage to old George Stephenson) with "them", as Peter put it "closing the boxes behind us." This historic line is not one I can claim to know well. It opened as early in the Railway Age as 1838 having originally been proposed as a canal. Time has been kind to it, many of the original station buildings surviving. One of its characteristics is the position of one or two signalboxes on gantries above the line to afford the signalmen a better view. At night they were lit up like low-flying aircraft and their signalmen waved enthusiastically at us, glad to be able to shut up their boxes and head for home.

Luminously, the Tyne accompanied us to Hexham and a surprising rash of factories. EWS uses the sidings here for loading timber from Kielder Forest, but Peter, Steve and I agreed that the town's industries had perhaps even more potential traffics for carriage by rail.

The line climbs out of Hexham, past the old Border Counties Junction - where the lovely route along the North Tyne once led to Bellingham - and on beside the South Tyne to Haltwhistle. It was pleasant just to trundle through the darkness and none of us found it necessary to make much conversation. Peter pointed out the opencast loading point at Melkridge which had closed a month or two before, and we wondered at the cost of jilting such expensive infrastructure. All over the railway network opencast coal loading points stand not so much mothballed as abandoned once mining operations have ceased. But there again there's perhaps not much of a secondhand market for this sort of stuff!

I have a soft spot for Haltwhistle. I changed trains here in 1972 and caught the Alston branch service down to the 'highest market town in England'. It was the first day of a week's hike along the Pennine backbone. Even as branchlines go, the Alston run was abundantly bucolic. The guard was on first name terms with most of the passengers, and two or three times stopped their two car diesel unit between stations to enable elderly couples to cross fields of waving grass to remote cottages and farms. Within a year, that sort of public service, woven into the landscape by well over a century of operation, had been ripped apart because it didn't *pay!*

According to the consist we had 790 tonnes behind us - quite a lot of lorries by anyone's standards, so we were a good advert for the EWS slogan "Loads off Roads". Steve reckoned there was a coating of grease on the line, a not unusual phenomenon up in this wild, wet and windy Wagnerian landscape, but *Caithness* seemed like a strong and willing shire horse on wet cobbles and obviously up to the job. At Greenhead, Steve tried to point out a bit of the Roman wall, but all I could make out was a bare outline of moorland. Midnight found us crossing the watershed

Wylam - George Stephenson country

between the Tyne and the Eden. I'd noticed that Steve was ignoring the lineside W signs which instruct drivers to 'whistle', or rather to blow their horns these days. More often than not these mark the approach of a public crossing, but between 23.30 and 07.00 this practice is waived so as not to invade the sleep of folk living within earshot of the railway. In any case, who but poachers and poets would be out in the wilds at such times?

From time to time a rough noise, like someone clearing a particularly sore throat, emanated from the locomotive's bonnet and I was told that these were the brake compressors coming on. Trying to assimilate all this information, expertise and technical data, together with railway lore, anecdotes and all the other ingredients of this night passage, hadn't left me with much time to take in the nuances and ambience of the locomotive itself. Oddly enough it reminded me of nothing so much as a Lancaster or Wellington bomber from the Second World War, a comparison emphasised by the roaring darkness outside and the sense of being elevated beyond generally recognised levels of consciousness. Steve compounded this feeling by pointing out the lights of Carlisle, still perhaps some fifteen miles away, and it felt for all the world as though the Border City was our target for the night. And in a way I suppose it was.

We went bucketing downhill past the old lead mining town of Brampton - 1 in 107 through How Mill and Heads Nook. "The Hardendale-Lackenby limestone trains struggle up here, even with a Sixty on," said Peter. Wetheral, with its high viaduct over the Eden, and curved pair of platforms linked by an attractively arched footbridge, brought us almost to the outskirts of Carlisle. I thought I knew the approach to Carlisle's classic Citadel station like the proverbial back of my hand, but it looked quite different from high up in our forward-facing eyrie. Its platforms were full of recumbent diesel units. Peter and Steve discussed whether or not I'd be better off spending the wee small hours with the wagons up at Kingmoor Yard, or in the relative luxury of the EWS signing-on point at the station. Stoically I opted to stay with *my* train, for which I was beginning to feel a proprietorial zeal. They acquiesced, though not without a knowing look passing between them, which I interpreted as meaning that a more appropriate

spot might be the nearest asylum.

Kingmoor lies a couple of miles north of Carlisle on a remote tract of land at the edge of Solway Firth. Opened in 1962, it was a belated attempt to rationalise movement of freight through a city which, prior to the grouping of the railways in 1923, had been served by seven different companies all with their own installations and infrastructure. In fact, at the beginning of the Sixties, nine different goods yards were still in use, linked by a procession of trip and transfer workings. British Railways' London Midland Region threw four and a half million pounds at the problem, laying 72 miles of reception, recessing, sorting and departure sidings within a 480 acre complex. Automated hump shunting techniques allowed wagons to roll into their required lines by gravity. Two control towers, which, judging by archive photographs of the spanking new yard, would not have looked out of place at Heathrow, overlooked the fan like spread of tracks, and they were linked (radio-telephonically) with the drivers of the ubiquitous diesel shunting locomotives that scurried about the yard like obsequious ushers at a society wedding. "It will pay for itself in ten years," was the general opinion of management at the time. Piffle - within ten years it was obsolete!

Steve dropped off the wagons and ran *Caithness* back to the locomotive siding at Citadel station. Peter telephoned for a taxi to take him back to Tyne Yard. Everyone so far had been so friendly and interested in what I was doing that I was ill-prepared for the reception I got in the shunters' cabin at Kingmoor. Their indifference was infectious. It infected me with dismay. For all they knew I might have been a *really* important person. Thankfully I didn't take it personally. "They're like that with everyone, mate," said a Knottingley driver who'd just arrived with coal empties from deepest Yorkshire and who had a couple of hours to kill before returning south with a loaded train of coal imported through Hunterston Dock in Ayrshire.

My new friend offered me the warmth of *Cairn Toul's* cab, coffee, and the sort of wide-ranging talk one has with a total, but amenable stranger in the darkest hours which come before dawn. About half past three he got clearance to commence his long journey southwards over the Settle & Carlisle and kindly dropped

"'It will pay for itself in ten years,' was the general opinion of management at the time. Piffle - within ten years it was obsolete!"

The 'Hoyer Train' runs alongside the River Tyne near Blaydon (*Peter J. Robinson*)

me off at Carlisle station where they were finishing unloading the London Travelling Post Office. For a couple of hours I shared the down side waiting room with a snoring cyclist, far too tired to sleep. By five o'clock they were preparing breakfast in the Virgin restaurant car on Platform 4. I felt like a tramp with his face pressed up against the window of *The Savoy*. I had a cup of vending machine coffee and lingered by the locked door of the EWS traincrew room. Eventually, someone coming off duty let me in and I waited in the mess room until the driver of the next leg of my journey signed on for duty. I relaxed in its relative luxury, finding myself coming over all emotional at the discovery of a loo with a seat on it.

I eavesdropped for half an hour on conversations laced with the procreative adverb. With boyish naivety I'd always imagined engine drivers enjoying their work. Or was their collective frustration characteristic of a greater malaise - the pressure of the modern workplace? All of us seem to be working harder and harder and longer and longer, just to stand still; just to tread water. In the future, we were lead to believe, technology would have rendered us all redundant, and the biggest problem we would face would be filling our leisure time. Science? - more like science fiction!

Driver Alan Wilson reported for duty at 05.23. I came as something of a surprise to him, and what we didn't have was a Standards Inspector to ride with us. An enterprising young man called Ronnie made some swift phone calls, but it seemed like I was the biggest mystery in these parts since Michael Kington's most recent encounter with a U.F.O. Just when it looked as though Alan would have to go off without me - "Sorry lad, if it was up to me, but ..." - Arthur Nelson materialised and we all relaxed.

So Alan, Arthur and I (plus Ronnie who was hitching a lift up to Kingmoor) jumped insouciantly off the edge of the platform, crossed the tracks, climbed (a little more easily now as far as I was concerned) into the cab of *Caithness*, started it up, and trundled along to the yard. Even though it was still dark, it looked a tad less forbidding at six in the morning than it had at one.

A few paragraphs back I'd left Kingmoor all but surplus to British Rail requirements. I had passed it often enough in recent

years, and seen what sidings remained empty of payloads, simply being used like an attic or an outhouse for the storage of unwanted items of rolling stock. Revitalised by EWS, it now receives and despatches in the region of fifty trains every 24 hours. My chemical train offered a perfect example of the sort of interaction of traffic flows increasingly taking place. To the eight container-carrying flats brought from Tees, *Caithness* added four tankers of china clay slurry and five timber wagons which had come into Kingmoor on the overnight Enterprise service from Eastleigh, near Southampton. The china clay and the timber were destined for the Iggesund board works at Workington.

Just before half past seven we pulled southwards out of Kingmoor with no less than seventeen wagons behind us, totalling 1255 tonnes. It would have taken upwards of thirty lorries - juggernauts at that - to carry our three commodities by road! I had my night's fourth encounter with Carlisle station. It was still opaquely dark, but, as we screeched round the tight bend on to the Cumbrian Coast line, bedroom and bathroom lights were flicking on in the old railway workers' terraces on Currock Road. Arthur pointed out an EWS wagon repair depot on the edge of town as we picked up speed. Halfway to Dalston we passed an early local from Whitehaven taking a load of workers into Carlisle.

There is an oil depot at Dalston which receives loaded trains of bogie tanks from Grangemouth on the Firth of Forth. Dawn had drawn its curtains wide enough to reveal an attractive little station with a half-stone, half-timber waiting room framed by conifers. *Caithness* picked up a bit of speed - forty perhaps - and began to roll like a marathon runner hitting their stride. In marshy fields beside the line we passed a dredger working a dragline by headlight on a gravel pit. It began to rain lightly. Signals came and went without any bells sounding reassuringly in the cab. Alan explained that this line wasn't fitted with the Advance Warning System. It was a bit of a throwback in other respects too: at Crofton we passed the remnants of a once private station built expressly for the local landowner's use (can you imagine that happening today?); whilst the growing daylight revealed the restricted dimensions of the line's overbridges which Railtrack had apparently had to tweak a shade to permit the passage of the

"Just before half past seven we pulled southwards out of Kingmoor with no less than seventeen wagons behind us, totalling 1255 tonnes. It would have taken upwards of thirty lorries - juggernauts at that - to carry our three commodities by road!"

Hoyer containers. We went through Wigton - Melvyn Bragg's home town - with a whoosh. A ruined windmill overlooks the station and there's another factory - making chemicals - which could offer traffic for EWS.

Whether or not lassitude was beginning to tell on me, I wasn't sure, but I could empathise with Alan's voiced concerns about accumulated working hours under the new regime. Towing management's line, Arthur responded by reminding Alan of all the extra days off the new working patterns were offering. Alan pointed out the trackbed of the old Solway Junction Railway, a long-forgotten shortcut to Lanarkshire's ironworks for trains of Cumberland ore. A cast iron viaduct, well over a mile long, carried it across the Solway Firth. It was brought down by ice floes in the Arctic winter of 1881. It was repaired, but the line closed in 1921, though the viaduct remained intact for another thirteen years, during which it became popular with the Scots who would walk over it to drown the sorrows of their compulsorily liquor-free Sabbaths.

Following that, we fell into a silence of sorts. Alan peered through the drizzle, Arthur chain-smoked. At Aspatria the Slumberland Beds factory taunted my tiredness. The line traversed an area of former coal mines and opencast workings; a kestrel flew across the track in front of us; beef cattle moved ponderously towards a muddy gateway. Prompted by me, Arthur recalled his railway roots. A Glaswegian, he'd spent the Seventies working out of Eastfield depot as a second man and had a soft spot for the 37s kindled by journeys up and down the West Highland line. Promotion had plucked him by degrees from such byways. Latterly he'd been based at York and had only been in Carlisle for a week or two before my trip. This was actually his first ride along the Cumbrian Coast line. He was waiting for Christmas to come and go before he started house hunting, reckoning that "something on the edge of the Lake District would do just fine." Oh Lucky Man!

A single yellow light slowed us for Maryport. We went down to 15 mph and passed a bare platform, a rusty siding with a track tamping machine stabled on it, an ancient signal box, and the former goods shed, bereft of tracks and optimistically offered "To Let". Round the curve came the sea, an unforgiving grey merging imperceptibly with the sky. White waves crashed against a stony

shore. Wind turbines gesticulated wildly like frenetic policemen on traffic duty. Keeping pace with delivery vans on the adjoining road, *Caithness* rattled through Flimby station. I spotted a roadside Body Repair Centre and felt like dropping in. I'd been awake for over twenty-four hours. There were more wind turbines, with black sheep grazing beneath them. Inland stood Iggesund's board mill where half our train load was destined after a short journey by road. Another Carlisle-bound local passed us, a single unit railcar. "Those Class 153s were built in Workington," said Alan, "at the Leyland bus works by the docks, I remember driving them out round the sharp curves with the wheels squealing." We passed the dock siding, but there being no crossover to the up line (though Arthur told me there was talk of one going in) continued across the Derwent which, judging by the unnerving proximity of the water to the bridge parapet, must have been close to high tide. At the far end of the bridge we ground to a halt, waiting for the signalman to 'pull off' the subsidiary signal guarding access to the yard. Seagulls swooped down on us. Perhaps to them we looked like a big grey mullet gasping for air on the bridge. Workington station is parenthesised by two antediluvian looking signal cabins which rejoice under the utilitarian nomenclature of *WORKINGTON MAIN No. 2* and *No. 3*. Railtrack's regeneration bandwagon had patently not hit town yet, though there was a latent dignity about the station's ochre-coloured brick buildings.

It was difficult to see the track for the weeds in the yard, and *Caithness* chugged to a halt just short of the steelworks which is famous, worldwide, as the place to go for rails when you're planning on laying new track for your railway or tramway. They no longer make their own steel here, of course - the blast furnace shut down in 1975 - nowadays raw steel slabs are trained in, along the same route as my trip, from Lackenby on Teesside, whilst finished rails go out to Bescot near Walsall; more remunerative traffic for EWS. At length a shunter strolled into view and uncoupled *Caithness*. We pulled forward, changed cabs, waited for the points to change, then moved slowly down the train to its other end. We coupled up again and paused to create the brake. Alan pointed out the remnants of Workington's once busy engine shed, recalling when it was full of steam locomotives awaiting their next turn of duty. I sensed his nostalgia for a busier railway, one where more than 6% of the nation's freight went by rail, and I hoped EWS's ambitions would materialise in time for him to savour the renaissance.

Back across the river we went, returning to the point which led into the docks. A shunter lent us a short wave radio, through which he proceeded to bark instructions, telling Alan when the end of our train had cleared the point, then guiding him cautiously round the curve into the sidings. "Keep coming, keep coming - OK, that'll do." There were four sidings. We backed the slurry wagons into one, the timber into another and divided the container flats into the other two. A fortnight before, local dignitaries and media people had assembled to witness commissioning of a new unloading facility specifically geared to the Hoyer container traffic, modestly congratulating themselves that several

thousand lorries would henceforth be absent from the North of England's roads annually.

Arthur got a call on his mobile urgently summoning him back to Carlisle, and I had a passenger train to catch back home to Derby, so we left Alan and *Caithness* to do a bit more shunting before returning to Kingmoor with the empties. We made our way into town via dockland streets and had bacon butties at a cafe near the station. Arthur considered this modest establishment 'a find', and I got the distinct impression that 'greasy spoons' were as important in the day to day holding down of his demanding job as signal boxes, locomotive depots and marshalling yards.

At the station a pretty booking clerk informed me that I could have a return ticket to Derby for the same price as a single. I mustn't have looked as tired as I felt. "One way will do fine," I told her, firmly but politely. "One way will do fine!"

Returning empties, Flimby *(Dave McAlone)*

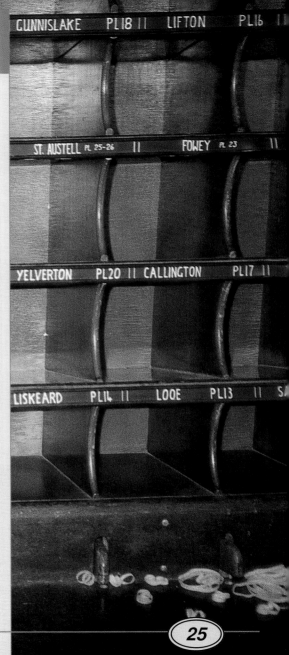

cornish posties & china clay

"*T*HE track talked to us. We couldn't use sight to see where we were, so we relied on our other senses. We *smelt* the brickworks at Leighton Buzzard, we *heard* the whoosh of the water troughs at Tebay." This was Paul Ruston, my host for the evening, remembering his days on the Carlisle TPO. TPO? They talk in abbreviations and acronyms these guys: Travelling Post Offices to laymen like us. They've been using them since the year after Victoria came to the throne, and Paul said that if one of the travelling posties from way back then somehow Dr Who'd himself into the present he'd immediately feel at home. "The job hasn't changed in a hundred and sixty years, and how many jobs can you say that about?"

"Platform seven, Temple Meads, midnight. He's a tall guy with a mop of white hair." These had been my instructions from Richard Yeo of the Post Office's Princess Royal Distribution Centre in London, and he was right, Paul didn't take much finding. Actually it was nearer half past twelve, courtesy of a delayed Virgin train from the Midlands when I leapt, two steps at a time, up the stairs from the subway and spotted Paul, a sort of human Mont Blanc, unmistakably loitering by a long red train of windowless carriages. A more flippant observer than I might have considered it a good job that Richard Branson isn't contracted to the Post Office. English Welsh & Scottish face financial penalties if any of the fifty plus post trains they run daily are behind time (though, by the same token, they receive bonus payments for exemplary time-keeping), and as my journey into deepest Cornwall with the Bristol-Penzance Postal progressed I saw how crucial scheduling is to the operation, and how time is, quite literally, of the essence in the relationship between English Welsh & Scottish and the Royal Mail.

The Cornish TPO leaves Penzance for Bristol, Monday to Friday at seven-thirty in the evening. Not so much a train, more an institution, people south of Saltash acknowledge that this is effectively their last link with 'Up Country' and, if they've missed their local post, will rush down to the stations where it stops to deposit their urgent, First Class post through the letter-box in the side of the sorting carriage. The train gets into Bristol at midnight where the team of twenty sorters is faced with a frantic turnaround before returning to Penzance at two minutes to one. Given the volume of mail which has to be unloaded for the Midlands and the North, and loaded from incoming connecting trains, every minute counts, and it was into a scene of controlled frenzy that Paul introduced me with about twenty minutes to go until departure.

We walked up the platform to see the locomotive. It was 47727 *Duke of Edinburgh Award*, a reassuring sort of title for an engine about to skirt the bare wastes of Dartmoor and Bodmin Moor. The train consisted of seven carriages: two POS sorting vehicles; three POT stowage vans; and two GUV vans. A similar train, almost a mirror image, was drawn up on the adjoining platform. "That's the Swansea-London TPO," said Paul and we wandered over for a quick word with some of its crew. He seemed to know everyone personally. But perhaps this just reflected how good he was at his job and that he had already accumulated the wisdom of thirty-five years on the travelling post offices.

Ten years ago this experience might have been consigned to the scrap heap. Men in suits and offices were contemplating a postal future in which the TPOs would be as obsolete as the pigeon post, but then every generation has its industrial assassins, those who would eliminate the past simply because it is old and has, infuriatingly as far as they are concerned, stood the test of time. But these whizz kids were ultimately faced with an unpalatable truth - there *is* no better way of sorting mail on the move, and no amount of mechanisation in hi-tech, purpose built centres could telescope the time that the travelling posties save on their overnight journeys.

The concept of sorting mail on the move dates back to 1838 when the Grand Junction Railway provided the Post Office with a converted horse box. The trial run was so successful that on the next occasion they removed the horse to create extra space. The idea caught on and with typical Victorian energy the country was soon criss-crossed by clandestine overnight trains; most connecting major centres, others tracing labyrinthine cross-country routes: York to Shrewsbury; Workington to Huddersfield; Peterborough to Crewe; towns with nothing in common except their TPO and, in more recent times, unfashionable clubs in the doldrums of the Football League.

To speed the mails up even more, lineside 'apparatus' was designed to effect collection and despatch of mail bags without stopping the train. Apparently there were precedents for this from stage-coach days, when rustics would have their mail hurled at them as the post galloped through. All of which was fine assuming the recipient managed to avoid decapitation. Needing something more reliable, and less dangerous, the railways developed a system of carriage-side nets to catch the mail and lineside poles from which to hang it on. The TPOs were brought to the public's attention in 1936 when the classic documentary *Night Mail* was filmed by the GPO. Romantic images of the train rushing through the night from London to Scotland were enhanced by Benjamin Britten's music and W.H. Auden's accompanying poetry. Hornby made a model of a sorting carriage complete with apparatus. I had one on my train set when I was about ten and spent hours watching the mail pouch being grabbed by the passing train on one side of the circle, and being hurled into a waiting receptacle on the other. Nowadays my pastimes are slightly more sophisticated, though not necessarily any more enjoyable.

Just to prove how effective the TPO could be, I'd brought a

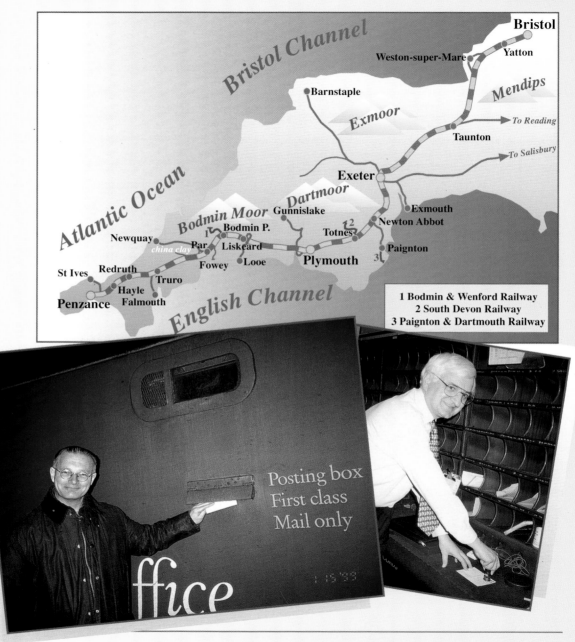

1 Bodmin & Wenford Railway
2 South Devon Railway
3 Paignton & Dartmouth Railway

postcard with me to send to my friends Eric and Ann Leslie in Barnstaple. Eric was a carpenter for the Eastern Region of British Railways before taking early retirement through ill health. Now he's a painter and illustrator of some renown in railway circles. We share an enthusiasm for railways and an off-beat sense of humour. The Leslies emigrated, and I choose the verb deliberately, from Sheffield to the land of Henry Williamson's 'Two Rivers' in the early Nineties and Eric now spends his days cycling along the 'Tarka Trail' imagining he's a Bulleid Pacific with the milk train from Fremington. I have a lot of friends in this mould - what's that old maxim about judging a man by the company he keeps? I got Paul to photograph me posting their card through the carriage's letter-box, then took a picture of him stamping it with the - much prized in philatelic circles - TPO frank, each stamp's inscription being unique to its train. Posted just before one in the morning, it was delivered to Eric's house just as he was pouring the milk on his cornflakes!

So busy had we been with this, that I barely noticed our 'on time' departure. Neither, apparently, did the posties, already busy at their sorting frames, or pigeon holes; rock-steady on their feet - despite the rolling of the train over points - like expert Cornish surfers. Paul introduced me to Chris Greenaway, the train's Acting Manager. Ten years in the job, he'd initially been attracted by the fact that it didn't involve wearing a uniform - a fact I found reassuring - and had quickly come to terms with permanent nights. Like all but four of the men on board, he hailed from Plymouth, and had the air about him of a man who wouldn't be in a hurry to swap his job. Chris quickly showed me over the train. Quickly, because we only had ten minutes before our first stop at Yatton where we were scheduled to meet a Royal Mail road vehicle with post that had been flown into Bristol Airport from Scotland. Chris explained how the two sorting carriages in the consist were individually assigned to Devon and Cornwall. Either side of them were stowage carriages where sorted and sacked mail could be stored, station by station, to expedite rapid unloading at their destination. At either end of the train additional containerised post was being carried in the GUV vehicles. On an average trip 800 bags of mail are sorted and something like 100,000 items of

post processed: in other words, each of the twenty crew members manage to get through 5,000 items en route!

All this brought us in the blinking of an eye to Yatton where I stepped down on to the windy platform with Chris and Paul to exchange banter with the postmen from the airport. A Wales & West railwayman had kept a lonely vigil to see us through and give the EWS driver the 'right away'. There was something almost 'American' in atmosphere about this brief pause at this wayside halt - a feeling emphasised as the station attendant waved his lamp along the platform towards the distant driver and we leapt aboard. It could have been some remote depot on the old Norfolk & Western. I half expected O. Winston Link would be lurking in the undergrowth, preparing to flood the lineside with a battery of arc lights. Instead there was just me and my compact camera - a bit of an anticlimax really.

Back on the train we picked up speed. Next stop Exeter. Paul talked of past and present posties; the patterns of their unusual working lives. "This is the only run where the men work an out-and-back shift. All the others are split so that, for example, London men will spend a day in Swansea and Swansea men will spend a day in London. So they find themselves some digs. I spent half my life in Carlisle. I played all the local golf courses: Powfoot, Dumfries, Brampton. The scenery at Brampton is breathtaking. There's one tee so high that it doesn't matter if you scuff your drive, the ball still soars away in mid air. Other lads had allotments or got involved in the local community. One ran a boy's football team. It's like leading a double life."

"And a wife in every port," I joked.

"I wouldn't know about that," he protested with a wry smile as between men of the world. "But in lots of cases it's more a matter of getting to know each other better than we know our families, and there's a great sense of camaraderie, and consequently a low turnover in people."

We rocked and rolled through the night. I hadn't a clue where we were. I kept having to stand aside as one postie after another dragged a sack of sorted mail through to one or other of the stowage vans. Frankly, I was becoming mesmerised by all the activity. It was impossible to focus on the sorters' hands, they moved so rapidly between the rubber-banded bundles of post and the designated pigeon-holes which filled one side of each sorting carriage. To clear my head I went walkabout, amused to discover that one enterprising member of the crew was operating a self-service tuck shop, whilst, in one of the stowage vans, the latest results of the crew's individual Fantasy Football league positions were displayed. Each of the sorting carriages contained a hot water urn and a small oven for heating pies, pasties and burgers. Naively I asked if these were provided for breaktimes, much to the amusement of the sorters in earshot. "Chance would be a fine thing," snorted one in a ripe West Country burr.

Down in the Cornish carriage I was introduced to Robert James, whose father, George, had worked on the TPOs for forty years and subsequently been honoured by the naming of a carriage after him. "Trouble is," quipped Robert, "we never seem to see it down here!" Cue for Paul to explain that EWS operates the Royal Mail fleet in a nationwide pool, a fact reinforced by the remnants of chalked East Anglian place names here and there along the carriage walls. All the sorting and stowage vehicles currently in use are Mk I stock dating, in design terms at least, from the late 1950s, though the carriage I was in - No. 80363 - had been built at York in 1972. A new generation of TPOs is due to go on the drawing board. The Royal Mail have invested £150 million in a network served by some zippy, dual voltage electric multiple unit mail trains, but these are designed for containerised post, and there is still a very real need for sorting vehicles. The Health & Safety Executive has quoted a retirement deadline of 2004 for all Mk I rolling stock, so, given the inordinate amount of time it normally takes for a fresh design to travel from blueprint to reality, something will have to be done soon; possibly the conversion of redundant sleeper vehicles. Likewise, EWS is taking delivery of a new high speed diesel locomotive design to replace the ubiquitous but ageing Class 47s which haul the TPOs now.

Meanwhile the Mk Is soldier on like elderly relatives, whose incarceration in a nursing home keeps getting postponed. They look like missing links in the history of carriage design. The exterior of the sorting vehicles is distinguished by recesses that are throwbacks to the apparatus once used to collect and despatch mail bags whilst on the move. Paul had been an apparatus engineer in his time or, more colloquially, an 'iron man'. Northbound from Euston he recalled the pick-ups at Harrow, Watford, King's Langley, Hemel Hempsted, Leighton Buzzard and Bletchley. At these points the local mail for the north was hung invitingly on a lineside post. As the train approached the iron man inside would lower a collecting net which would snatch the bag into its clutches as the train shot by. Further north, there were dropping points at the likes of Lancaster, Carnforth, Oxenholme and Penrith. Paul showed me a photograph of him (without the white hair) manhandling a pouch of sorted mail on to an arm which he would swing out into the rushing darkness at the appropriate moment for it to be plucked into a waiting net and peddled away by some whistling postman into the surrounding fells. "We had to have five weeks solid training to get the knack of operating the apparatus," reminisced Paul, admitting that he was "petrified" at first. "The pouches weighed sixty pounds and there wasn't much margin for error. It was funny, we got to be good friends with postmen we had never seen, let alone talked to. We'd send each other notes, we'd become pen friends. Penrith was the last dropping point to operate. It outlasted all the others. I think it was in seventy-one. We'd had to keep it going for the local MP who liked to open his Parliamentary post over breakfast!"

We were held up by signals on the outskirts of Exeter. Paul reckoned it would be the Great Western TPO, which runs between Willesden (on the outskirts of London) and Plymouth, blocking our path. But we didn't linger for long, and a few minutes later we decanted ourselves on to Platform 1 at St David's station. It was half past two in the morning. Little red tractors were scurrying about yanking trucks and trolleys laden with post as the local men hurried to load consignments of mail for Cornwall flown into Exeter Airport. They also had to unload post destined both locally and, curiously enough, for Truro and district which arrives a crucial thirty minutes faster by road. Paul and I stretched our legs, admiring the station's art deco architecture, passing beneath the Dixon of Dock Green-like Transport Police's blue lamp, and peering into the Post Office's purpose-built transhipment depot, a hive of activity as they hurried to get all the contents of

"Paul had been an apparatus engineer in his time or, more colloquially, an 'iron man'."

Sorting in the Cornish carriage - only another eighty thousand items to go!

two trains loaded on to local road vehicles. I'd changed trains at St David's dozens of times but never seen it in its nightshirt before.

We got away from Exeter at quarter to three. In midsummer there might have been a hint of dawn about the sky, but this was January and it would be pitch black for hours yet. Back inside, the carriages were a fuggy mix of orange peel and beefburgers, but there was no sense of slackening off on what was, for the bulk of the team, the last lap down to Plymouth. On the contrary, everyone appeared to be working faster and faster to ensure that every last item of mail was sorted. Paul boasted that the travelling posties were 99.7% accurate in their sorting. "How does that compare with state of the art mechanised sorting equipment?" I wondered.

"Don't ask," he grinned. Just then, as if to prove the point, a sorter called Keith turned to show me an envelope wrongly postcoded PR. "It should read TR for Truro," he said, "a machine would send this to Preston! It just goes to show how important the right postcode is now."

Paul was called away for a moment, so I wandered into stowage van No. 80404 to do some thinking. In the subdued half light cast by low wattage naked bulbs it had the look of a submarine about it. Groups of sacks lay piled neatly, waiting to be unloaded at wayside stations as we worked our way down through The Duchy. I went into W.H.Auden mode: *letters for the rich, letters for the poor, the shop on the corner, and the girl next door.* It dawned on me, in a way I had not appreciated, let alone thought of before, how much our lives are shaped by the routine act of the morning's post landing on the mat, and how we all, to lesser or greater extents, consciously or unconsciously, divide the mail up into good and bad. Holiday confirmations, building society windfalls, amusing postcards, and letters from far-flung friends in one category; larger than expected bills, tax demands, interview failures and deaths in the family in the other. And the guys in the sorting carriages, either side of me, were significant and essential cogs in the machinery which seals our fate, for better or for worse.

To regain some equilibrium, I flattened my nose against one of the small head-high windows which ran along the carriage wall. At first all I could make out was a gloomy reflection of the interior behind me, so I did my best to cover the rest of the window with my hands. That was an improvement, but there was nothing to be seen apart from a line of distant lights. Then it occurred to me that we must be running along the banks of the Teign estuary, and that I was looking across an invisible mass of water towards Shaldon and Ringmore. Soon we were slowing round the curve into Newton Abbot and I had a fleeting mental picture of a much younger version of myself posing for my father's camera in front of one of the early Warship class diesel hydraulic locomotives once so indigenous to this part of the world.

My father never exactly shared my passion for railways, but he humoured extravagantly my enthusiasm, going out of his way on business trips to drop me for the day at busy railway centres like Banbury, Wolverhampton and Slough. I remember him quizzing the foreman at Newton Abbot diesel depot here as to the likely whereabouts of the locomotive carrying the last number I needed to complete the Warships. But in those far off, pre-computer days there was no readily available knowledge as to the location of D852 *Tenacious*.

Up and down the Devon banks we went - Dainton, Rattery and Hemerdon, difficult terrain for a railway even in the diesel age; no wonder they can get the first class post to Truro quicker by road. Back in the sorting carriage Chris Greenaway had produced a lap top and was busy tapping in data to provide an analytical summary of the run: actual times against schedule; staff attendance figures; volume of mail processed; technical hitches with the rolling stock; and so on and so forth. Now there was a genuine sense of journey's end. The Devon carriage had to be totally cleared. The labelling strips extracted from their channels beneath the pigeon holes, all the rubber bands and tags and labels and spare sacks stored away for the evening's northbound trip back to Bristol. The sixteen Plymouth-based sorters were coming to the end of their shift. A few hours sleep, a meal or two, and they would be back on the next evening's northbound postal.

Paul was due to leave me here, but before hurrying back to his hotel, he pointed out the London-Plymouth 'Great Western' TPO

Who said there was no time for a break? Robert James disproves the theory!

already empty and silent in one of the bay platforms designated specifically for Royal Mail use. He showed me how it was slightly higher than a passenger platform to enable trolleys to be wheeled easily on and off the vans. Then he disappeared into the night, taking with him the ephemeral sense of friendship one shares with a hitherto total stranger on a long journey.

Plymouth had memories to haunt me too: of my mother reduced to hysterics by the bucolic West Country tones of the station announcer with his Liskaards, Badmin Roads, Lastwithials and Saint Oarstulls; and of my boyhood trainspotting chum, Robert Lathbury, who somehow managed to get himself invited on to the footplate of *Blackmore Vale* at the head of 'The Brighton' while I obliviously munched my way through a Bowyer's pork pie at the platform end.

Interlude at Plymouth

We pulled out of Plymouth at quarter past four. There were just four posties on board now: Robert, Keith, Nigel and John. I looked over Keith's shoulder as he sorted the Off Islands mail for St Mary's, Tresco, St Martin's, Bryher and St Agnes which would continue by helicopter from Penzance. Rumbling over the Royal Albert Bridge, and getting up speed beyond Saltash, I struck up a conversation with Robert concerning the imminent clash of Penzance & Newlyn and Launceston at Rugby Union. Both teams were near the top of the league and Robert was anxious that Penzance should steal a march on their old rivals, who were currently three places above them. Robert gave me his dad's number to ring. "He'll be able to tell you all about the old days!"

George James began work as a telegram boy in 1942. After a spell in National Service he joined the travelling posties in 1948. For the next forty-four years he worked on the Penzance-Bristol postal, clocking up an amazing 2,311,272 miles. "I loved every minute of the job, boy," he told me over the telephone. "We worked double shifts, three days a week. The Post Office worked every day of the year except Boxing Day. We had a Salvation Army man in our team called Clifford, who played the cornet beautifully. On Christmas Eve all the boys from South Wales, Birmingham and London would join us in singing *Silent Night* on Temple Meads with Clifford playing his instrument. On New Year's Eve we'd be passing through Bridgwater at midnight. We'd take a bottle of whisky out, line up the glasses along the sorting frame, wish ourselves a happy New Year, then get back to work." Up until the early Sixties George's TPOs would have been steam hauled. "We used to change locomotives at Newton Abbot. Course we couldn't see who was driving, boy, but we'd know by the speed we were going. There was one bloke who'd leave Newton like a bat out of hell. When we got out at Penzance he'd be frying up his breakfast on the shovel in the fire box." There was only one apparatus in Cornwall, at Liskeard. "You counted nineteen beats of the wheel across the viaduct then put the net out. One night we had a supervisor with us. The Liskeard boys had got wind of this and hung out a turnip shaped like a human head. The net scooped it up and it rolled on to the carriage floor. The supervisor went white, turned to us and said: ' Oh God lads, I

Northbound Cornish Postal catches the last of the sunlight on St Germans Viaduct

think we've topped someone.' On the way back we hung out a bunch of flowers with the pouch and a note asking the Liskeard boys to 'put them on the poor soul's grave'."

First stop in Cornwall was Bodmin Parkway. I gave Keith a hand to unload sacks labelled for the likes of Padstow and Tintagel. A postman appeared out of the shadows, some brief badinage, and we were gone. The old Great Western branchline to Bodmin has been preserved and re-opened as a steam railway. Unlike most tourist lines, however, this one carries goods again, in the shape of light fittings for a local company called Fitzgerald. Twice a week the Bodmin & Wenford line shunts some covered wagons into the exchange siding at Bodmin Parkway to be collected by an EWS engine. The wagons are worked north on an Enterprise service to Fitzgerald depots at Birmingham, Warrington or Leith. Former EWS supremo Ed Burkhardt was greatly encouraged by this sort of collaboration between private 'short lines' and the main network.

Down the luxuriantly wooded Fowey Valley we went, past Restormel Castle, invisible to us in the racing darkness, and on to Lostwithiel from where a branch line, busy with china clay trains operated by EWS, hugs the river's west bank down to the port of Fowey. The main line, however, heads inland through Treverrin Tunnel to Par, where I was due to leave the posties and join the driver. I spent the last few minutes trying to fix a mental picture of the still busy scene inside the Cornish sorting carriage. I'd been intrigued by the romantic names displayed on the pigeon holes: Mousehole, Long Rock, Nancledra and Prussia Cove. I'd even wondered what part of Cornwall Missorts was in until the penny dropped. Watching the posties incredibly rapid sorting technique for the last time they reminded me of experienced touch typists - though possibly not as pretty - who had no need to read the keyboard. These guys barely looked at the pigeon-holes, seeming to know instinctively where each place name was. Perhaps the most unique facet of the Penzance TPO is that the mail is sifted and sorted down to individual walking postmen's beats.

We pulled into Par - not to unload post but to change drivers. I was changing too, from the carriages to the cab. I hurried up to the end of the platform where Rail Services Manager, Huw

Mike Smith

Philips, was waiting for me. There wasn't time for pleasantries. We bundled into '727 and set off for St Austell. Now we were in the heart of china clay country. Huw pointed out the sidings at Par Harbour. I glimpsed a clutter of warehouses and the floodlit prow of a coaster before we were swallowed up into the night.

Driver Mike Smith was beginning his shift. He would take the TPO to Penzance and return with the empty stock to St Blazey for stabling and routine maintenance. Then he was rostered to drive two light Rail express systems locomotives up to Plymouth for the evening's two mail trains to London; one purely a van train, the other the Great Western TPO. He would return from Plymouth 'on the cushions', as generations of railwaymen have described a trip back by passenger train with their feet up. Huw was Mike's boss, but they seemed on companionable terms. After a brief pause to unload more sacks at St Austell, we were off again, past the clay dries at Burngullow and on to a section of line myopically singled some years back. Late-running can be exacerbated by this bottleneck and Huw hopes that Railtrack might consider re-doubling the route in the not too distant future. One is always hearing horror stories in the railway media about Railtrack's recalcitrance, but at the sharp end railwaymen seem to recognise a common purpose, and Huw readily acknowledged several recent examples of worthwhile collaboration between Railtrack and EWS.

As the main line singles, the goods branch to Drinnick, Kernick and Parkandillack curves away into a moonscape of china clay workings, the lifeblood of EWS's Cornish business. Huw was bullish about the year just ended, traffic figures being up a significant 10%. He recommended I should call a certain Sue Sargent of English China Clays with the confidence of a child knowing that things would go well on parent's evening.

"Huw? - oh yes, he's brilliant," came a West Country giggle from the other end of the phone.

"So he warned you I might ring!" I teased, and was treated to a reprise of that infectious laugh. Sue, it transpired, edits ECCs house journal and wanted to pinch the title of this book to caption a photograph featuring the first run of a new Class 66 on a clay train down to Fowey. In return for the favour she put me in touch with Derrick Yeo, ECCs logistics expert, who was able to tell me something of the shipping patterns from Par and Fowey. Par is the smaller of the two ports and access to its quay is restricted by tides. Maximum tonnage here is around the three thousand mark and regular traffic flows include Spain, Portugal and Greece where the china clay is used in the ceramics trade. Fowey is a deep water port and regularly loads vessels of up to 12,000 tonnes capacity. The Great Western Railway developed Fowey as a port; and, perhaps not surprisingly, given the close links between the railway and shipping, Huw represents EWS interests on the Board of Harbour Commissioners. Scandinavia features strongly in destination terms from here, most of the clay to Finland, Sweden and Norway being destined for paper making. EWS also handles much of ECCs land-based transport, the flow to Irvine in Scotland even features in the *Guinness Book of Records* as the UK's longest regular freight haulage by rail. Other long distance rail workings include Cliffe Vale in the Potteries and Italy via the Channel Tunnel.

I was just asking Huw and Mike if we'd pass any oncoming trains when the rails round the curve in front of us suddenly gleamed in a beam of light and the 'up' *Golden Hind* ricocheted by. A lengthy, lofty viaduct carried us into Truro past the floodlit cathedral. "I only recently discovered that it wasn't finished until 1910," said Huw, a third generation railwayman of Welsh stock, but whose childhood roots are in Duffield, Derbyshire. Both of these men, raised in the North, relish the lifestyle in England's big toe. Huw even keeps a sailing dinghy, though, being 'on call' three days a week, bemoans that he has little time to use it.

Truro is another unloading point for the postal train. Huw and I got down on to the platform for a moment or two, saying a quick hello to Lee Woodall, an EWS employee who was travelling with us in the loco's rear cab to attend to shunting movements and to give the 'right away' after station stops. I hadn't stood on Truro platform in thirty years. Last time I'd been here - exploring Cornish branch lines - the main line trains were hauled by diesel hydraulic motive power.

Three decades may have elapsed, but I still remembered the deep curving cutting south of the station which leads to the

China clay country I - near St Austell

Falmouth branch junction. We were exchanging the land of china clay for the land of tin. Tin is largely talked of in the past tense in Cornwall now, but the week before my trip, apparently, one of the old mines had optimistically been re-opened. Huw would be keeping an eye on it as potential traffic. Already, in the relatively short lifetime of EWS, he and his team had attracted several new commodities to rail: oil rig chains, seaweed, seed potatoes, and even orange juice.

Later, attempting to make some gist of my notes at home, I remembered that one of Cornwall's busiest, albeit seasonal, rail-based traffic flows had been the carriage of broccoli. Writing in *Trains Annual 1966*, R.C.Riley had outlined the arrangements for carrying this perishable cargo and gone on to describe a journey from Penzance to York aboard a 'Grange' class locomotive hauling thirty-two wagons of the dark green stuff. On March 15th 1960, no less than seven special broccoli trains were despatched from Penzance and Marazion to London, South Wales, the Midlands and the North. What EWS wouldn't give for those sort of tonnages

now; what Cornish growers wouldn't give for them!

It is a steep 1 in 80 climb most of the way from Truro to Redruth, but our Class 47 seemed to have the measure of its load. The talk, as usual, got round to motive power. Mike had just had a run up to Okehampton and Meldon with the first Class 66 to reach St Blazey for crew training. In common with drivers I'd met 'up north' he was reserving judgement, finding it peculiarly different that the throttle worked in the opposite direction, needing to be pushed away from you to increase power. On paper it reads like a small alteration, but imagine how your feet would cope if the accelerator and clutch pedals were swapped in your car! Being originally from Doncaster, Mike was a big Deltic fan and had enjoyed a nostalgic drive on *Royal Scots Grey* when it was down in Cornwall on a railtour. Personally I was quietly thrilled just to be in a Forty-seven. Back in my spotting days we knew them as

China clay country II - loaded china clay hoppers head past Golant on their way to Fowey

ades

Brush Fours. My first encounter with one is etched in my memory. It was stabled beyond the coaling plant at York, and in those days I was barely tall enough to see over the palings of the fence on Leeman Road. But the sight of this new design, resplendent in two-tone green, with a yellow face and a red bufferbeam, subliminally and erotically reminiscent of a well-lipsticked mouth, took my breath away. It was love at first sight, and because five hundred and twelve of them were built, there was a lot of scope for love-making. By the time I hung up my spotting book I was just seventeen short of the set. If only I'd been as numerically successful with girls.

At Gwinear Road Mike pointed out the former junction of the branch to Helston which the local authority is considering re-opening. Gwinear Road reminded me of Quiller-Couch's amusing short story, *Pipes in Arcady,* which relates the strange sequence of events leading up to the point when the story's narrator passes in a local train and catches a glimpse of eight naked men watching a gang of platelayers waltzing to the strains of a flute and concertina in a lineside meadow. I will not spoil the story for you by expanding on the complex plot here.

Our last booked stop before Penzance was due to be at Hayle. Huw told me the story of a little girl who habitually stood on Hayle station and waved to the drivers of the northbound postal. Somehow or other he had got to hear of her impending tenth birthday. On the evening in question she was astonished to be beckoned over to the locomotive and invited to ride up the line with them. Nice touch, EWS, nice touch! Apparently the posties are a tad particular as to the exact pulling up point of the TPO at each station. The drivers try to memorise marker points in order to get as close to the preferred point as possible. Mike was having difficulty remembering where to stop at Hayle. Innocently enough I asked him when he last drove the TPO. "Err, yesterday," he joked. At least I think he was joking. In the end he stopped with the front of the locomotive parallel to a 45 mph speed marker and got the thumbs up from the postmen back down the platform who'd reversed their van almost up to the carriage doors. All part of the service!

Accelerating out of Hayle on the last lap, we crossed the River Hayle and saw the lights of Lelant reflected in glassy pools abandoned by the ebb tide on the saltings. The St Ives branch hugs the coastline here through Carbis Bay to its seaside terminus, but it's a long time since the *Cornish Riviera Express* ran a through coach to the picturesque fishing port, resort and artistic community.

In daylight the run past Long Rock and the view of St Michael's Mount would have been intoxicating. In darkness the most imposing view was the High Speed Train servicing depot and Sainsbury's. But Penzance station appeared unaltered by time. We were signalled into the platform nearest the sea wall and braked smoothly to a halt by a lump of granite bearing the inscription: PENSANS A'GAS DYNERGH, which I presumed must be Cornish for: "Penzance Welcomes Careful Engine Drivers". We were pleased to see that, being a few minutes early, we'd beaten the collecting post office vans to it. Mike was more laconic: "They'll be fining us for getting here *before* them!" Soon, though, a couple of postal vans roared on to the platform in a cloud of dust, like something out of the Keystone Cops.

Mike and Lee shunted the carriages out of the platform and ran round them, waiting to follow a sequence of passenger train departures back up the main line to St Blazey. Huw twisted my arm in a vicelike grip to join him at a neighbouring 'greasy spoon' for a bacon butty. In its warm fug I experienced the pleasurably guilty feeling of truancy. Back home my wife would have to make her own cup of tea to drink in bed; my daughter would have to chase herself to be dressed in time for the school bus; and my son would have to talk incessantly about football to anyone else prepared to listen in place of me. Here I was, 'seeing life', or at least what passes for it in Penzance at six in the morning.

I'd had a 'great night out'. Not in the way most people would think of amusing themselves, but more enlightening, perhaps, than a night on the tiles. And at least now I have a foolproof method of getting back to sleep if I've woken in the small hours worrying about my bank balance. I don't count sheep, I try to remember all those Cornish names on the pigeon-holes of the sorting carriages: Camborne, Helston, Perranporth, St Agnes ...

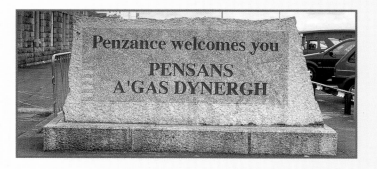

trans-pennine trash

IN a previous existence, Paul Bayman's Grade II listed office was part of Peak Forest station on the Midland Railway's long defunct direct line between Derby and Manchester. At eight o'clock on a January morning a pale imitation of daylight seeped half-heartedly through the Gothic trefoil window. Outside, across the rimy tracks, a pub called "The Midland", some quarry workers' cottages, and what was once the village school clung tenaciously to the grey hillside. Paul is Traffic & Train Crew Manager at Peak Forest, and he had organised my passage on the Bredbury to Roxby Gullet 'binliner'.

Not a lot of Mancunians know, let alone care, that a sizeable percentage of their household waste is taken by train across the Pennines and buried in a big hole on the outskirts of Scunthorpe. Were I a script-writer for a second-rate comedian, I might score cheap gibes at Scunthorpe's readiness to handle Manchester's detritus. In fact, it's an arrangement which suits everyone involved. Greater Manchester gets rid of rubbish not easily disposed of locally; UK Waste, who handle matters at the Roxby end, make a 'tidy' profit; Scunthorpe gets an old iron ore mine filled in; and EWS finds itself with a lucrative traffic flow.

Proffered coffee, I pleaded for half a cup, not yet having attained the average engineman's level of bladder control. Jim Eccles, the Standards Inspector from Warrington who'd drawn the short straw of accompanying me, had scurried off to find our

Scunthorpe Skyline - the Bredbury-Roxby Gullet 'binliner' nears its destination.

locomotive, so Paul gave me a quick summary of Peak Forest's background and activities. How it had devolved from British Rail's Buxton depot, being more handily located for the area's quarry workings. That it has forty-six drivers and eight shunters on its staff roster, and prepares around eight locomotives a day; mostly for the hectic aggregates traffic, but also for cement from Hope, limestone from Tunstead to Northwich for ICI, and, of course, Manchester's waste trains. Paul's own railway career had commenced at Buxton in 1970 as a 'number taker'. This had nothing to do with trainspotting. On the contrary, it was a very necessary chore in those pre-computerised days; Paul's task being to wander around Buxton's then numerous goods yards recording details of each and every wagon in sight. Desk-bound now, with a computer monitor replacing sheaves of handwritten numbers, Paul seemed nevertheless at ease with his work and bullish about the benefits of privatisation. "You were embarrassed to say you worked for British Rail," he remembered.

A thrumming noise outside led me to the window. Below, alongside what is left of the old platform, stood our locomotive, a Class 60 called *Samuel Johnson* - I looked forward to the company of such a witty and erudite fellow traveller. Jim and I hurried downstairs and got aboard. 60062 was still in Transrail grey, the livery of one of three shadow franchises which rose out of the ashes of British Rail prior to full privatisation. It is a dowdy colour scheme at best, inferior to the dark blue of Mainline and the bold orange and black of Loadhaul, the other two shadow franchises, and certainly second best to EWS's 'sexy' maroon and old gold.

Paul had promised me the company of a senior driver with "lots of historical knowledge," so I guess I did a double take when a shaven-headed, thirty-something bounded into the cab. I began to think that the Peak District air must contain astonishing powers for delaying the ageing process, or that English Welsh & Scottish had initiated a programme of hormone replacement therapy to coincide with the issue of its trendy new uniforms. It transpired, somewhat anti-climactically, that there had been a last minute change of roster, and that this 'youngster' with a Lothian accent was Colin Campbell, who'd cut his teeth at Edinburgh's Haymarket depot, gone to Millerhill, Sunderland and North Blyth,

Paul Bayman at Peak Forest.

then come south "to find work" when the latter bit the dust. Not that he missed the north - save perhaps for Hibs home matches - and found The Peak: "A great place to walk the dog and bring up the kids."

Ideally, I would be making all these cab rides twice. Once with what the Irish would call *the craic,* once in total silence; for I was finding it incredibly difficult to listen to and to watch simultaneously. So we were through the one and three quarters miles of Dove Holes Tunnel, through several precipitously rocky cuttings, and on to the curving viaducts at Chinley before I had time to take stock of my surroundings. I'd been on 60s before, on the Settle & Carlisle coal run. They are immensely comfortable engines; wind and soundproofed; and one gets a terrific view ahead through the two large, almost square, front windscreen windows. All the drivers I've met swear by them. Like most classes, they had their teething troubles when introduced in the late Eighties, but alterations to their computer software seem to have eradicated these, and EWS regards the hundred members of this British-built design as front rank motive power

Jim Eccles, Colin Campbell and *Samuel Johnson*

"Drivers, it seems, share the enthusiast fraternity's predilection for motive power that is distinguishable from rolling stock."

for their heaviest trains.

We waved to Chinley's signalman and continued, light engine, on the old Great Central & Midland Joint through New Mills Central, Marple and Romiley to Woodley. This is a line I know quite well. In the early Seventies I would travel home from Manchester Polytechnic to Derby on Friday afternoons in Peak-hauled, steam-heated compartment stock which oozed hot vapours from fractured pipes like Icelandic geysers. Or, if we'd been let out from letterpress early, on the Harwich Boat Train in a Gresley buffet which must have been one of the last wooden-bodied carriages still earning its keep for British Rail.

At New Mills Jim pointed out the mouth of the old tunnel which formed the egress of the branch line out to Hayfield. One of the antiquated Metropolitan Cammell diesel multiple units, which still trundle - like Teddy Boys who've never grown out of their drainpipes and winkle-pickers - around Manchester for First North Western, passed us on its way over to Sheffield via the big tunnels and moorland vistas of the Hope Valley line. I think of them as 101s, but to Jim they will always be 'blue squares' on account of the old colour-coded coupling systems. The more I thought about it, the more I figured Jim was on HRT himself. Setting up the ride by telephone, he'd sounded like a man looking sixty in the face. In the flesh he looked a decade younger. I was flabbergasted to hear he had started on the railway in 1955. "I began as a knocker-up at Springs Branch, Wigan. The gaffer'd send me round to drivers' and firemen's houses to tell them when to sign on. Then I became a cleaner - ashes out of the smokebox, lots of elbow grease, that sort of thing. I helped the fitters too and learnt my way around the locomotives. I did a few years of firing then passed out as a driver in 1964. I had three or four years with steam up until the end."

That morning the six o'clock weather forecast had spoken optimistically of sunshine followed by rain in the afternoon. In reality, the weather was running, like many an EWS goods train, a tad early, and Greater Manchester was already looking characteristically murky. The morning rush-hour's last commuters watched us impassively from Spartan suburban platforms. We encountered more archaic multiple units, one with a lady driver. I asked Colin if he was glad to be 'divorced' from passenger

trains, and in as much as it meant he could continue to drive locomotives, as opposed to Sprinters and Pacers, his reply was affirmative. Drivers, it seems, share the enthusiast fraternity's predilection for motive power that is distinguishable from rolling stock.

We clattered over Marple Wharf Junction and glimpsed the Rose Hill branch curving steeply and enigmatically away into the woods. Then, momentarily, it seemed as though we were in mid air, as a high viaduct carried us over a steeply wooded valley with the River Goyt far below. Alongside, at a slightly lower level, a canal aqueduct spanned the same chasm. Both Jim and Colin, keen walkers, knew the geography of the local canal network, but having spent the last twenty years researching and writing about inland waterways, and consequently having become a bit blase about them, I was loathe to get drawn into any conversation regarding their finer points. "You'll see plenty of canals on this journey," smiled Colin, and I replied with an equivocal: "Yes, I know!" Jim chipped in with some propaganda about his local Sankey Canal, and how well it had been smartened up, and how nice it was to walk along now. And so as not to appear churlish I made some propitiatory noises about the benefits of canal regeneration, their recreational value, and their economic contribution to regional tourism and trade.

If the truth were known, I had become slightly intoxicated by the power of rail over water. The canals had been abandoned as serious freight movers because they lacked the inherent puissance to compete, or at least in their 18th century, narrow gauge, unimproved guise they did. I suppose that, high up in my cab, in my high-visibility vest, waving regally at trackworkers, I was experiencing the same sensations as Toad of Toad Hall when his horse-drawn caravan was swept aside by a 'magnificent, immense, breath-snatching' motor car. "Oh what a flowery *track* lies before me, henceforth," Kenneth Grahame's words; my italics.

So I was glad when the talk reverted to railways as we reached Woodley, where we would reverse off the main line onto the branch leading to the refuse loading point. We had to swap cabs to reverse, and it was easier to get down on to 'The Cess' and to clomp along the ballast than negotiate the ear-splitting confines of the engine room. Ensconced in the other end, we waited for the signal to change to yellow. The indicator showed a B, denoting that we were routed on to the branch. Branch! Once this had been the Cheshire Lines Committee's strategically important Manchester avoiding line, carrying Trans-Pennine expresses from Hull to Liverpool via Stockport's Tiviot Dale station. Jim could remember it as a busy goods route. Not so much a branch now, it's more a twig serving two terminals: a Tilcon aggregates depot; and our own destination, GMW's Bredbury refuse works.

Colin drove *Samuel Johnson* cautiously over indifferent track. Gingerly, we approached a hand-operated point dividing the direct Tilcon line from the spur into the refuse works. Although the point appeared to be in our favour, Colin brought the locomotive to a halt and Jim leapt out and gave the blades a good kick. "The kids round here wedge stones between the blades," explained Colin. "If Jim wasn't here I'd have to get out myself and check that the blade was home. A derailment could cost EWS thousands." It seemed immensely sad that children, who would once have come to watch the trains with a mixture of pride and envy, now come just to trespass and vandalise. Colin, it transpired, had been 'bricked' recently. In other words, tomorrow's citizens had flung a brick through the cab window from an overbridge. "I had a sliver of glass stuck in my eyeball for two days," winced Colin.

The rails were slippery. "Sun's not out yet," said Jim. "Don't get sun round here," quipped Colin. At the entrance to the refuse depot there was another point to kick. There in front of us stood a long line of bogie flats bearing yellow containers. Colin tapped out a sequence of numbers on his mobile and telephoned to check the whereabouts of the mobile shunter. "Hello Ken, Colin here, where's the tapper?" Then he rang control at Doncaster to tell them we'd arrived, so that they could fax our 'papers' through to the refuse depot office. "The shunter - sorry, Rolling Stock Technician - is driving over from Guide Bridge," said Colin. So we got out to stretch our limbs and get a bit of fresh air before the journey ahead. Colin expanded on the day ahead of him. "I signed on at 08.09 and I'm due to finish at 18.55. I'll drive the loaded 'binliner' as far as Healey Mills near Wakefield and come back with a train of empty waste containers for GMW's Northenden depot. Then I'll go to the cement works at Hope to shunt as required." Peak Forest's drivers work a wide variety of routes,

driving as far as Crewe, Leeds, Birmingham and Bletchley on a daily basis. "Tomorrow I'm off to Warrington for some Class 66 training," he added.

Belying the advance of privatisation, the shunter rolled up in a yellow van bearing the legend 'British Rail'. I learnt that his name was Abdul Hannan as I accompanied him from wagon to wagon conducting the brake test. Then we drove down to the other end of the train to place the tail lamp on the rear vehicle. A veteran of twenty-six years on the railway, his job involves driving all over the Manchester area: Bredbury, Northenden, Glazebrook, the Airport, Stalybridge, Hope Street, Castleton and Trafford Park; wherever a train needs coupling or uncoupling, Abdul's your man. On the day of my trip, however, he was a man with a problem. Despite Colin's call, the consist hadn't been faxed and it looked as though we were going to miss our booked departure.

The refuse depot is massive and had a surreal, sci-fi sort of feel to it. Sitting in the van while Abdul went to the office, I was suddenly taken with the thought that Sigourney Weaver might materialise out of the shadows in a remake of *Alien*. But it was Abdul who appeared round the back of a dustcart, waving the papers like Neville Chamberlain returning from Munich. He thrust them at me and I flicked through them: a clearance to proceed certificate from GMW; a Railtrack 'routing sheet' with notices regarding width restrictions affecting our 8ft 6ins containers; and EWS's consist which had finally come through. Abdul drove off in search of more wagons to shunt. Feeling like a team player, I swaggered back to the locomotive.

We left at 09.57, seventeen minutes adrift. Colin telephoned Romiley signal box to get permission to join the main line. We were train number 6E06 and we were hauling sixteen wagons, each laden with three containers, totalling 446 tonnes. Jim evinced surprise at the comparative lightness of our load, but then we remembered that the compacted refuse we were carrying would be relatively lightweight compared to most commodities in the ever expanding EWS portfolio.

Jim was miffed, largely on Colin's behalf, I sensed, about the delay. He phoned Paul, back at Peak Forest, to ensure there were

Abdul Hannan -
Rolling Stock Technician

"But it was Abdul who appeared round the back of the dustcart, waving the papers like Neville Chamberlain returning from Munich."

GMW refuse container, Frodingham

no recriminations when the time sheets came to be analysed. Colin was due an hour's scheduled stopover at Healey Mills, including a thirty minute 'facility' break for attending to calls of nature and for eating his 'snap', so he didn't think his return roster would be delayed, but he reckoned we might have lost our 'path', and his pessimism was to prove well founded. At Hyde North a red signal forced us to kick our heels while a Hadfield electric went by on its way into Manchester. In the enforced interlude, Jim and Colin discussed EWS's defensive driving initiative. In effect, Jim was working his passage, quietly assessing Colin's performance as we went along.

A decent interval behind the electric, we 'got the road', and powerfully pulled away on to what had been the Eastern Region's showpiece 1,500 volts electrified main line between Sheffield and Manchester, opened with a flourish in the Fifties. Metaphorically, but unashamedly, we wept nostalgic tears for the Promethean Bo-Bo and Co-Co locomotives designed to haul its heavy goods and express passenger trains respectively. Jim had encountered them whilst working goods trains into Dewsnap Sidings from the Warrington area in his driving days. Colin had had to make do with encountering the sole surviving Bo-Bo in the National Railway Museum. How rapidly railway history moves on. Because the voltage used was non-standard, British Rail abandoned the line in the early Eighties, and now the route beyond Hadfield's outer suburban terminus has become a public footpath and cycleway, though from time to time groups campaign for its re-opening as a railway. From my strictly amateur perspective, I admired that dramatic line through Woodhead as much as anyone. Its last regular passenger workings ceased in 1970. With pent up emotion, I'd journeyed sentimentally from Sheffield Victoria to Manchester Piccadilly and back to savour the line for last time. I was so sad - and I'll leave it to the sympathies of each reader to decide on the intended emphasis - that, as soon as I alighted back at Sheffield, I got on the next westbound train and repeated the return journey immediately.

Jim was crestfallen to see Dewsnap Sidings eradicated and replaced by housing and business units. It must be galling for railwaymen to revisit once vibrant installations reduced to wasteground or redeveloped for non-railway use, a bit like returning

to fields where you played as a child only to find that they have been *modernised* into a motorway. We came to Guide Bridge, where several rail infrastructure companies make use of a 'virtual quarry' supplied with Penmaenmawr ballast by EWS. From a cursory glance at the Ordnance Survey map I had assumed we would branch off here in the direction of Stalybridge, not much more than two miles away. Frustratingly, however, track rationalisation had rendered this route inaccessible. So off we plodded on a peregrination of Manchester's somewhat unsavoury eastern periphery; adding perhaps a dozen unnecessary miles to our itinerary.

Down through Fairfield and Gorton we went, encountering a procession of oncoming diesel and electric units sporting a variety of post privatisation colour schemes. No one can argue that the railway isn't a brighter place than in the insipid days of British Rail's 'corporate image', when, to paraphrase Chelsea's 1970 FA Cup song, blue was the colour, boredom was the game. Another red light at Gorton served to emphasise our late running status. Presently the point blades moved and the route indicator, or 'feather' in railwaymen's vernacular, allowed us access via the down goods loop to the Ardwick Branch. Briefly, in the Eighties, a few passenger services ran this way on a circuitous route between the East Midlands and the North West, largely as a sop, it was claimed, to appease protests at the running down of the Settle & Carlisle. Personally I relished such mystery tours of a part of Manchester generally perceived as being 'beyond the pale', having always preferred the steak and kidney pudding architecture and ambience of Victoria station to Piccadilly's green salad. Now the line is purely for freight, and we proceeded carefully over the jointed, twenty miles an hour, speed-restricted track. Rubbish lined the rails. More, it seemed, than we were legitimately carrying. "Sofas, cookers, cars - you get them all along here," sighed Colin, prompting Jim into a tale of a journey down this line when he'd had to telephone the signalman and report a burning car by the track. "What's odd about that, then?" had come the reply. Not to be outdone, I told them how holidaymakers on the Cheshire Ring canal route were regularly given a police escort along the Ashton Canal through Droylsden.

Resignalling had seen the semaphores at Philips Park replaced by fibre-optic-operated colour lights. Colin rolled his train carefully round the curve to Baguley Fold Junction where another red light barred our way. This time Colin got down on to the ballast and used the telephone on the signal post to ask the nearby 'box when we would be allowed on to the main line. I glanced at my watch - it was ten-forty. Colin returned to the cab. "We won't get away from here before eleven," he said with raised eyebrows. We waited patiently as Pacers clattered by in both directions. "Toy trains, nodding donkeys," said Jim gloomily. "I couldn't handle that." Colin nodded his agreement. All of which launched Jim into a 'changes I've seen' diatribe. Listening to him, I didn't for a moment doubt the authenticity of his experience. It seemed as though the whole of his railway life had been one long reorganisation after another: the phasing out of steam; the Beeching Report; Serpel; sectorisation; and privatisation.

Shortly after eleven we got the go-ahead and moved out on to what had once been the London & North Western Railway's main line across the Pennines via Standedge Tunnel. We had the River Medlock for company now and one or two boggy fields grazed by shaggy ponies. "We're coming up to 'Hanging Dog Crossing'," said Jim. "Least that's what railwaymen call it, it's actually Clayton Moor. Just after they'd replaced the old swinging gates with lifting barriers this old chap comes along, walking the dog, stops to light his pipe and hooks his dog's lead on to the barrier. When the train's gone past ..."

We were still laughing when we came to the junctions at Ashton Moss and roared through Ashton-under-Lyne's island-platformed station. Beyond it Colin reduced speed to pass our containers safely through Katherine Street Tunnel. "It's got a bit of a bevel in it," he explained. We continued through a Lowryesque landscape of back-to-back terrace houses and gaunt textile mills. Then yet another red light stopped us just short of Stalybridge station. All Colin's doubts regarding our pathing had come home to roost. We'd spent the best part of an hour trundling round from Guide Bridge, barely two miles away from where we now stood. Colin went to 'phone the signalman again, but this time the telephone was out of order, so he returned to the cab, consulted a thick directory of Railtrack telephone numbers, and rang through on his mobile. Of course we were waiting for another passenger

Stalybridge Station Buffet.

train to clear the line. They average four trains an hour through Standedge now, which doesn't leave much capacity for freight. Such is the volume of Trans-Pennine traffic entering the new Millennium, that Railtrack has included the route in its Network Management Statement for a fifty million pound upgrade, subject to outside investment from interested parties. Meanwhile, separated from their former colleagues in the passenger sector, Jim and Colin reflect EWS's corporate frustration that lightly-loaded, off-peak railcars benefit from historical priority over freight trains carrying far more profitable payloads.

Eventually we rumbled down into Stalybridge past a siding of turquoise coloured tanker wagons carrying, as Jim put it: "Something very dangerous!" But it wasn't tank*ers* of gas so much as tank*ards* of beer which occupied our minds as we passed the famous "Station Buffet", a mecca for serious beer drinkers. I thought fondly of two foaming pints of Moorhouse

"We'd spent the best part of an hour trundling round from Guide Bridge, barely two miles away from where we now stood."

"Now in competition no longer with the canal, but with the M62, the railway's advantage is not to be measured so much in terms of time as in its negligible effect on the environment."

Bitter from Burnley shared here with Jackie, my wife, on a jaunt in the early Eighties, and the pie and black peas which it so agreeably washed down. Jim had sampled the buffet's idiosyncratic delights as well, and we all expressed regret that we hadn't been stopped alongside the platform instead of half a mile outside the station. "Only for the pies, though," insisted Jim, towing the company's strict no alcohol line.

Emitting a steady throb, like an irritated blood vessel, *Samuel Johnson* entered Stalybridge Tunnel, 668 yards long; followed by Scout Tunnel, a baby at only 202 yards. We were in the foothills of the Pennines now, climbing a gradient of 1 in 125, and travelling due north through the Tame Valley. Colin was enthusing over the scenery; somehow I couldn't see lorry drivers being so poetical. "This is a great bit of railway. On frosty days with crisp sunshine the air is unbelievable." Unfortunately, I could only take his word for it, because cloud had come down and the spire of Woodend church, above Mossley, was in a meeting with the angels. Colour light signalling was being put in. Little knots of dayglo orange engineers came and went out of the mist with rueful waves. They were replacing semaphores which would have been raised and lowered over the smoke trails of Black Fives and Jubilees. Jim told me to look out for Greenfield Junction box, an authentic LNWR signal cabin of timber construction. Presently it loomed out of the murk and I had time to see that it still sported a London Midland red enamel name plate. Pessimistically we reckoned that the new signalling would hurry the box's closure and, doubtless, the sign would soon function ornamentally over someone's fireplace.

A high viaduct on a curve took us over the Huddersfield Canal which is being re-opened with Millennium monies. Ironically enough, it was abandoned by the LMS Railway in 1944. The last recorded passage across the summit was a party led by the canal campaigners Robert Aickman and Tom Rolt four years later! It took them five days to cover the twenty miles and seventy-four locks, not least because the canal was by then virtually derelict. Even so, when restored, the new generation of pleasure boaters drawn to sample what will be, by definition, an energy-sapping journey, will do well to accomplish through passage under three days, statistics which serve to emphasise the impact the 19th century railway must have had on Trans-Pennine transport. Now in competition no longer with the canal, but with the M62, the railway's advantage is not to be measured so much in terms of time as in its negligible effect on the environment.

The western end of Standedge Tunnel lies at Diggle about 650 feet above sea level; high, but not that high, given that the surrounding moorlands ride the horizon at 1,500 feet and beyond. It's grim up here, as they're forever reminding themselves, and anyone who has ever trudged the Pennine Way will tell you that these black and boggy moorlands represent the nadir of that particular journey. Jim had walked it twice: once rapidly as a youth; the second time, more measuredly, to mark his fiftieth birthday. But it is as a railwayman that he knows Standedge best. Cocooned in our Class 60 cab, the 3 mile, 66 yard tunnel was still awesome, yet imagine it in the days of steam. I was intrigued by the presence of a distant signal two-thirds of the way through. A colour light now, of course, but Jim had heard old drivers talk of it being a semaphore with a 'clapper' attached so that it could be heard when rendered invisible by swirling smoke and steam. At 45mph, it took us about four minutes to negotiate the darkness. There are, in fact, *four* Standedge tunnels: the canal, dating from 1811; the original single track railway bore of 1849; a second single track built in 1871 to augment the first; and the one in use now, built in 1894 to double track dimensions. Curiously, the railway tunnels were linked by side galleries, or adits, to the canal bore, causing smoke to issue eerily from the canal portals.

Once, all of Standedge lay in the West Riding. Nowadays eastbound trains go into the tunnel in Greater Manchester and emerge in West Yorkshire. Robert Aickman, a writer of ghost stories when he wasn't campaigning for the retention of the post-war waterways, was much taken with a tale told to him by a porter at Diggle about a girl who would wave to engine drivers from the upstairs window of a lonely moorland house near Marsden. The extraordinary thing was that the tradition of waving to this girl continued from generation to generation before it became known that it wasn't a girl at all, but a demented old woman. Aickman was inspired to pen *The Trains*, one of the most chilling of all railway stories of the supernatural.

Samuel Johnson coasted all the way down the Colne Valley

Returning empties at Slaithwaite

Healey Mills

on a ruling gradient of 1 in 105. The landscape was fundamentally Pennine, a gory collision between nature and industry. Temperamentally, I'm beguiled by such antagonisms and juxtapositions in land use. Numerous railway photographers apparently share my enthusiasm, for this has always been a well chronicled stretch of line. This was one of Eric Treacy's (the late Bishop of Wakefield) stamping grounds, though I find it frustrating that he, and his contemporaries, rarely panned out from the railway to picture it in its wider setting of textile mills, terraced housing, washing lines, cobbled streets, viaducts and moorland ridges.

Colin raised the interesting matter of the Bredbury binliner's return route. Apparently, because of the nature of the track layout at Woodley, the empties are worked back via Sheffield and the Hope Valley to facilitate easy reversal into the depot. Later, whilst polishing up this chapter, I spoke to John Bird, Market Manager for EWS Construction at its head office in Islington, and he told me of a new binliner which had started operating as a combined train from the depots at Brindle Heath and Dean Lane on the northern side of the city. John was enthusiastic about the prospects for the carriage of waste generally. Already it had increased by fifty per cent on British Rail days. Other cities, such as Bristol, Bath, London and Edinburgh were using rail for long distance disposal of their waste, and he was optimistic of securing new contracts and doubling tonnages again within the next few years.

Tunnels took us into Huddersfield, one of the great railway stations, architecturally and atmospherically, in the British Isles. I should add gastronomically, all three of us being able to vouch as to the excellence of the sausage sandwiches at the cafe on platform 4. I was just beginning to grasp the obvious truth, that EWS employees are not so much productivity driven, as stomach led. Jim's railway career, it emerged, had been one long round of visits to butcher's shops in railway towns. "When I was training on the Class 90 electrics to Carlisle I'd go to the covered market and order twelve pounds of Cumberland Sausage, wrapped individually, for the lads back at the depot. I did that two or three times a week for six months and the tight bugger never offered me a penny discount!"

At Heaton Lodge Junction the lines of the once rival London & North Western and Lancashire & Yorkshire railway companies merge for two or three miles through the Calder Valley as far as the outskirts of Dewsbury. Old maps reveal an astonishing density of lines in the vicinity of Mirfield, once an important interchange station, which, the story goes, went to the trouble of providing a billiard table for passengers with time to kill. There was a busy engine shed here too. We caught a glimpse of it in an advanced state of decay, but still more or less intact. Well aware now of my companions' interest in food, I pointed out a corner shop discovered on my canal travels which purveyed the most incredibly tasty corned beef and baked bean pie, served hot in thick square slices from a big tin tray on the counter. Three tracks run through the long since unstaffed and largely demolished station: one for 'down' eastbound traffic; and fast and slow 'up' for westbound. Briefly, at Thornhill Junction, the centre track becomes bi-directional. Colin pointed out how disconcerting it can be to, when travelling eastwards, to see an oncoming passenger train little more than a hundred yards ahead of you on the same track, until you realise that it is being held by a signal on the westbound platform at Ravensthorpe station.

Clattering across the points on to what had been 'The Lanky' line to Wakefield, Jim remembered long unfitted trains of coal wagons running into the precincts of the now demolished power station at Thornhill. I recalled how coal had also been brought in by barge along the Calder & Hebble Canal until as recently as 1981. Both forms of transport have shed vast tonnages with the rationalisation of the power industry. A surviving traffic in the neighbourhood, however, is cement to Blue Circle's depot at Dewsbury, a Monday-Friday trainload from Earles Sidings on the Hope Valley line running here via Sheffield; a regular driving job for Colin. In railway circles, Healey Mills was synonymous with shunting, as The Kinks once put it, *All Day and All of the Night*. Here, in the early Sixties, the North Eastern Region lashed out on one of their trademark multi-million pound marshalling yards; not knowing - how could they? - that the coal, steel and textile industries whose freight it was designed to speed, would all contract dramatically. When Healey Mills opened something in the region of a hundred and thirty trains passed through it every weekday. Now the number averages thirty, most of which stop to change drivers and/or locomotives, rather than perform any shunting. Yet such figures represent an improvement on the Healey Mills of the early Nineties when it looked likely to close altogether.

We rumbled over the River Calder whose course was diverted when the yard was built. The main running lines bifurcated around the sidings which, at the western end, were filled with melancholic rows of withdrawn locomotives and rolling stock. One whole train, formed by a Class 37 and a rake of what once might have been Network SouthEast carriages, looked as though it had been shunted into its siding and left to rot. Beyond it stood 31s and 47s surplus to requirements. It was like going to the RSPCA shelter - you wanted to find good homes for them all. There were signs of life, however, further on. A Class 37 was undergoing maintenance in the diesel depot ("One of the best designs ever," opined Jim) and to the south, across acres of sidings, stood not one, but two returning 'binliners'. One of these was Colin's return trip to Northenden, near Stockport, and with a quick goodbye and good luck he made a bee-line for it. More pertinently, as far as Jim and I were concerned, Control had decided to hoick *Samuel Johnson* off for a maintenance examination, and we were going to get, not only a new driver but a new locomotive as well: Kevin Beresford and *Kinder Scout* respectively.

Some yard staff effected the engine change. As with our previous Class 60, 60080 still sported Transrail colours. Jim went to talk to an old acquaintance, I wandered around looking for a loo. A shunter called Nick suggested I use the engine shed wall, which I did as discreetly as anyone could whilst wearing a dayglo vest. My own personal 'facility break' completed, I returned to the train, now coupled up to its new locomotive. Jim and I introduced ourselves to Kevin, a Doncaster driver, and flung ourselves at the mercy of his local knowledge. "I'm a Lancastrian, miles from home in a foreign country, be gentle with me," begged Jim, or words to that effect. Kevin took all the usual Lancashire and Yorkshire irreverential banter in his stride, notched up the regulator, sat back in his comfortable driving seat, and proceeded to devour his lunch. I have a female friend who won't accept that trains don't have to be steered like road vehicles. Watching Kevin

use both hands to munch his way through a gargantuan bap as the train rumbled out of the yard, she would have had a nervous breakdown. We ran past the site of Horbury & Ossett station where the traffic was once so dense over four tracks that a special signalling system had to be devised.

A Virgin passenger train was pulling out southwards from Westgate station over the ninety-nine arches which carry the Doncaster line across the rooftops of Wakefield. I wondered how many of its passengers, variously concentrating on their laptops, mobile phones, personal stereos and all the other paraphernalia deemed necessary to assassinate time on a journey nowadays, noticed the long yellow train passing beneath them, let alone bothered to question what it might possibly contain.

Architecturally, Westgate, Wakefield's premier station these days, is not a patch on the unstaffed, down at heel and seedy, though Grade II listed, Kirkgate. *Kinder Scout* lurched across pointwork on to the Pontefract line, passing Cobra's hugely successful, privately-owned goods yard, busily being shunted by their own Hunslet diesel. In a loop beyond the bridge over the Calder a new Class 66 on a train of steel coil was the cynosure of perhaps a dozen enthusiasts with cameras.

"There's a lot of railroad round here," said Jim, trusting Kevin to elucidate, and for a few minutes the talk was of arcane railway geography - Goose Hill, Fryston, Wath Road and Curdworth - nodal points in a railwayman's mental map, yet as unlocatable as Timbuctoo to anyone else. Soon we reached Hare Park Junction and the electrified main line from Leeds to Doncaster. As if to prove the status of our new surroundings, a GNER express wooshed by, leaving us rocking in its slipstream. Jim had a memory of an opencast loading point hereabouts. He thought it might be called Wintersett, and sure enough we soon came upon it, mothballed, and looking like an awfully expensive piece of infrastructure to be written off.

The talk turned to Kevin's career. He joined British Rail from school in 1978, having had his attention drawn to an advertisement

Kevin Beresford

Medge Hall

in the local press. It seemed a preferable alternative to mining. In his early days he was a secondman on King's Cross-Newcastle duties, becoming familiar, amongst other diesel types, with the celebrated Deltics. "I spent half my life tinkering with the steam heat boilers," he explained: "the drivers wouldn't look at them!" Jim empathised, and they engaged in an esoteric discussion over the finer points of Stones, Clayton, Spanner and Laidlaw-Drewery boilers. One of Jim's claims to fame was that he once kept the Royal Family warm - not personally of course - whilst on Royal Train duty. Kevin passed as a driver in 1984: "Right in the middle of the miners' strike." It was not a good time to attain such seniority. He went a year without driving a train; eventually moving to Knottingley depot in desperation. Jim had had similar experiences at Wigan, for in his time the railway operators had wallowed in the luxury of up to twenty spare links. The resultant inactivity had obviously been anathema to him. In the end, like Kevin, he was forced to move to another depot to find more meaningful employment. Such patterns of overmanning, as tolerated by British Rail, would give EWS accountants nightmares now.

Imperceptibly, or perhaps we'd just been too busy talking, we had left the Pennines behind and progressed into a flat, sort of fen-like, countryside drained, almost geometrically, by dykes and navigations. We had turned on to the Skellow Loop at Adwick Junction, crossed the East Coast Main Line and passed the remains of Thorpe Marsh power station. Only the 'binliners' regularly use this line to avoid Doncaster now. Jointly constructed by the Great Central and Great Northern railway companies, it connects with the Doncaster to Grimsby and Hull lines at Hatfield & Stainforth, under the headstocks of Hatfield Main Colliery. Jim wished he'd brought a camera, his grown-up children having been raised in the Lancashire coalfield, yet hardly having seen a working mine.

After being held on the 'up' slow at a signal, we took the Grimsby line at Thorne Junction and made our way across the Isle of Axholme, former territory of the Axholme Joint (and its mellifluous progenitor, the Goole & Marshland Light Railway), an agricultural line which briefly thrived by transporting the fats of these alluvial flatlands: potatoes, flax, carrots, peat and celery. The Stainforth & Keadby Canal kept us company, though it is no longer plied by bluff keels with billowing sails.

Some splendid Great Central signal boxes punctuated the line's progress. At Medge Hall and Goodknow Bridge there were level crossings still protected by traditional gates. This is a busy stretch of railway, hosting hourly Northern Spirit services from Scunthorpe to Doncaster and Cleethorpes to Manchester Airport, together with EWS Enterprise, petrochemical, metals and waste trains. At Keadby there's a unique sliding bridge which carries the line across canal. Kevin told us that they have great difficulty with it in summer when heat expands the steelwork and it refuses to slot back smoothly into place. Similar problems bedevilled the King George V Bridge over the River Trent. Opened in 1916, to a design patented by the Scherzer Rolling Lift Bridge Co. of Chicago, it was a lift bridge providing segregated road and rail crossings and the capacity to rise for the passage of high-masted vessels on the River Trent. It rose for the last time in 1958, though the river still hosts commercial shipping. We glimpsed a sizeable coaster berthed on the east bank downstream at Gunness Wharf.

A long viaduct carries the railway over the suburban outskirts of Scunthorpe. We saw Scunthorpe United's ground, where Kevin Keegan once graced the turf. This is a very lucrative part of the world for English Welsh & Scottish. Scunthorpe was hooching with Class 56 hauled trains of HAA hopper wagons carrying coal imported for the steelworks via Immingham Docks. The station dates from LNER days and has the redbrick simplicity of style one associates with a model railway. Beyond it the tracks blossomed into a phalanx of sidings. Against a backdrop of steelworks, we pulled into the Trent Reception Line. A shunter quickly uncoupled us and we ran round our train, looking an incongruous payload in this setting of steel. As well as coal, considerable tonnages of iron ore are brought to the Santon ore terminal from Immingham.

I was looking forward to the climax of our journey, the last leg over the route of what had once been the North Lindsey Light Railway, opened in 1910, to the remote village of Whitton on the banks of the Humber. The shunter, Charlie Parkinson, joined us for this recherche ride into the interior. It wasn't clear if he was coming to do some shunting or to act as bodyguard and interpreter. We moved slowly away from Trent Junction along a zig-zagging line seemingly trying to find an escape route from Scunthorpe's periphery of bingo halls, scrap yards and tar works. At Dawson's

Lane Crossing Charlie got out to work the barriers by depressing a plunger on a board beside the track. The rest of the lads were talking Rugby League, which Jim had played semi-professionally for Leigh - "Until I broke my ribs!" - but I had one eye on the landscape, growing drearier in the half-light of a dull January afternoon, and beginning to bring to mind the Siberian tundra.

The curves got tighter. Well, not so much curves, as a series of angled straights, as though some railway modeller had run out of curves and simply bent his fishplates. *Kinder Scout* staggered round each of these illogical angles like an inebriate finding their way through the vegetable patch to the outside privvy. At Dragonby Charlie pointed out the exchange sidings for traffic hauled by private shunter to Flixborough Wharf. Roxby Gullet doesn't appear on the Ordnance Survey map. To me the name suggested a malevolent squire in a Sherlock Holmes story. But the dictionary was more accurate, for the approach to the waste disposal sidings felt exactly like an oesophagus, the way into a stomach.

Appropriately it began to rain. Seagulls moaned in the distance. The depot, operated by UK Waste, loomed ahead. We ran on to the head of the loop and, once again, Charlie quickly uncoupled us. The containers would take a couple of hours to unload using giant forklift trucks. Empty containers would be placed on the bogie flats ready for the train's return departure at 17.40. Kevin had arranged to take Charlie back on the engine to Scunthorpe. Jim and I were to be collected by car - always assuming we could be found in this back of beyond location, where even mobile phones were sinisterly dead. I'd enjoyed the ride immensely. I'm glad it's such a lucrative traffic for English Welsh & Scottish. But I still think Manchester's got a nerve. Or am I just talking a load of rubbish?

Main picture: **Dragonby**
Inset: **Brian Robinson with the Roxby 'staff'.**

moving the mendips

IF faith can move mountains, then so can EWS - ten million tons of them annually on current figures. It's good business, but it's not without irony, much of this aggregates traffic being destined for the construction and maintenance of - roads! Almost half of this 'ammunition for the enemy' originates from quarries in Somerset's Mendip Hills, a yellowish limestone much prized for its hard wearing qualities. I might equally well have gone to Leicestershire, Derbyshire or the Yorkshire Dales to experience, first hand, the carriage of construction materials, but Construction Manager, Chris Pendlenton, recommended the Merehead to Purfleet run because it regularly features some of the heaviest trainloads worked anywhere in Britain, and because he also thought I might find the American built, Class 59 design, dedicated to this traffic flow, an interesting precursor to the Class 66 now being acquired by EWS in large numbers.

An unusual aspect concerning the carriage of Somerset stone is that the locomotives and wagons are privately owned by a company, known as Mendip Rail, which has pooled the logistical, rail-based resources of two businesses: Foster Yeoman and Hanson. They have quarries at Merehead and Whatley respectively, reached by branches off the Great Western main line either side

of Frome. Though booked to leave Merehead just after seven in the morning, the first Acton-bound train of the day often departs considerably earlier to free the sidings for later trains to be made up. Bearing this in mind, Standards Inspector, John McBurney, had suggested we start from Westbury, where the train would change drivers.

I didn't ask, but I guessed John was in his early thirties - a rough calculation extrapolated from the fact that he'd served fifteen years on the railway and had joined it straight from school. "I went to the careers centre in school. I told the woman I wanted to work in a bank. She said there was no YTS scheme for banks, but she could get me one on the railway."

It reminded me of the careers officer I'd been to see in a Dickensian office up several gloomy flights of stairs in the backstreets of Leicester. He looked like a retired military man: a clipped moustache and a clipped vocabulary. I told him I was interested in books. He looked out of the dusty window for a moment, seeking inspiration, grappling with my destiny, then turned and said: "What about working for W.H.Smith?"

Main picture: Eastbound aggregates near Little Bedwyn *(K. Goss)*
Inset: Foster Yeoman 'switcher' at Merehead even dwarfs a Class 59

John investigated the contents of his in-tray. Visits to his office, if not exactly infrequent, are dependant on his work load elsewhere. Standards Inspectors, like NCOs, are expected to be all things to all men. One moment they might be embroiled in the finer detail of a management meeting, the next filling in for an absent shunter at some remote, rain-sodden, windswept siding. John cast an eye over the previous day's Production Leaders' Log, a sort of daily newsletter detailing the salient points of need-to-know data. Simultaneously, he provided cogent answers to my probing questions concerning Westbury's sphere of operation. The depot may be about to lose its TOPS function, but by all other criteria business is booming. A section of the sidings has been adapted for use as a virtual quarry, or ballast stockpile, for infrastructure work, whilst, with the closure of nearby Swindon as a signing-on point for drivers, Westbury will face an increasing workload. Currently there are forty-six drivers at Westbury. Most of their work derives from the quarries, but they also drive infrastructure trains on Railtrack's behalf and deliver coal imported via Avonmouth docks to the local cement works.

Departure time approached, so we got our stuff together. John checked his briefcase, and I couldn't help noticing that it was crammed, not with the to be expected sheaf of vital documents, but with a considerable quantity of Tunnock's Caramel Wafers. Just as I was deliberating the niceties of commenting discreetly on this confectionary bullion, our driver, Des Gringell, popped

his head round the door and announced that it was time to go. We were scheduled to follow in the footsteps of a Paddington express. It came round the corner from the west as we crossed the tracks to where 59004 *Paul A. Hammond* stood at the head of our train. I reckoned by now to have evolved a foolproof and dignified method for climbing into cabs from rail level, but this monster from Illinois was in a different class. It was like having mastered The Munros and finding oneself on the North Face of the Eiger. I'll gloss over my ungainly ascent. Once through the outer door, a dogleg turn to the left gave access to the cab itself. "One end of a 59 is roomier than the other," John explained. "Most American locos have only one cab, so the one at the other end is a bit of a bolted on afterthought. We're lucky to have the larger one with you on board." Embarrassed by an accumulation of excess weight in recent months, I scarcely realised matters had gone so far.

59004 was built by General Motors in 1986. Disillusioned with the lack of power and unreliability of British motive power, Foster Yeoman had ground-breakingly shopped abroad when purchasing a dedicated fleet of locomotives in the mid Eighties. That in itself was unprecedented. No customer of British Rail had ever attempted to run its own motive power before. BR might

> "I couldn't help noticing it was crammed, not with the to be expected sheaf of vital documents, but with a considerable quantity of Tunnock's Caramel Wafers."

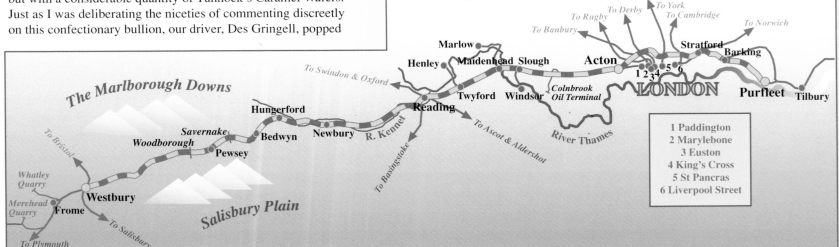

"I asked Des if he admired the 59s. 'I like anything that keeps going,' he responded philosophically."

Des Gringell and his teapot in the Woodborough Loop

have been typically reactionary faced with such radical proposals had not an annual contract for over four million tonnes of aggregates been tossed temptingly on the table.

We pulled out at 08.12 in the wake of the Great Western High Speed Train. I asked Des if he admired the 59s. "I like anything that keeps going," he responded philosophically. To the south, on a neighbouring hillside, Westbury's 'white horse' gleamed in the wintry sunshine. It was going to be a good day for travelling in a warm cab. We could ignore the trackside 110mph maximum speed limit sign - with three thousand tonnes in tow there was no danger of us breaking the sound barrier. In fact, all EWS goods trains run to self-imposed speed limits carefully monitored by the company's Standards Inspectors like John McBurney. Random checks are made with 'speed guns' similar to those used by the police, and woe betide any driver found over the limit. EWS locomotives are also progressively being fitted with Q-Trons, the equivalent of a lorry or coach tacograph or an aeroplane's black box. Thus, data from every journey can be down-loaded and analysed, both as a means of interpreting performance or, in the event of an incident, clarifying exactly what happened.

John had printed me out a copy of the train's consist before we left. We were train number 7A09, hauling thirty-eight wagons totalling 1,544 feet in length. At Acton, on the outskirts of London, the train would split into three: twelve JYA wagons being destined for Foster Yeoman's own depot at Purfleet; twelve JHA wagons bound for Day's at Angerstein Wharf on the south bank of the Thames; and fourteen MEA wagons which would be taken on to Tolworth, near Chessington, for use by Railtrack.

Like employees everywhere, Des evinced a mixture of pride and resentment. I sensed tensions beneath the surface of his banter with John, though nothing you wouldn't encounter in any factory, shop or office in the land. Des joined the railway in 1973 and has worked out of Westbury Depot ever since. His father was a ticket collector and shunter, the railway providing much of the town's employment, but following in his footsteps was more coincidental than deliberate as far as Des was concerned. Until 1979 Des was a secondman. In those days much of the Western

Region's motive power was still diesel hydraulic. Des spoke of his experiences on the 'Thousands' and 'Seven Thousands', locomotive classes which enthusiasts would more readily refer to as Westerns and Hymeks. "The Thousands had two engines. The steam-heating boiler was between them and the noise was unbelievable! We weren't issued with earplugs, so I used to stuff bits of rubber into my ears. We did Westbury-Paddington-Exeter-Westbury turns: six a.m. to two-forty-five. They gave you mileage payments for anything over a hundred miles, and that was a three hundred and fifty mile round trip. Good money!"

Between Salisbury Plain and the Marlborough Downs we ran - between The Ridgeway and Wansdyke. We may be more sophisticated, we might be at the 'cutting-edge' of technology, but the haulage of stone across this particular landscape goes back as far as Stonehenge. More or less level with another white horse, gouged out of the chalk escarpment, we pulled in to the Woodborough Loop for the *Golden Hind* to overtake us. There was time for a cup of tea taken from a silver pot simmering on the hob. John told me that the 66s, pretty much derived from the 59s, were designed with sloping side panels to prevent drivers from resting their mugs on them. "So much sugar gets spilled that it filters down into the works and literally gums them up, bringing the whole locomotive to a stand still." Behind us the locomotive's two-stroke engine ticked over, reminding me of my lawnmower. John was flicking through a copy of *Rail* magazine. "We're tenth in the table for driver's basic salary," he told Des which, predictably, led to more sparring. "I don't know what you're worried about," said John at one point, "my basic's a grand less than yours."

"Well at least they've got something right," responded Des.

"I've worked 156 hours this month," John confided to me, "plus 84 overtime. When I got home the other day the missus said: 'Who are you then?'"

Thankfully, the *Golden Hind* swept imperiously by and put an end to contentious talk of hours and overtime. Des had already gone to the signal controlling the loop and telephoned the signalman to confirm our whereabouts. So, almost as soon as the express had left us in its slipstream, the point moved over in our favour, we got a single yellow followed by a green, and Des opened the throttle. The figures of a woman, a child and a dog were silhouetted against the light on the adjacent road bridge. Mother and child waved vigorously as we rumbled below, just as folk would have been waving to the passing trains at Woodborough since the earliest days of the Berks & Hants line in the 1860s. The intrinsic drama of a passing train - especially a long goods one - still delights the child in us all. We don't go and stand by the M4 and wave at lorries do we!

EWS has brought extra tonnages to its aggregates portfolio by a willingness to cater for short-term flows. Recent examples include stone from Merehead to Exeter for renewal of the Honiton by-pass, and rocks along the preserved West Somerset Railway for sea defences at Minehead. The latter is of particular interest as it shows how the company is prepared to make innovative use of otherwise tourist-orientated lines to extend its sphere of operations. The American influence is clearly perceptible in this way of thinking, numerous 'short lines' existing within the USA railway network for the despatch and delivery of local goods.

We had been climbing steadily, with the Kennet & Avon Canal for company, to the summit of the line at Savernake. Another 59 had passed us hauling empties back from Acton. The initial order for Class 59s from Foster Yeoman had been followed by one from the Amey Roadstone Company, and it was one of these, 59104, decked out in the mustard-green colour scheme familiar from ARC operations throughout the country, at the head of this westbound train. Though owned by their separate companies, and maintained and managed by Mendip Rail, all eight Class 59s currently available (a ninth member of the class works in Germany) are operated in a common pool. In terms of reliability, their 98% availability record makes them amongst the most dependable traction anywhere in the world.

Savernake was the junction for a branch line to Marlborough, and it was also the point at which the Midland & South Western Junction Railway made its way surreptitiously northwards and southwards across the downland landscape, linking Cheltenham with Southampton. I belong to the wrong generation to have tasted the joys of railways like these: the Somerset & Dorset; Midland & Great Northern; Stratford & Midland Junction; lines constructed not so much out of commercial expediency as political intrigue.

Leaving the loop at Woodborough

Had I been a Hamilton Ellis, a Bryan Morgan or a Gilbert Thomas I might have written of perfect days in the solitary confinement of compartmented carriages, redolent with what Philip Larkin called "the reek of buttoned carriage-cloth": compartments with the window lowered by a leather-strap to let in an intoxicating cocktail of new mown hay, wild embankment flowers, creosoted sleepers, oil and soot and steam; compartments with luggage racks as commodious as hammocks and mahogany bulkheads decorated by framed prints of faded seaside resorts. And I would have traced such journeys on one inch, linen-backed Ordnance Survey maps: Sturminster Newton to Shepton Mallet; Melton Mowbray to Melton Constable; Fenny Compton to Moreton Pinkney; and Foss Cross to Savernake. What would those doyens of railway literature have made of our American diesel and its massive train? I like to think they would have stood on Savernake's long vanished station and waved with the fervour of the child at Woodborough.

My colleague, Keith Goss, who'd got up early - very early - to give me a lift down to Westbury by car, had arranged to photograph our train passing the handsome canal pumping engine buildings at Crofton, just over the summit. The light was perfect.

The sun was at an obliging angle. Des considerately tooted a fanfare on the horn to warn Keith of our approach. Anyone who takes their photography seriously will tell you - at length, if you give them the chance - how rare it is that everything falls into place: the location, the content and, above all, the light. But this had the makings of a perfect picture, at least it would have done but for the absence of one ingredient - the photographer! We scanned the canal bank, the fields beyond, the adjoining hillside. No Keith. There was, of course, nothing we could do, except have a little cry. I tried to get him on his mobile phone, thinking that perhaps he'd gone on to Little Bedwyn, another location we'd discussed the potential of. A fatuous female voice intoned infuriatingly: "The person you have called is not responding - please try again later."

It was pretty much downhill all the way from Savernake to the outskirts of Reading; in terms of gradients that is, not morale. Sunlight had percolated the cuttings. We blew our horn to warn an Amey track gang that we were bearing down on them. Des pointed out white patches in the 'four foot' between the rails. "After a lot of rain the clay beneath the ballast becomes waterlogged and the weight of passing trains forces it up between the sleepers. The gangs have to rake the clay off the surface and re-ballast the track, though the only permanent cure is to put in a damp course and a waterproof membrane."

At Great Bedwyn a Thames Turbo was waiting to reverse and follow us up the main line. There was no sign of Keith at Little Bedwyn either, a spot favoured by photographers and artists owing to the picturesque juxtaposition of the railway and a canal lock. I could only assume he'd got lost in the mazy Wiltshire lanes, suffered a breakdown - mechanical or personal, either was plausible - or been overtaken by sleep in some remote lay-by or other.

In a 59, the main control desk is located in the centre of the cab between the driver's and secondman's seats. The driver sits on the left hand seat and operates the throttle to his right by pushing it forwards to increase the power. On his left, parallel to the sliding side-window, are the brake controls, horn, Advance Warning System re-set button and a control to operate the valve which sprays sand onto the track to aid adhesion when it's slippery.

In front of the driver, the equivalent of a motor car dashboard features a variety of dials and gauges indicating speed, brake pressure and power. The 59s have a Co-Co wheel arrangement, that is there are six wheels to each of its two bogies. They weigh 121 tonnes, are 70ft in length, and have a maximum speed of 60mph. Their 16 cylinder engine develops 3,300 horsepower giving a tractive effort of 114,000lbs. They have fuel tanks capable of holding a thousand gallons, and if you think your car guzzles petrol, these monsters average a mile to the gallon. Statistics apart, I can summarise for the technically illiterate - the 59s are a big piece of kit!

Coasting down into Hungerford, we crossed the High Street watched, I later learnt, by a drop-jawed Keith. Apparently he'd waited and waited for us at Crofton, then panicked into assuming that we'd either already passed, or been diverted on to a different route, his grasp of railway geography still being in its infancy! Later we playfully chided him for his lack of endurance. I made a mental note to send him out to photograph a steam special, then he'd know what patience was all about. We slid through the station and got switched on to the loop. Such side-lining is far from tedious. There's the chance to gather one's thoughts, to mash some tea, or simply to commune with nature in the shape of Hungerford's spiralling lineside rabbit population. For some reason or other we began to talk about cricket. Des opens the batting for Trowbridge, though he's fearful that, at forty-two, and being so often at the beck and call of EWS at weekends, his place in the first team is no longer a sinecure. "At the end of last season we were promoted from the Bristol Alliance into the South-west Premier League. This summer we'll be playing the likes of Bath, Gloucester and Cheltenham, all of who have an ex-professional and an overseas player in their line-ups. It won't be easy!" I was not convinced. Des had appraised all my questions as carefully as he would each ball of an over to see if I'd put any 'spin' on them.

The Turbo swanned by. I suppose Hungerford marks the extremity of the commuter-belt. The sort of place where estate agent's adverts would boast of desirable residences being "75 minutes from Paddington". Signal R849 turned to green and we regained the main line. As 59004 gained power I felt a sort of

"Statistics apart, I can summarize for the technically illiterate - the 59s are a big piece of kit!"

The Merehead-Acton-Purfleet aggregates train runs alongside the Kennet & Avon Canal near Kintbury

"They are impressive trains and they have been enormously successful, but I suspect most railway observers find them too homogeneous to be admired with anything approaching affection."

'snatch' at the back of the locomotive reminiscent of the effect one feels when an automatic car changes gears. Des said it was something to do with the field-weakening in traction motors. He might as well have been trying to explain relativity to me. Strange how we can make the same journey as the person next to us, yet experience it quite differently. John and Des's antennae were receiving signals pregnant with gradients and curves, traction motors and brake pressures, I was watching reedbeds swaying in our wake, and glimpsing snowdrops in the woods. Not that I was impervious to the engine's mastery, it was just that I was largely ignorant of the science involved.

The Downs were behind us now and we were traversing a watery landscape which owed much of its character to the River Kennet. The main channel was canalised, but there were numerous backwaters and mill races which the railway was constantly bridging. A westbound HST shot past us like a missile. They are impressive trains and they have been enormously successful, but I suspect most railway observers find them too homogeneous to be admired with anything approaching affection. We want our motive power and rolling stock to exude heterogeneity, and it's no coincidence that many of the staff now employed by EWS chose the freight strand of the post-privatisation railway business simply because they wanted to be involved with locomotives and 'real' trains rather than ubiquitous multiple units and Sprinters. Des echoed these sentiments when I asked him why he'd chosen to go with EWS as opposed to say Wales & West or First Great Western. "I liked driving DMUs on the Weymouth-Bristol route. It was interesting changing the gears. But Sprinters? I don't think I could have coped with the monotony."

At Newbury we went through the station on the middle fast line. This is George Behrend territory, another of the old railway writers I grew up admiring. I must have been twelve or thirteen when I first read *Gone with Regret,* his erudite and mellifluous tribute to the GWR. Newbury has a chapter of its own in my well-thumbed copy. When Behrend knew it a branch sprouted up the Lambourn Valley into racehorse country, whilst the eponymous Didcot Newbury & Southampton line made its unhurried way across the grain of the countryside, climbing steeply, northwards and southwards out of the Kennet Valley.

Behrend wrote lyrically of Paddington-Weymouth expresses, Saint or Star hauled; of slip carriages, horse boxes, race specials and milk trains. I admired his prose style, and shared his love of the railway as a social and aesthetic entity. More than this, I envied him the variety which progress has diluted to the extent that now less than half a dozen different kinds of train pass through Newbury on a daily basis.

Outer suburban stations came thick and fast between Newbury and Reading. Thatcham first, followed by a pretty GWR timber signal box at Colthrop, overlooked by a paper mill and a vast ordnance depot. Des remembered working passenger trains along this line and the influx of youthful passengers at the end and the beginning of term at Midgham, where the station nameplates still advise one to alight for the nearby Douai School. Des may miss the variety of passenger working, but he doesn't miss the passengers and their infuriating helplessness. "I pulled into Westbury the other day with a train of stone empties and this woman called through the cab window to me: 'Is this the train for Castle Cary?'!"

EWS does good business at Theale: Foster Yeoman has another distribution depot here, served by a daily train from Merehead, and petroleum is railed into Murco's terminal from Robeston, near Milford Haven. 59101 *Village of Whatley* stood in the down loop with two drivers on board. John put this down to an aberration in crewing timetables, one man covering the other's physical needs or facility break. They were Westbury men and a fanfare of horns marked our passing. Beyond Theale the countryside gives up the ghost. In fields on the frayed hem of Reading's outskirts I counted eight burnt-out cars, joy-riden out of the town, abandoned and set alight. Blocks of grim, Eastern European looking flats overlooked the railway at Southcote Junction, and you don't need a degree in sociology to draw conclusions regarding the reasons for some extremes of vandalism.

A red signal held us while a Turbo from Basingstoke crossed our path and went ahead of us into Reading. Running through Reading West, John and Des took turns to lecture me on the propensity of drivers to 'drive through their bums'. Really technical, I thought, but even I could grasp what they meant. Like horsemen, their posteriors respond to rhythmic messages as subtle as a distant jolt as each wagon's air brake is released. Snaking over elaborate pointwork, we went through on what Des reliably informed me was the "up relief". Numerous 165 and 166 Turbos populated the bays. We raced one of them heading off on the old Southern line towards Wokingham. No contest - it left us for dead. I caught a glimpse of Reading Gaol, thought of Oscar Wilde and wondered flippantly if he had taken to trainspotting. More productively, I thought of all the gaols I knew overlooking stations: Shrewsbury, Wakefield, Armley (Leeds), Strangeways (Manchester) Pentonville and Wormwood Scrubs; and tried to remember A.E.Housman's line about prisoners being kept awake all night by the 'groaning rails' or some similar imagery. Des was prompted by the sight of the prison to relate the story of a Westbury driver who'd shunted a stone train: "Somewhere down Ascot way. He'd had three hours to kill before returning with the empties and had gone round the town for a walk in the middle of the night. Trouble was, there'd been a burglary and the police arrested him for acting suspiciously. Luckily CID accepted that a goods train wasn't the most likely means of escape, though it brought a new definition to the term 'getaway vehicle'."

We came to Sonning Cutting, classic territory for railway photography since Maurice Earley's heyday in the era of box cameras and glass plates. Early February and the gorse was already in bloom, at least we were doing our best to put the brakes on global warming. A lengthy straight section of quadruple track - slow lines to the north, fast to the south - took us through Twyford and on to Maidenhead. I had explored the Western Region's Thames Valley branchlines in the late Sixties, trundling by single unit railcars through Wargrave and Shiplake to Henley-on-Thames, and by way of Bourne End on the now abandoned line through Loudwater to High Wycombe.

In their role as tour guides, John and Des drew my attention to Brunel's bridge over the Thames at Maidenhead, but seemed far more excited to show me where Rolf Harris, Billy Connolly and Terry Wogan lived in sumptuous riverside residences. Passing traffic had increased noticeably since Reading. Virgin Cross Country trains went by in either direction, still hauled by the classic Brush Type 4 design of the 1960s, though not, sadly, for much longer. There were First Great Western HSTs and Thames

Turbos too, emphasising the increasing competition for paths. Near Taplow a shallow cutting was strewn with new concrete sleepers waiting to go in. At Slough, Horlicks' big redbrick factory overlooked the junction of the Windsor branch. We passed an oil terminal at Langley, a destination I'd considered (but later dropped) for another of my journeys. Sometimes, Des told me, the stone trains are routed into the loop at Iver, but we got a clear road. We saw evidence of two more significant traffic flows for English Welsh & Scottish: domestic coal at West Drayton; and petroleum, carried along the old Staines branch to Colnbrook for use as fuel by aeroplanes at Heathrow.

Having passed beneath the M25 we were now in Greater London. We got talking about Railtrack. I asked the other two if they had noticed changes in the standard of track maintenance and signalling since privatisation. Both seemed conscious of a steady improvement. "We haven't had any temporary speed restrictions all the way from Westbury," said Des. "Yet I can remember runs to Acton in British Rail days when there might have been four or five checks for maintenance work." John was similarly bullish. "They're finding their feet and they're certainly spending some money," he summarised. Suddenly, we were under electric wires, put up recently for the Heathrow Express service with its sleek silver trains, yet somehow a strange apparition on what was not so long ago the electrification-free territory of the Western Region. We went through Hayes & Harlington and into what John called the 'suicide country' of Southall. I didn't ask him to elaborate. Partly because I froze at the thought of the gory details, but also because I didn't want either of them to have to relive the sort of 'incidents' that are an inevitable part of an engine driver's life. Quite what right those committing suicide have to involve third parties in their suffering is beyond me, but possibly, by definition, it is beyond them too.

The tube trains of Ealing Broadway emphasised how close we had come to the capital. Acton Yard presented a busy scene. There were rakes of aggregate wagons and several stabled locomotives; among them no less than four members of Class 66. John considered it likely that the other two portions of our train, bound for Angerstein Wharf and Tolworth, could well go out behind examples of this new design. Not, apart from their

John McBurney at Acton

EWS livery, that they looked much different from our 59, though I had already been taught the trick of differentiating between a 66 and a 59 by the provision of a centrally located headlight above the cab windows on the former. Des left the cab, as I could imagine him leaving the crease, with the minimum of fuss. He was due to work empties back to Westbury, then work another train down to the quarries, before returning to Westbury and ending his eleven hour shift at 18.35.

John and I had about quarter of an hour to kill before we were due out of the yard with an Acton driver. As far as John was concerned, the journey to Purfleet was tantamount to a tumble off the edge of his mental map. Some attempt had been made to find a local Standards Inspector to accompany me, but the man in question had just had a baby - or at least his wife had - and so John manfully agreed to continue as my minder into what was, for both of us, unknown territory. He forewarned me what to expect of the natives. "At Westbury we take a pride in our appearance, we wear the uniform. You wait and see, this London guy will be in jeans and a tee-shirt." In all respects but one it was an accurate prediction. Only there wasn't one sartorially challenged Acton driver. There were two!

There are three different ways of getting a goods train from Acton to Purfleet, but the width of our JYA wagons restricted us to the North London line. Our driver, Robert Welstead, had drawn forward twice for a shunter to uncouple the other two portions. Then, with a brusque blast on the horn, we rumbled off across a bewildering complex of lines and junctions at the commencement of what was to prove a fascinating journey into deepest Essex.

The fourth man in the cab was Mike Lang, a driver new to Acton, and consequently on route learning duty. We passed through Willesden Junction, Kensal Rise and Brondesbury Park stations. I plucked an Ordnance Survey map from my bag and spread it prominently in front of the window to try and get some notion of the way we were going. Goodness knows what the signalmen made of me. I imagined a message going from box to box: "Allo 'Arry, do yer know them EWS geezers are usin' maps to find their way over the Norf Lunnon now!"

High up in our 59, we were treated to an ever better view of the A5 and Kilburn High Road than commuters on the twenty-minute-interval purple and green Silverlink 313 electrics which kept swishing past us. I peered voyeuristically into back gardens and bathrooms, but saw nothing untoward. Every half mile or so we encountered little knots of passengers waiting impatiently on platforms, and could almost read the disappointment in their eyes that we were transparently not their train. Beyond Finchley Road & Frognal a long tunnel led to Hampstead Heath. For someone reared on Betjeman, it felt like a homecoming. At Gospel Oak it began to drizzle. An elderly 'heritage' multiple unit of Class 117 stood waiting to provide a connection to Barking; weeks away, probably, from the cutter's torch.

Everything was happening so quickly that there wasn't much time for talk. I urged Robert to act as a guide, to tell me what to look out for on my left and on my right. But that was unfair - driving on yellows and double-yellows he had his work cut out to concentrate. I did, however, get out of him a brief resume of his

Class 66s basking in Acton sun

railway career to date: that he was made redundant by British Telecom, who'd honed him in certain telephonic skills before announcing that they were obsolete; and that he'd responded to a British Rail advert for drivers in the local press. "I went to Old Oak Common. I quite liked the idea of driving a train. They just didn't tell me it would take two years!" That was seven years ago, and several changes of employer later he seemed to be happy working for EWS. His colleague, Mike Lang, was a Devonian who'd been on the railway twice as long. Though from Newton Abbot originally, he'd begun his career working on Oxford station, transferred to Reading, then gone to - but I missed where he'd gone next because there was a sudden thump on the windscreen and, as a consequence, one pigeon less on the rooftops of Kentish Town. All I do know is that he'd just been transferred from Willesden, where he'd driven postal trains to Acton, hence the need for route learning which, he reckoned, given the sphere of operations expected of Acton drivers, would take about twenty days. At Camden Road Junction I caught a glimpse of St Pancras station and the adjoining gasholders. Minutes later we were crossing over the East Coast Main Line, on its way out of King's Cross, and I can almost swear I saw Alec Guinness trying to dump a body out of a wheelbarrow over the portal of Copenhagen Tunnel. What I did see, without a doubt, was the Castle Cement terminal served by EWS block trains from the same company's works at Ketton, near Stamford.

We ran through dank cuttings of sombre brick retaining walls to Highbury & Islington where a colour light signal was flickering unnervingly from green through yellow to red and back again. To be on the safe side Robert stopped the train and telephoned the signal box for clarification. "The fault's been reported," he said, returning to the cab, " and they're waiting for some blokes to come out and repair it. They've said it's OK for us to go through." As we slowly regained our momentum, a lengthy container train passed in the opposite direction behind a couple of Class 86 electrics - one bearing the name *Aldaniti,* a reminder of the old London & North Eastern Railway's inspired tradition of naming engines after racehorses. An element of abstraction enhances a name. Good public relations they might be, but *The Magistrates Association* or *Rotary International* are not charismatic names for locomotives. Personally - and I realise I might be out on something of an about-to-be amputated limb here - I have always thought that classic song titles would be motive power friendly: imagine *Strawberry Fields, Bohemian Rhapsody* or *Wonderwall* powering past at the head of a lengthy train; spotting could'nt possibly be considered half so nerdy if you only needed *Jumping Jack Flash* to complete a class.

The North London line was spellbinding, both in its busyness and topographical gratification. As John said, it reminded him of

a game of *Monopoly.* At Hackney Central there were red Routemaster omnibuses in the wet streets below. Come Hackney Wick we were crossing the River Lea and moving over a tangle of lines into Stratford. John and Mike were reminiscing about Stratford depot's famous silver-roofed locomotives. "They had about four hundred drivers here back in the Eighties," Mike said: "Now there's about forty!" An Anglia Railways turquoise coloured Class 86 electric sped past us on its way into Liverpool Street. Stratford's platforms were populated more by trainspotters than commuters. As we went through Maryland station the clock was turned back by the sight of one of the earliest English Electric Type 3s, 37023, in the dark blue livery of the shadow franchise Mainline, bearing down on us with an EWS intermodal train. Almost forty years ago it would probably have been working out of Stratford depot pulling passenger expresses to the Norfolk coast. Almost invariably, admiration for a locomotive design follows an inverted arc. When first introduced their novelty value appeals. Then, as a class grows more numerous, indifference sets in. Withdrawal brings sentimentality and as, one by one they are consigned to the breaker's yard, we weep crocodile tears of nostalgia for a paradise, perhaps not so much lost, as temporarily mislaid until time takes its toll of the next threatened class.

Before the railways promoted the spread of suburbia, the part of East London we were travelling through must have been overwhelmingly rural. And so the fox at Forest Gate, which nonchalantly disentangled itself from some saplings, to pick its way across the tracks almost beneath our buffer beam, was either a figure from a time loop, or a streetwise urban fox with nothing but contempt for trains. We went over the River Roding, its glutinously muddy banks indecently exposed by low tide. Then a railway flyover brought us to Barking and the end of the Underground as far as we were concerned, for our route lay along the line of the old London, Tilbury & Southend Railway into the land of marshy football fields, car factories, trailer parks and descendants of the Dagenham Girl Pipers.

Ford is one of EWS's biggest customers. There are flows of finished cars to Garston on Merseyside, Mossend near Glasgow and Eastleigh near Southampton. Components are conveyed to other Ford plants in South Wales and Merseyside. We were through Dagenham Dock almost too rapidly for me to take anything in. Besides, John and Mike had turned from trains to cars and were enthusiastically discussing the new Ford Focus, which *Top Gear*'s Jeremy Clarkson had described as 'faultless' and I wondered what epithet he'd apply to a Class 59. Another set of eastbound empties went past behind 59102 *Village of Chantry*. John reckoned it was the Thameshaven-Whatley. I reckoned that sighting gave me a complete set of 59/1s in a day - pretty good trainspotting by any standards.

We had nearly reached Purfleet, but first we had to cross Rainham Marshes with their rifle ranges, criss-crossed by electricity pylons and drained by boggy runnels. Mike had turned the tables and was asking me the questions - where was I going next; what had I done so far? Most railwaymen I had met on my travels had been tactfully incurious about the project, so it was nice to put it all in context. I was able to emphasise the pressures of journalism, the deadlines, the fear of writer's block, how no-one understood me, how I suffer for my art. I think he got the message - he laughed a lot anyway.

It had been agreed that John and I would jump train at Purfleet station, Foster Yeoman's depot being out beyond the back of beyond. Someone had warned John that Purfleet was like Chile, people went there and never came back. So John had asked Robert to drop us at the station and Robert was worrying that he'd not get the train started again on what would now be a wet, tight curve. We slowed down past a derelict oil depot backed by a crumbling chalk cliff, which seemed to be in the process of being demolished by a solitary man with a crowbar. The rain was more like sleet now, and the sky beyond the widening Thames the colour of ballast. Robert's fears were exacerbated by the presence of a level crossing carrying a busy road across the line immediately beyond the platform's end. If he couldn't re-start from here he'd be front page news in the *Essex Examiner*. We all shook hands, swore eternal brotherhood, then John and I leapt onto the platform like secret agents parachuting into unknown territory. Possibly by luck, more probably with Robert's expertise, 59004 kept its feet and drew its train off-stage through a curtain of hail. Not wishing to become another statistic - not wanting to be two more of the 'missing in Purfleet' - we bolted for the up platform and were soon sinking gratefully into the comfortable cushions of an elderly 310 electric unit, which took us back to Fenchurch Street, democracy and the known world.

Rainham Marshes

Steve Bell and Clive Rooker

*T*HERE was a 'but' coming, I could sense it, in Clive Rooker's voice at the other end of the phone. "We've got the EDs, Michael; we've got some traffic; *but* it doesn't look as though we can go round via the coast!"

"Well, two out of three's a distinct improvement on last week," I thought to myself, as I put down the telephone. The previous week I'd gone all the way down to Eastleigh and found that the train had been cancelled on account of a derailment at Hoo. But it was definitely disappointing to hear that we couldn't go the 'scenic' way, through Fareham, Chichester and Worthing, and on past Brighton to Three Bridges, where our Tuesdays, Wednesdays and Fridays Infrastructure trunk service from Eastleigh to Hoo was scheduled to call in and shunt as required.

EWS's Infrastructure Services business wasn't meant to be riddled with such uncertainties anymore. Post-privatisation there was to be a dynamic, timetabled series of trunk services designed around the location of 'virtual quarries' and 'local distribution centres' to ensure the most cohesive use of resources. The main players were to be EWS and Railtrack, supported by a cast of engineering contractors whose job it would be to take 'possession' of stretches of line earmarked for maintenance or renewal, usually at night and weekends to minimise disruption to passenger traffic.

Infrastructure - or to give it its old name, departmental - was always the poor relation of railway operations. The equivalent of domestic housework, it was perceived as a chore which you wore your oldest clothes to do or, in the railway's case, you used your oldest wagons and locomotives. Pre-privatisation, no money changed hands, and consequently it wasn't always necessary that departmental workings should bear close financial scutiny. Privatisation altered such *laissez-faire* attitudes, radically. Far from being an afterthought, civil engineering activities

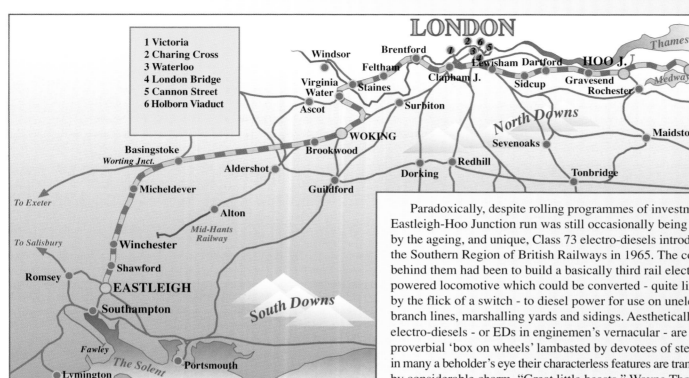

1 Victoria
2 Charing Cross
3 Waterloo
4 London Bridge
5 Cannon Street
6 Holborn Viaduct

suddenly represented 15% of EWS's annual turnover, rendering it, overnight, the most lucrative account in the company's portfolio. To reflect such newly acquired significance, a fleet of wagons was ordered to replace designs going back half a century and beyond. Kim Jordan, Infrastructure Services General Manager when I was working on this book, but since retired from the railway industry and replaced at EWS by Neil Smith, put it thus: "We inherited over seven thousand wagons, nearly all being too old, too small or too slow to provide a sound product for the future." Some of the railway system's last vacuum-braked wagons could now be replaced by modern air-braked stock and, by the same token, older, dual-braked locomotive designs, retained to work with vacuum-braked trains, could be withdrawn.

Paradoxically, despite rolling programmes of investment, the Eastleigh-Hoo Junction run was still occasionally being hauled by the ageing, and unique, Class 73 electro-diesels introduced by the Southern Region of British Railways in 1965. The concept behind them had been to build a basically third rail electric-powered locomotive which could be converted - quite literally by the flick of a switch - to diesel power for use on unelectrified branch lines, marshalling yards and sidings. Aesthetically, the electro-diesels - or EDs in enginemen's vernacular - are the proverbial 'box on wheels' lambasted by devotees of steam. But in many a beholder's eye their characterless features are transcended by considerable charm. "Great little beasts," Wayne Thompson, one of the drivers I met at Eastleigh, had called them, with evident sadness that they were gradually being withdrawn.

My previous week's aborted trip hadn't been entirely unproductive. I sat in the office Clive Rooker shares with Operations Standards Inspector, Chris Galloway, munching chocolate digestives, sipping hot, strong tea and listening to Wayne Thompson outlining Eastleigh's spheres of operation while Clive - a Standards Inspector with one foot in Didcot and the other in Eastleigh - attempted to rescue something from the wreckage of our plans by telephone. To railwaymen, professional and amateur, Eastleigh needs little introduction. It is the former Southern Railway's equivalent of Crewe, Swindon and Doncaster; a greenfield site eaten up by the railway age and spewed out as a redbrick railway town devoted to the manufacture and maintenance of locomotives and rolling stock. Here Richard Maunsell built his stylish and

"Aesthetically, the electro-diesels - or EDs in enginemen's vernacular - are the proverbial 'box on wheels' lambasted by devotees of steam."

elegant Lord Nelson and School class locomotives and Oliver Bulleid his inimitable Merchant Navy and Light Pacific designs.

We had looked out on gleaming, after-shower-wet rooftops of regimented housing built for the thousands once employed in Eastleigh Works. Wayne succinctly outlined Eastleigh's role in the EWS scheme of things. "We're largely involved in infrastructure these days, and so we tend to be at our busiest at weekends. Monday to Friday we ferry materials to and from the LDCs - local distribution centres. Then from Friday night onwards, we work out to where Railtrack and the civil engineering companies like Balfour Beatty have taken 'possession' of a section of line."

"Not that we don't do freight as well," he'd continued, "our biggest job is the Furzebrook-Hallen Marsh gas train. There's usually five drivers a day on that job, carrying propane and butane which are bi-products of the oil farm at Wych. It's taken in tankers to Avonmouth for export, and, interestingly, that flow has two routes, via Westbury or Swindon. We also do Ford Vans - built here in Eastleigh - to Dagenham or Garston; crude oil from Alton to Fawley and bitumen, twice a week, from Fawley to Bromford Bridge. Then, of course, there's the military traffic too"

Between urgent, and increasingly frustrating telephone calls, Clive had shown me round Eastleigh depot. I'd been surprised to see two or three Freightliner Class 47s 'on shed'. Potential Wooden Horses of Troy? No, Clive had explained that EWS has a contract to maintain their rival's motive power and the nearby docks at Southampton are one of Freightliner's busiest terminals. Elsewhere we'd seen examples of Class 37 and the new Sixty-sixes coming on stream to replace them. But it was the electro-diesels which caught my eye, two or three pairs of them being in situ, and I'd urged Clive to do his best to persuade control to provide a pair of them when we finally got to make the trip to Hoo.

*   *   *

A week later, on Eastleigh station, encumbered with photographic gear and scribbling notes in a pad, I must have looked like just another of the trainspotters gathered at the end of Platform 3. Minutes later, however, a pair of electro-diesels pulled up and plucked me from the throng. It was a defining moment, pre-ordained, but pure showbiz all the same.

Clive had a driver called Steve Bell with him. We pottered up the line to the East Yard and stabled the two locomotives on one of the few bits of siding space available. Theoretically we were scheduled to leave just before three, but it was already twenty past, and our train had yet to be assembled. We headed for the Ground Frame where Traffic Inspector, Joe Hosking, was filling in as general factotum in the face of an acute staff

73136 and 73108 prepare to leave Eastleigh for Woking and the 'mysterious east'

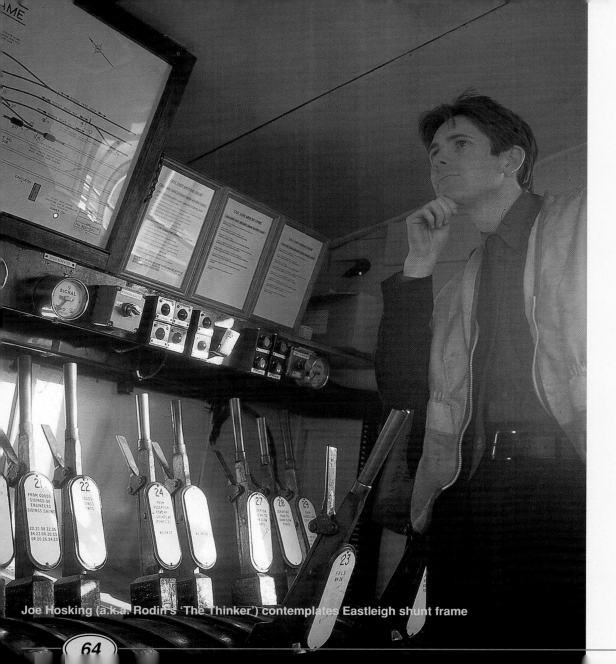

Joe Hosking (a.k.a. Rodin's 'The Thinker') contemplates Eastleigh shunt frame

shortage and, as he put it: "Having a last ditch attempt to make some sense of the muddle." An old head on young shoulders, Joe gave every appearance of making a fist of it. His problems were exacerbated by a lack of siding capacity. "I put in a request to Railtrack to let us have the disused down carriage sidings," he explained. "That was six months ago, and I guess it got lost in the property department, but there's no doubt the extra space would be a great help." The wisdom of his words was about to be graphically demonstrated.

Doncaster had faxed a consist requiring us to take four 'Bass' materials wagons to Woking and sixteen 'Sea Urchin' spoil wagons to Hoo. Rather romantically, infrastructure rolling stock is classified and categorised by the names of fish, a tradition apparently inherited from the Great Western Railway. There are 'Salmon' bogie wagons for carrying sleepers, 'Dogfish' hoppers for ballast - Clive gave me a data sheet containing more fishy nomenclature than an angler's basket.

Our task appeared reasonably straightforward, but Joe was relying on the services of a mobile shunter, called Pat, who was unfamiliar with the layout of the yard, and everyone was literally having difficulty locating the wagons in question. To add unnecessary pressure to the proceedings, a train of gypsum empties had called to collect extra wagons, and priority was being given to getting this timetabled service away on schedule. So we sat in the cabin and chin-wagged, waiting for the metaphorical mists to clear. Pale shafts of sunlight filtered through the blind and gilded the point frame. Clive tried to fob me off with the notion that the frame and its levers dated from the London & South Western era, but I hadn't studied industrial archaeology for nothing, and I pointed out politely the embossed lettering proclaiming it to be of British Transport Commission, Southern Region vintage - much hearty laughter ensued. But whatever its provenance, the frame, its red and blue levers and the track diagram above it, exuded considerable charm and evoked a timeless sense of railway heritage.

Pat returned from his one man mission to find the wagons. "It's not a shunter they need here," he declared, "it's Fred Dibnah!" He had a point - we'd noticed some ancient looking wagons with builders' plates on their solebars dating from 1957, and in the distance was stuff looking a good deal older still. "I've got two

"This anorakisation of railways is a peculiar business. One wouldn't get very far in, say films or football, if one affected an indifference to the culture, history and tradition of either subject."

Bass," continued Pat "but I haven't a clue where the others are." It was a start, but it didn't solve *our* problem. Time was ticking away and we were up against various constraints, not least the loss of an appropriate path and the parameters of Steve's twelve hour shift.

Meanwhile, the gypsum empties had left behind a Class 66 for Southampton Docks and Joe was able to give us his undivided attention. A few phone calls later the gist of things was that we would just take the two Bass we'd found to Woking, then come straight back to Eastleigh. As a dispassionate observer I tried to rationalise the pattern of events leading up to this disappointing compromise. Disappointing to me, for sure, in that for the second week running, little was going according to plan. But more importantly, disappointing for English Welsh & Scottish that its resources were so ineffectively stretched. Everyone involved, or so it seemed to me, had worked conscientiously to achieve to our goal, and what shortcomings there were lay more in the nature of the working conditions - the restricted capacity of the yard and the lack of an on- site TOPS 2000 terminal in particular. Ironically, Steve had worked the previous afternoon's train via the coast and Three Bridges without so much as a hitch - something which Clive failed to see the funny side of.

A Class 09 shunting locomotive, which had been perpetual motion personified throughout our extended sojourn, positioned our two wagons for us. We backed down on to them, coupled up and left the yard as train 6Y40 just before six o'clock in the evening. We chugged across the main lines, relatively noisily, in diesel mode. But as soon as we'd joined the 'up slow' Steve depressed a button on the console which lowered the current collector shoes on to the third rail and suddenly calm descended.

Used by now to varying degrees of cab noise in different diesel designs, I was astonished by the unearthly quiet. The fact that we had two locomotives didn't mean that we needed two drivers; jumper cables between the inward facing cabs carry control information from the leading locomotive to the one behind. Steve was driving 73136 *Kent Youth Orchestra* in the dark blue colours of the shadow franchise Mainline. The other engine, in British Rail's Civil Engineering 'Dutch' livery of grey and yellow, was 73108. Ambiently, the atmosphere in the cab reminded me

of nothing so as much as a tram!

We trundled along the slow line in the dying light of what had been a welcomingly sunny afternoon in the wake of a procession of cloudy days. Steve pointed the Itchen Navigation out to me. It transpired that he was a canal buff and possessed an impressive tally of my books on the subject. Inland waterways, it appeared, would come back to haunt me wherever I went on this rail freight odyssey. Beyond Shawford, four tracks merged to two, and soon we were rattling through Winchester where Steve had been brought by his dad to watch the last years of Southern steam. For the first time in my travels I was with railwaymen who openly admitted to an enthusiasm for railways beyond the call of duty. Clive had been inspired to join the Western Region because of the charismatic diesel hydraulic designs he'd seen as a boy. There had been times, both men agreed, when they had had to keep their love of railways in the closet to avoid ridicule. Now, though - and not least because Ed Burkhardt himself had publicly 'confessed' to being fascinated by trains - EWS's employees exist in a culture where railway enthusiasm, as long as it doesn't compromise professionalism, is nothing to be ashamed of.

This anorakisation of railways is a peculiar business. One wouldn't get very far in, say films or football, if one affected an indifference to the culture, history and tradition of either subject. In most activities enthusiasm and commitment is everything. What Gilbert Thomas once wrote of as "an absurd fear of seeming childish," has inhibited generations of railway minded people from wearing their hearts on their sleeves. We're stigmatised like gays, we're ghettoised like blacks; we're forced to feel our way in conversations, lobbing knowledgeable hints over a metaphorical net to see if they're returned.

During a lull in the conversation I took stock of my surroundings, most noticeably the dual controls, reminiscent of the set up in a driving instructor's car. Apparently the provision of two control modules was peculiar to the Southern Region whose Class 33 Crompton diesels were similarly fitted. As Steve moved his control arm through its notches, so the secondman's in front of me moved spookily in unison. I had to be careful where I put the tea, thoughtfully provided by Clive, to avoid the arm spinning round and sending it flying.

Clive pointed out that with the smooth running of our EDs, and the lightness of the load, we wouldn't get a full sense of the gradient we were climbing. "That Freightliner up ahead will be feeling it though," added Steve. We had waited for it to clear the section before leaving Eastleigh and followed at a respectful distance. In fact I had an ancient memory of my own concerning the 1 in 252 climb to Litchfield when, back in 1967, the rebuilt Bulleid Pacific *Tamar Valley* had hustled me up the bank in fine staccato style on an ochreous April evening. Back then, the EDs were perceived as usurpers, progenitors of a steamless era which filled us with dread. How bizarre, then, that little more than thirty years later I should be travelling over the same track, espousing regret that the electro-diesels' future was equally insecure.

We went through Wallers Ash Tunnel, beyond which Steve thought we might get looped to let some South Western Trains services overtake. But we weren't, and got a clear run on to Micheldever where completion of the London & Southampton in 1840 was celebrated with a "cold collation of delicate viands and rare wines". We celebrated the summit with another cup of Clive's tea and freewheeled down to Worting Junction, confluence of the Southampton and Salisbury lines on the outskirts of Basingstoke.

At Fleet the station clock read 19.14. We had left rural Hants for the fleshpots of suburban Surrey. Steve, something of an authority on local railway history, pointed out where the Brookwood Cemetery Railway had once curved away from the main line. Apparently coffins were loaded on to mourners' specials at Waterloo and worked, with due regard for the circumstances, to Brookwood for burial. "Did the corpse require a ticket?" I asked flippantly. "Just a single," laughed Steve.

If you've been following the plot, you will recall that the evening's task had been simplified to its bare bones - sorry, I can't seem to shake off the cemetery - all we needed to do, or so we thought, was drop the two Bass off at Woking and return to Eastleigh. Privately I was wondering whether to return with the lads and the locos or make my way by passenger train to London where I'd arranged to spend the night with a friend on Clapham Common - sorry, I'll rephrase that, my friend, Angela, whose address is Clapham Common. Naturally, I regretted not reaching Hoo, whose marshland remoteness and echoes of *Great Expectations* appealed to the geographer and literary student in me respectively. However, I appreciated that Clive had already gone out of his way to organise this second trip for me, and the cards seemed stacked impossibly against us. Besides, Steve had hinted at the existence of a choice fish & chip shop in the vicinity of Woking yard, which I was beginning to think would make an appropriate climax to the trip. All these fishy wagons had whetted our collective appetite.

We reached Woking at half past seven, puzzled by the fact that we weren't signalled into the yard. Steve brought us to a shuddering halt and we phoned the signalman who phoned the shunter who claimed to have no knowledge of the two Bass. Not wishing to block the up line, Clive and Steve came to a quick decision, and I'm still not clear if it was for my benefit, or because they couldn't think of anything else to do. Whatever the reasoning, they decided, spontaneously, to continue on to Hoo and see what transpired. I had a frightening vision of us becoming the Flying Dutchmen of railway infrastructure, doomed to haul our two wagons around the south-east for eternity. Clive contacted Westbury TOPS on his mobile to acquaint them with our increasingly unpredictable itinerary and to get them to confirm the wisdom of our new destination.

Meanwhile we went on, what was for me, a mystery tour of leafy Surrey, through stations I'd only ever seen in timetables: Chertsey, Virginia Water, and Egham, then over the Thames into Staines. This had been Steve's home patch for a time when he'd driven third rail electrics from Farnborough. Clive had worked them as well, out of Charing Cross, and they shared a nostalgia for Bulleid EPBs. Westbury rang back confirming we should proceed to Hoo. While they were talking to Clive, Steve suddenly rammed the brakes on. He'd seen a signal go to red a split second *before* we passed it. Probably it was just a 'trigger-happy' signalman, but on the railways, unlike the roads, you never take risks. He rolled his train gently up to the next signal - which was indicating double yellow - and got out to telephone the signal box. While he was away, two Class 37s growled past with a car train. He returned with his eyebrows visibly in orbit. "The

"I had a frightening vision of us becoming the Flying Dutchmen of railway infrastructure, doomed to haul our two wagons around the South-east for eternity."

Eastleigh - the boys in the bothy

signalman's no knowledge of the incident," he intoned with a dash of irony.

So on we went, through Feltham, where saplings are transforming the once massive marshalling yard into urban woodland. By Hounslow the signal at the far end of the platform was red and its phone was ringing. It was the signalman again, clarifying what had happened back at Staines, so that his paperwork could be completed accurately. If only motorists faced the same stringent procedures at traffic lights, I thought whimsically, the steeply graded 'playing field' might be lowered a bit in public transport's favour.

Duty done, and seen to be done, we set off once more, traversing suburb after suburb. The density of the railway network in the South-east emphasises the magnitude of Railtrack's workload if it is to keep these routes maintained, let alone modernised. Oddly enough, most of the ballast used in this corner of England comes from a remote quarry on the west coast of Scotland. It's sailed in by ship to Southampton, Purfleet or Grain where 'virtual quarries'- or storage points, for those not familiar with current jargon - have been established. To EWS falls the task of ferrying it to local distribution centres at Eastleigh, Westbury, Hoo and Temple Mills in East London, from which, in due course, it is sourced as required.

We crossed the Grand Union Canal at Brentford, ran briefly alongside the M4, and bridged the Thames in the Boat Race environs of Barnes. Incandescent stations, depopulated between the end of rush hour and the return of theatre-goers, punctuated our progress. Clapham Junction laid no obstacles in our path. There were people here, at least, and how comic we must have looked to those who bothered to note our passing - two big, box like locomotives and two four-wheeled wagons; like a brace of burly bouncers manhandling a pair of misbehaved midgets out of a nightclub.

It was nine o'clock and Steve reckoned we would be at Hoo within the hour. A red light stopped us briefly near Stewart's Lane depot - a pale shadow of its former self - but soon we were over Factory Junction and through Wandsworth Road on a quadruple stretch of track which Clive told me was separated colloquially into the 'Chatham Line' and the 'Atlantic Line'; the latter, apparently, after some 'boozer' beside the railway arches in Brixton. Steve

Night-time shunting at Hoo Junction with 73108 and 73136

Brixton. Steve reckoned we'd get a glimpse of The Dome from Denmark Hill or, failing that, from Lewisham. At Peckham Rye Clive showed us where there had been coal drops in the days when 'The Smoke' relied on domestic coal for its winter warmth. I was thinking it would take me a month of Sundays to fathom the geography of the third rail network south of the Thames, though I knew I'd never again get the sort of 'ringside seat' which the view from the cab of a Class 73 afforded me. Our silent progress through the night had taken on a dream-like quality, which even the side windows, vibrating from time to time in synchronous resonance with the brake compressors, could not dispel.

In the vicinity of Hither Green, the EDs home depot, we passed a couple of oncoming goods trains: a Class 60 with empty stone wagons followed by the unusual combination of a Thirty-seven and Seventy-three hauling something we were unable to distinguish in the gloom. At night the drivers' of passing trains flick their interior lights on and off by way of a greeting. Sidcup always makes me think of *The Caretaker* and the character 'Peters' who was trying to get there for his 'papers'. It occurred to me that Harold Pinter might make an equally surreal and symbolic drama out of our evening's journey. Also of dramatic potential, was the story Clive and Steve told me at Bexley, where a dodgy car dealer was exposed to the police when the viaduct above his premises collapsed.

An old electric multiple unit, delegated to de-icing duties, brought nostalgic sighs from my companions at Crayford. Beyond Dartford, where lines of Networkers were stabled in sidings for the night, there was a real sense of having left London behind. I'd been down to Sittingbourne once, years ago, to write a piece about someone restoring a Thames sailing barge on Milton Creek, but otherwise this was decidedly a foreign land to me. As we ran through Gravesend, Steve brought the diesel engines to life to smooth our passage from the main line into the yard at Hoo. Remnants of the Thames & Medway Canal run parallel to the line and we passed a remote concrete platform once used for access to the rifle ranges on Denton Marsh. Hoo Junction affords access to the Isle of Grain branch, a line confined to goods use now, albeit busy with a variety of traffic flows: intermodal, infrastructure and construction. In the mists of time it led to two back-of-beyond Southern Railway termini - Port Victoria and Allhallows-on-Sea.

"What you doing here with this lot!" the shunter goaded us when we'd crossed the 'up' main line and entered the yard. We drew up on the reception road and, almost immediately, a Class 09 shunter coupled up to our two much-travelled Bass and sped them away, like tired children well past their bedtime. Frankly, it was past my bedtime too ...

*   *   *

As a parting shot, Kim Jordan had suggested I try and attend a possession. I'd told him I had an uncle who went to one once. My aunt had passed away suddenly and he needed to know where his clean socks were kept. "You're getting mixed up Michael," laughed Kim. "Your uncle probably went to a seance, a possession's something quite different, in railway terms it's where the engineers take over a length of line for a night, a weekend or, in some cases, even longer to undertake improvements or maintenance."

Standing corrected, I asked Clive Rooker to try and fix it for me to visit one of these possessions in the Woking area, but the weeks went by and nothing materialised; much like my uncle's socks. Then I read in *Rail* magazine that some of the Hoo Junction-Grain ballast trips were being worked by EWS's last handful of operational Class 31s, pretty much the only diesel type in current operation that I hadn't encountered on my travels. I had a soft spot for these unglamorous machines. Originally known as Brush Type 2s, they had been among the first designs of British Railways' mid Fifties Modernisation Plan, so some of the survivors had been trundling round the system for forty years. It seemed somehow 'meant' that I should catch up with them in a remote corner of Kent, not a stamping ground one traditionally associates with the class. In the beginning they were largely confined to the Eastern Region - south of the Humber and north of the Thames. One once took me on a boat train to Harwich, others I'd see in the glare of Sheffield and Rotherham steelworks. In the Seventies they were re-engined and spread their wings, finding work in the West Country, the Midlands and the North-west. I'd ridden behind them from Salisbury to Bristol, Oxford to Worcester, Birmingham to Norwich and Crewe to Holyhead. It was their unfashionable looks I liked; the over-preponderance of grillwork, the perpetual 'frown' on their face produced by the reduced depth of the cab's centre window. They were artisans mingling with aristocrats, foot-soldiers compared to cavalry; and I guess I just admired their guts. Ah yes, give me a Thirty-one, a compartment carriage and a view across some forgotten corner of England and Civilisation has reached its apotheosis as far as I'm concerned.

So I telephoned Neil Hickman, Traffic & Traincrew Manager at Hither Green depot, Lewisham, and asked if I could ride from Hoo to Grain and back on a ballast trip with an "oh and by the way, wouldn't it be a nice coincidence if they happened to be using a pair of Class 31s that day." Neil was helpfulness and enthusiasm personified, and tacitly 'promised' some Thirty-ones "as long as they haven't blown up by then."

Hoo Junction at eight on an August morning looked a smidgen more civilised than on my previous encounter with it, though there was still no denying its remoteness. This time I arrived by road, for only bona fide railway staff are allowed to use the tiny, concrete built halt beside the marshalling yard. A shame, that, because the marshes between the railway and the Thames Estuary have become a popular nature reserve, the towpath of the Thames & Medway Canal is in the process of being refurbished, and the *Saxon Shore Way* traverses the locality on its way from Gravesend to Rye.

I repaired to the enginemen's lobby where the air was blue but the mood mellow. Like enginemen everywhere since the days of *Novelty, Sans Pareil* and *Rocket*, they were debating the foibles of the traction at their beck and call. As a stranger - halfway between paradise and purgatory - I was welcomed with interest and courtesy. "Are any of you booked to drive the 09.19 to Grain?" I asked, and a guy called Colin Kerswill pointed me in the direction of Harry Bath, a driver of Asian descent, sitting in the corner. No-one, least of all Harry, was cognisant of my trip, but some phone calls were made and we discovered that we were awaiting the arrival of one Dennis Donovan, Hither Green driver and steam inspector.

With less than ten minutes to go before the booked departure, Dennis swept into the lobby, exchanged banter with all and sundry and kissed one of the men - Jim Bannister, an old colleague - on both cheeks, much to the delight of the assembled throng. Neil Hickman had been as good as his word. He had promised me a loquacious companion, and, in Dennis, I'd obviously got one. But the other rabbit I'd wanted conjuring from the hat, was not to appear. In that infuriatingly unreliable way of rabbits, my wished for Thirty-ones did not materialise, though, tantalisingly, a pair of the machines *were* tucked away in one corner of the up yard with a couple of Bass behind them - possibly the recalcitrant pair we'd towed from Eastleigh a few months before.

A delightful lady shunter called Barbara Drewery attended to our departure. "Are you ready for the brake test Harry?" she chortled down the radio. And in spite of Dennis Donovan's last minute arrival, we reversed on to the up main at 09.17 on the footplate of Loadhaul orange and black liveried Class 37 number 516. In terms of longevity, I privately admitted, this was the next best thing to a Thirty-one, but Dennis was dismissive of the design. "All bark and no bite!" But then he would be, no veteran of Bricklayers Arms (the South Eastern Division motive power depot, a lump of coal's throw from the Old Kent Road), which

Dennis had joined from school in 1951, would publicly admit to an interloper from the north being as powerful as the Southern Region's own, lamented Thirty-threes.

We spent the thirty minute journey to Grain oscillating between the end of the twentieth century and its dreamlike middle, between two quite different, yet not entirely dissimilar railway worlds. One moment we'd be discussing the finer minutiae of present day operations, the next Dennis would have us steaming down to Dover on the *Night Ferry* or the *Golden Arrow*. He himself had contrived to travel full circle from his £2 5/- a week days as an engine cleaner to a Steam Inspector due to footplate preserved Standard Class 5 73096 from Alton to Canterbury the following weekend.

37516 was towing a load of fourteen empty bogie box wagons, designated JRA, which would be left at Foster Yeoman's terminal at Grain to be loaded with ballast to add to the stockpile at Hoo Junction. The Grain branch dates back to 1879. In its original manifestation it was endearingly known as the Hundred of Hoo Railway (an EWS locomotive had just been so named) but before passenger services began operating the line had been assimilated by the South Eastern Railway Company. Fascinatingly, for the first few years of its life, the route boasted a service of continental boat trains connecting with railway steamers between Port Victoria, on the eastern extremity of the Isle of Grain, and the Belgian port of Flushing. A number of supplementary branches sprouted from the line: one to the vast cement workings in the neighbourhood of Cliffe; another to a naval depot reached via exchange sidings at Sharnal Street; a third for passenger traffic to the ambitiously promoted, but ultimately moribund, holiday resort euphemistically christened Allhallows-on-Sea, where Allhallows-on-*Mud* might have been more strictly accurate.

George Behrend journeyed over the line in the Thirties and wrote of the experience with typical lyricism in *Don't Knock The Southern.* Even then the service was so sporadic as to necessitate use of an omnibus part of the way, a preamble which came to an abrupt halt when the "bus swerved off the road and planted itself in the adjoining marsh." Eventually Behrend and his companion caught up with the train - a two-coach push & pull affair - at Stoke Junction Halt, being harangued by the communistic driver

"... Dennis swept into the lobby, exchanged banter with all and sundry and kissed one of the men - Jim Bannister, an old colleague - on both cheeks, much to the delight of the assembled throng."

Opposite - **Hundred of Hoo images**
Top left: **Harry Bath and Dennis Donovan;**
Centre top: **37516 at Grain;**
Top right: **Harry gets the token;**
Lower left: **Hoo Junction Staff Halt;**
Centre lower; **Middle Stoke;**
Lower right: **Cooling Bank**

Behrend would have got on altogether better with Dennis who was busy relating the story of some soldiers engaged in a mock exercise to blow up one of the branchline's overbridges. "They were in full camouflage, blackened faces, the lot, but they were all wearing high-visibility vests. They signalled me to bring the train to a halt and an officer came up to the footplate. I said. 'You ought to be more careful, I had a job to see you blokes!'"

About a mile from Hoo Junction we stopped to pick up a token for the single line to Grain. The siding to Cliffe veered off to the left, still used for the carriage of sea-dredged aggregates, but once, famously, the route of a daily train of cement from Cliffe to Uddingston on the outskirts of Glasgow which took Southern Region diesels as far north as York.

The gradient climbs from Hoo Junction's sea level, marshland setting to the Hundred of Hoo's two hundred foot plateau. On photographic reconnaissance the previous day, I'd followed the line's progress as closely as possible by road, finding myself with time to inspect St James's church at Cooling, inspiration for the opening passage of Dickens' *Great Expectations* where, in the swirling marshland mists of the graveyard, Pip first encounters the escaped convict Magwitch.

Flat out, 37516 dragged our 477 tonne load up Cooling Bank at a steady thirty miles an hour. "This wooded cutting may look picturesque", Dennis confided, "but in the autumn the leaves mulch down and make the rails extremely slippery." Harry nodded in agreement and added how difficult it had often been to get the heavy oil trains from Llandarcy over the summit. Wybourne Crossing marks the ridge of the escarpment and the site of High Halstow Halt. We slowed to take account of the crossing's 15mph speed restriction. "On the way out we'd order potatoes here," Dennis reminisced. "Half a hundredweight sacks of reds or whites grown beside the line, and they'd be ready for us to collect on the way back."

Harry shut off power and we free-wheeled down the bank in a shallow cutting of ragwort and rabbits with orchards on the horizon. We passed the sites of Sharnal Street station and Beluncle Halt, the latter deriving its mellifluous name from a nearby farm.

There are still sidings in situ, where coal was worked in recent memory to Kingsnorth Power Station, but these days it all comes in by sea. The line arced around the edge of Stoke Saltings and the graphically named Stoke Ooze, beyond which I'd watched coasters and barges navigating inland on the River Medway the day before. It is a landscape - seascape might perhaps be a better term - of low horizons and low cunning: twice each twenty-four hours the tide reaches out and tweaks the land's green cummerbund. In one creek an old steel barge lay tethered with an improvised line of washing fluttering incongruously along its rusty deck. Dennis joked that the limp clothing was arranged, naval fashion, to read 'England Expects'! Serendipitously, I had been reading Roger Deakin's *Waterlog,* a narrative of the author's swims around Britain, cocking a snook at authority's increasing aversion to 'wild' swimming. One chapter is devoted to his swim across the "brakish" Medway from the Gillingham shore to the island of Hoo Salt Marsh and its abandoned mid-nineteenth century fort, one of two built to protect Chatham Dockyard from would-be invaders. The other, Darnet Fort, was visible to us, beyond the power station's long jetty.

As our train rumbled by the scattered communities of Stoke, Middle Stoke and Lower Stoke, Dennis spoke regretfully of an oil train which derailed so violently here that many of the tanker wagons split their skins, spilling their sticky black liquid cargo out into the adjoining maze of creeks and inlets; a miniature *Torrey Canyon* of an environmental disaster thankfully rare in railway circles. We passed a lineside airstrip where microlites are built and tested and reached the site of Stoke Junction. "That's where the line to Allhallows ran," pointed Dennis. I saw its course curving away to the north and tried to imagine how differently things might have panned out if the holiday resort, gleaming in its developers' eyes, had flourished as hoped. Probably there would be a half-hourly service of electric trains from Charing Cross catering for a subtopian hinterland of bungalows and villas. Somehow we can all be glad that their grandiose schemes came to nothing.

Conjecture, nostalgia, I am whistling in the wind. The Grain branch flourishes today for hard-headed reasons based on

"Flat out, 37516 dragged our 477 tonne load up Cooling Bank at a steady thirty miles an hour."

economics and not whimsy. Indeed, its single track, however romantically threaded across the marshlands and orchards of this remote, saltwater-surrounded corner of Kent, is worked hard enough to warrant twenty-four hour operation. In addition to English Welsh & Scottish infrastructure ballast shuttles, there's a nightly Foster Yeoman aggregates train to Theale near Newbury, occasional trains of imported Polish coal for use by Guinness at its Park Royal plant, and heavy tonnages of intermodal traffic to and from Thamesport. Somehow, it seems, that each time the Isle of Grain loses traffic, like oil, bitumen and the Channel Tunnel associated construction traffics which have also disappeared in recent years, it's flexible and durable enough to throw up a new one. And I judged by the weight of road traffic using the parallel A228 that there is undoubtedly scope for more traffic to be transferred to rail if extra paths can be found.

Nearing its terminus, the line crosses the main road twice; the outermost level crossing being protected by automatic barriers, the innermost by good old fashioned hand-operated gates. We were met here by Ken Morrison, who took the token from us and inserted it in the drum inside the diminutive, cream-painted crossing box. Just before reaching this second crossing, we'd passed through a pair of flood gates. Following the Great Flood of 1953, British Petroleum didn't fancy being held to ransom by the sea a second time.

Grain is 38 miles and 22 chains from Charing Cross and 11 miles and 3 chains from Hoo Junction. Shunting space is at a premium and 37516 was held in a loop for twenty minutes until an intermodal train had overtaken us and pulled cautiously into the adjoining sidings at Thamesport. Harry went off for a smoke, Dennis regaled me with more tales from the footplate. "The diesels made us soft, now we moan if there's a draught from the window, in steam days we'd work all weathers in exposed cabs."

Presently we proceeded cautiously into Foster Yeoman's yard at the present extremity of the line, just short of the site of Port Victoria's pier from which the ferries for Belgium departed all those years ago. We left our empty wagons in the loop and drew forward to collect another train of empties requiring maintenance - not the loaded ballast train I had expected; though by now I had learnt to expect the unexpected where infrastructure was concerned. Of the return journey to Hoo Junction there is little to relate. Dennis and Harry were convivial company, the scenery splendid and the weather benign. At 'The Junction' we reversed our box wagons into the down yard and crossed to the up yard to stable the locomotive. Under supervision, I was given the task of applying the hand brake, which took so many winds of the handle that I suspected Dennis of winding *me* up. Harry went off to check about his next duty - possibly a trip up the Cliffe spur for aggregates - and Dennis checked his watch · to see when the next up train would respond to a the wave of a high-visibility vest from the staff halt. I went back to my car. The Thirty-ones had departed into the ether - if not history - not only was I not going to get a ride on them, I wouldn't be getting a photograph either.

A Class 37 returning from Grain with infrastructure box wagons - with Thamesport and the Medway beyond the creeks of Stoke Ooze

ayrshire coal

**Curving round the
Killoch Branch
near Drongan**

AYRSHIRE! High rolling hills, sweetly named watercourses, sleekly eponymous cattle, Burns Country; the stuff of tourism. Only there's a darker side - literally - black blotches on the braes; opencast coal, and lots of it. Take the A70 (which you'll share with a steady stream of coal lorries) and, past Ochiltree, you breast a rise to be confronted with Scottish Coal's Killoch Opencast Distribution Point. It hits you like a punch on the nose in a beer tent; great heaps of coal and a high utilitarian building; a Marcel Duchamp-like collision between brick and concrete. Once Killoch was the jewel in the National Coal Board's modernisation crown, a deep mine with a cast iron future. So they thought when they sunk the first shaft in 1953. Within thirty years it was shut - progress, privatisation and, I daresay, a fair amount of political skulduggery brought deep mining to an abrupt end. It might have been an end to the carriage of coal by rail as well had there not been a Utopian - if not economic - requirement for the black stuff from the power industry.

I suppose in my typically untypical way I eschewed the obvious when choosing a journey for the chapter devoted to Old King Coal. Obvious, would have been a Merry Go Round train trundling between the Selby coalfield and an Aire or Trent valley power station. But traffic patterns are changing rapidly. Large tonnages of coal are being imported and worked longer distances, more profitably for English Welsh & Scottish. Also there were geographical criteria to fulfil. The emerging map of my travels looked threadbare beyond Hadrian's Wall. Besides, I had once drunk a treacly black stout with my father and his father in the Miners' Welfare at Brocketsbrae, so this Scottish journey would be something of a 'hamecoming'.

One tends to think of Ayr - if one thinks of it at all - as a seaside town with a view, called Arran, that you'd die for. But substantiating the county's Jekyll and Hyde tendencies, there are boils on its backside, one of which is a phalanx of loops and sidings within stone-skimming distance of the seafront. This is Falkland Yard, point of dispatch for upwards of fifteen lengthy coal trains a day to places as distant as Staffordshire, Yorkshire, Merseyside and Fife. An increasing proportion of this coal is imported through Hunterston Dock between Largs and Ardrossan. The rest is opencast mined in the hills behind Ayr and 'tripped' down to

Falkland Yard along surprisingly scenic branch lines, which, elsewhere would undoubtedly feature tourist-orientated steam operation.

There had been an element of confusion - a commodity which seemed to anticipate my movements - and my plans had been changed. I'd had it in mind to follow the fortunes of the daily Falkland-Methil Power Station coal slurry train. You may remember Methil featured in The Proclaimers' song *Letter from America* as one of a list of unsavoury Scots towns for which it was difficult to believe in a benign future. It was a coal and docks town, 'was' being the operative word. But anyone who has read my canal guides will know that I enjoy a perverse affinity with such places - the Walsalls, Wigans and Worksops of this world - and I also relished the reverse symmetry of a West to East, coast to coast run to contrast with my earlier journey with chemical containers from Teesport to Workington.

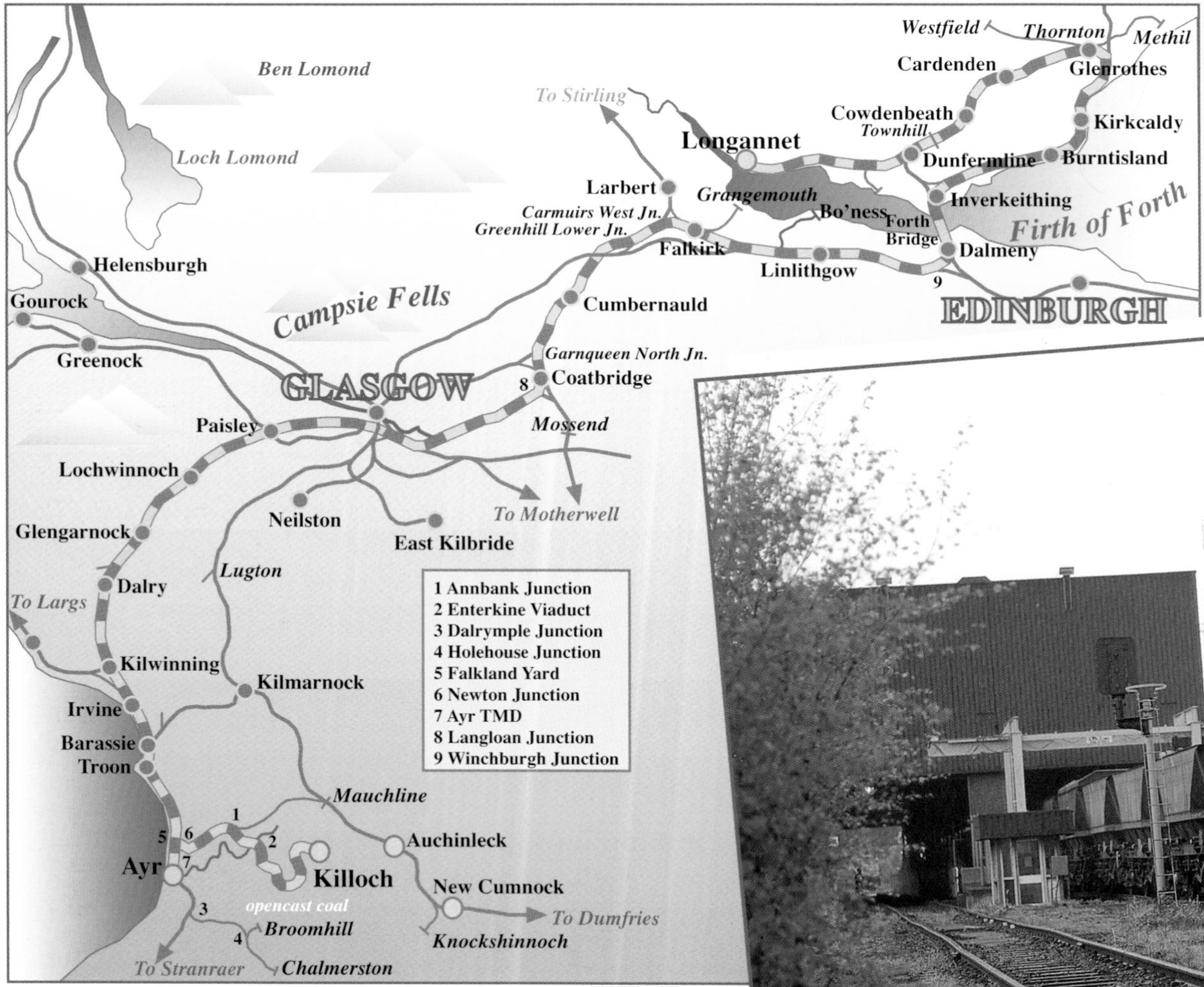

The slurry train's a Thornton duty - Thornton being a once huge and now small, but still significant, railway centre to the north of Kirkcaldy - and it's booked to run from Methil to Falkland with empty wagons in the morning and return with loaded ones after lunch. The slurry itself comes down from Killoch the previous afternoon, and George Small, of EWS Motherwell, had arranged for me to travel over the branchline with an Ayr driver so that I

Discharging at Longannet

1 Annbank Junction
2 Enterkine Viaduct
3 Dalrymple Junction
4 Holehouse Junction
5 Falkland Yard
6 Newton Junction
7 Ayr TMD
8 Langloan Junction
9 Winchburgh Junction

John Hunter at the regulator of 56078

would make the same full journey as the box wagons. Unfortunately, when I'd reached Falkland Yard, on the back of a five hour drive from Staffordshire, they'd told me that, due to circumstances beyond their control, "the slurry was nae running the day".

Nae slurry, nae bother. I had a driver, I had a minder, we had a path, so we hooked on a train of hoppers and hot-footed it up the branch from Newton Junction while the 'gannin was guid'. We were immediately beyond the widespread limits of Paisley's power box, and under the mechanical control of Mauchline's signalman. Alongside Ayr's motive power depot, home to around forty local drivers, we had stopped at Black House to acquire an electric token for the single track as far as Annbank, four miles to the west.

I had better introduce my fellow conspirators: John Hunter, Robert McInally, and locomotive number 56078; a machine of early Eighties vintage, still 'dressed down' in Railfreight grey. Its colours suited Ayr's periphery. The single line was strewn with litter and cast oots. At Annbank Junction we were met by a shunter called Gary Withers. It was his job to pass us up the branch and see to uncoupling and coupling at Killoch.

From Annbank, which the Ordnance Survey shows confusingly as Mossblown, the direct line to Mauchline and the former Glasgow & South Western main line from Glasgow, through Kilmarnock and Dumfries to Carlisle, continues due west. The Killoch branch, which originally ran through to Muirkirk, as

part of a once incredibly dense network of local lines built to serve the coalfield, veers off to the south and snakes its way through some charming countryside to its black terminus, a dozen miles from Ayr and, according to one of the yellow mileposts which stand trackside on the branch, 51 miles from Glasgow.

We needed a fresh token from the groundframe at Annbank to let us on to the branch. Only one train is allowed on the branch at any given time. It takes the best part of an hour to travel from Ayr to Killoch in each direction. Add shunting in the colliery precincts, and it means a minimum return journey time of around three hours. Thus there are currently paths for half a dozen round trips a day, but everyone would like more. Killoch has become a distribution point for several opencast sites and it also acts as a washery, some coal being brought in by rail to be cleaned. A number of independent mining contractors are involved and demand for their product is high. EWS, in consultation with Railtrack, is being encouraged to provide extra capacity. This could come from new methods of train working, or some upgrading of the signalling. It's a nice problem to have.

I confess to somewhat predictably expecting the crossing of the Forth Bridge to be the highlight of my two part journey. It certainly proved a fitting climax, but along the way I fell in love with Enterkine Viaduct, astonishingly unknown, even amongst the *cognoscenti*, rarely photographed and unscripted in railway literature. It spans the River Ayr, south of the former colliery village of Crawfordston, its flat iron deck supported by a sequence of slender masonry piers. "It looks even better from below," Rab had said, and the following day I took him at his word and was rewarded by the accompanying photograph.

Beyond the viaduct, we plunged into a fir plantation, and came back into the open in pursuit of a particularly mad March hare. We were doing twenty, it was limbering up for the leporine olympics. Here and there were spoil tips - or 'bings' as they call them in Scotland - left over from deep mining days. 56078 lumbered by remnants of the old stations at Trabboch and Drongan, which sounded more Irish to me than Scots, and wouldn't have looked out of place in the timetable of the Cavan & Leitrim. Passengers must have been conspicuous by their absence, but

A Class 60 locomotive heads across Enterkine Viaduct with loaded
coal hoppers for Falkland Yard

**Rab McNally
on point duty at Killoch**

"Aye, I ken the
steam boilers,
sonny, I mind
them weel!"

presumably the revenue from coal more than compensated the Sou' Western's coffers.

John and Rab are both thirty-somethings. You know you're getting old, I thought, when it's the engine drivers, rather than policeman, that are younger than you. They've worked nineteen and seventeen years on the railway respectively. In neither case had they been drawn to the railway out of interest or enthusiasm. John, in fact, had worked in a shoe factory. "I was a leather upper cutter," he told me, which made him sound like some sort of boxer, and he had the square jaw to go with it. Redundancy forced him to look for another job, and it was his father-in-law, a locomotive driver, who suggested he try British Rail. In his early years as a secondman at Ayr, John, like others we've met on these wanderings, spent half his time grappling with those devils incarnate, otherwise known as steam heat boilers. John, something of a 'wee comic' in his dour, Scots, deadpan way, mimicked the querulous tones of an old man: "Aye, I ken the steam boilers, sonny, I mind them weel!" He's laughing now, in another thirty years railway publishers will be beating a path to his door for reminiscences like these.

Rab had joined the railway straight from school - or, rather, he'd gone home to change first. He became a lamp man. "They needed a monkey to climb all those ladders," John had interjected. Rab had trawled round the district's signal boxes, filled a drum with paraffin from the oil house, then shinned up each signal ladder to replenish the sumps in the spectacle lamps. "It was a brilliant job," he told me, with ill-concealed enthusiasm and nostalgia. But there was no future in it, the march of modernisation rid Ayr of most of its semaphores, the few survivors being lit electrically.

The Muirkirk line had headed in a south-easterly direction from Drongan - a village of unmistakable coal mining provenance - I glimpsed its melancholy earthworks diminishing in perspective across miry ground watered by the Taiglum Burn. The colliery line, of comparatively recent construction, turns in a big arc back towards the north. There's a shallow cutting governed by a 10mph speed limit. Apparently it's susceptible to landslips. "They should let it collapse and lay the track over the top," Rab suggested before

dramatically lugging open the cab door and beckoning me to look at Ben Lomond, all of fifty miles away, but exposed by a sudden gap in the clouds. "You ken by the shape," he insisted, and I wasn't about to argue.

Gary, having driven up from Annbank in a hired van, let us into Killoch sidings, where a catch point is installed to prevent any headstrong wagons from taking it upon themselves to escape from the yard and head off for a day on the coast. Rab showed me where there had been a bothy for the shunting staff when there'd been a colliery here: "I used to ride shotgun with the manager when he came up here on Thursdays with the wage packets." The single line fans out into eight tracks, or 'roads' as they call them, two of which are largely moribund with discernibly rusty rails. I was surprised to see two shunting locomotives, a Class 08, busily positioning wagons, and a hired Sentinel diesel as well.

We drew slowly along road number six until our thirty-six HAA hopper wagons were clear of the rear points. Rab rang Doncaster to tell control we'd arrived. We uncoupled, then, gingerly the locomotive proceeded past the washing and blending plant to the headshunt. The track was all but buried by coal dust made glutinous by the winter's heavy rains. I asked if I could get out and do some photography. "Nae bother," said John, "only watch where you put your feet or we might have to come and pull you out by the ears!" I got the message.

I'm not sure I subscribe to the theory of reincarnation, but collieries send a shiver down my spine which a passing interest in industrial archaeology barely accounts for, so possibly I was a miner in a former life, how else can I explain that recurring fantasy of having my back scrubbed in a tin bath? Abandoned wartime aerodromes have a similar effect on me, as do one or two other things which belong in a different and, I daresay, better selling book. Suffice it to say, I was in my element, stalking 56078 around the yard, trying to capture it in the lens against the almost surreal backdrop of the washery, seeing it reflected in puddles and against the glow of a fiery brazier. Killoch is one of four Ayrshire coal railheads currently in use. Of the other three, Knockshinnoch lies off the Glasgow & South Western main line near New Cumnock; Broomhill is awkwardly located on a spur off the

Fire and brimstone at Killoch washery

this is just a formality, but occasionally, perhaps if the coal is wetter than usual, a wagon may be overweight and require the removal of some of its load before it can proceed. We had 1,537 tonnes, loaded in thirty-six HAAs, and learnt from the print-out faxed quickly through from Doncaster that they were destined for Drax Power Station in Yorkshire. Rab telephoned control again. "Hello Mr Boyle, I'm just coming oot o'Killoch the noo." I'm not exaggerating his accent for effect. I remember being told by Knottingley drivers, regularly driving up to Ayrshire now over the Settle & Carlisle, that they found the local patois impenetrable. Being half Scottish by birth, and wholly so by affinity, I didn't expect to have too much trouble with my compatriot's vernacular. But en masse, in the mess room at Falkland Yard, they might have been speaking the Gaelic for all I could mak oot.

There followed one of the most idyllic sequences among my rail freight journeys. Down the branch we went with the sun setting over Arran, the rail joints resounding to the rhythmic clang of each passing four wheeled wagon. The side windows were down, oystercatchers called over the adjoining fields, lambs bleated and watched us inquisitively. Prompted by the sea view, Rab regaled us with fishing talk. A keen sea angler, he bemoaned the pollution which was diminishing the stocks of bass, flounder and coddling historically indigenous to the Ayrshire coast. Whitewashed farms glowed in the golden light. Silhouetted figures moved with heightened symbolism along traffic denuded roads.

We recrossed the Ayr and returned to Annbank. Rab phoned Mauchline box to see if we'd get a clear run into Ayr, but there was another coal train on its way down the 'main' line and we knew we'd have to bide a while at the junction. It's not always a good place to be marooned. As the old playground taunt would have us believe, sticks and stones won't necessarily break our bones, but they can clang resoundingly on the cabside. "It should be a designated hard hat area," John suggested laconically. A new shift had begun, and a shunter whose name I didn't catch was waiting to see us off the branch. A toddler in a pink coat walked by waving with her mum. John studiously ignored her. "Do you nae wave at wains?" Rab challenged him. "Is waving written into the job description?" I said, just about my funniest contribution of the afternoon compared with the other wee comics.

A Class 60 in Loadhaul livery swept by on the line from Mauchline. It would need to be clear of Black House before we could follow in its wake. The smell of fish suppers frying filtered into the cab from Mossblown's tightly-packed streets. Rab was telling me that this was his second of three consecutive six-hour shifts on the Killoch Branch. The day after next he was due to drive a Yorkshire bound coal train as far as Carlisle. The coal train ahead took its time to clear the section, but eventually the semaphore governing access off the Killoch line rose, and we drew forward on to the Mauchline-Newton line until, with reference to some trackside marker boards, we judged our rear

Dalmellington branch, necessitating the use of a guard's van (an old Southern Railway bogie vehicle) to facilitate the working; and Chalmerston sits near the end of what's left of the old Dalmellington branch; another highly scenic line, which wends its way delightfully up the Doon Valley to where the National Coal Board had its extensive Waterside system of mineral lines. The late railway photographer Derek Cross once described these as "elemental lines in an elemental landscape." Quite honestly, I could have stayed put and written a whole book about these fascinating coal lines. Something of their history can be gleaned from a visit to the admirable Dunaskin Heritage Centre at Patna.

Returning to the yard throat, we backed down on to a train of loaded hoppers, paused to create the brake, then drew forward slowly over the weighbridge. Usually

Glenn Elvin

wagon to have cleared the point. Now the token could be released and we could proceed to Black House. Dusk had drawn its curtains on the landscape. We ran past the backs of houses whose inhabitants watched television between robotic bites of supper. At Black House Rab kept an eye open for the local kids whose chief joy in life is to race down on to the track, while drivers are otherwise engaged with the token machine, and steal the tail lamp.

We rang Paisley power box, to get permission to proceed, and were told we would be routed on to the harbour branch. A modicum of local coal is exported through Ayr Harbour to Ireland and some opencast coal is loaded on to railway hoppers in the harbour precincts, but mostly the harbour sidings are used by EWS to increase the capacity of Falkland Yard. We were waiting to cross the main line alongside Ayr's motive power servicing depot. A splash of light revealed the identity of one of the Class 56s on the fuelling road as none other than 56004, the last member of the class still wearing British Rail blue livery at the time. When finally we crossed over to the harbour, Rab introduced me to "the best shunter ever at Falkland!" This accolade went to John Skilling, ex-miner, ex-merchant seaman, a flat-capped sexagenarian just commencing his twelve hour shift. We uncoupled quickly, Rab drove 56078 back to the depot, I drove back along the A70 for a fish supper in Ochiltree. Floodlights bathed the purlieus of Killoch as I passed - there was still work to be done.

*   *   *

Six or seven weeks later I was on the A70 again, only this time there were no coal lorries, probably because it was three o'clock in the morning. It was still dark when I reached Ayr, though there was a hint of daylight hanging beyond the floodlight gantries of Somerset Park, Ayr United's decrepit football ground, which stands alongside the EWS traction depot. John Hunter and I arrived simultaneously. "Alright?" I grinned. "No, I don't like getting up this early!" This time I knew he wasn't joking.

All thoughts of Methil had been abandoned, I was heading for Longannet, a bigger power station on the north bank of the Firth of Forth. John had been asked to accompany me, but when we got to the office there was an urgent message for him to call Rosters. For a moment, judging by the look on his face as he came off the phone, I had visions of a second cancellation. "Don't tell me the train's not running again," I begged him. "No, the train's running, you're going, but I'm not. I'm off tae Lugton." Such was the shortage of drivers that, given the choice between accompanying a journalist and working a revenue-earning train of fertilizer, there was no contest. Fortunately, regulations were to be 'relaxed' and it had been tacitly agreed that I should ride with the driver on my own. The driver, Glenn Elvin, had 'nae problem' with this arrangement, all he wanted was for us to get on our way as quickly as possible. "The sooner we're gannin the sooner we'll be back!"

Our engine, number 56088, was stabled in the shadows of the shed. So deep was the gloom, and so weatherstained its paintwork, that it was a moment or two before I realised that - hallelujah! - it was in EWS red and gold colours. Ten locomotives down the line and finally I'd 'copped' a red one! Glenn scurried aboard and got it going by turning the key and pressing the starter button in a routine personally reminiscent of many a narrowboat coaxed into life on misty, early morning canals - only the roar inside the engine room was a tad noisier.

Glenn busied himself expertly, satisfying himself that the locomotive would get us to Fife and back. "These are the best engines of the lot," he shouted out of the engine room. "Loading power, acceleration, ride - I don't know why they're doing away with them." Not exactly charismatic, the Fifty-sixes date from 1976, the first batch - of what eventually numbered a hundred and thirty-five locomotives - being built, somewhat bizarrely, under licence in Romania. They are big lumbering locomotives, given to emitting a high-pitched whine when extending themselves, and they have spent their working lives handling the traditional train loads of heavy industry: coal, oil and steel. I thought Glenn was being a trifle pessimistic in believing their days to be numbered. True, a few have been withdrawn - particularly from the non-standard Romanian ranks - but I'm sure EWS will rely on their sheer brute power for a good few years yet.

Though there are a number of coal trains shuttling between Ayrshire and Fife daily, Ayr drivers are only rostered on one, booked to leave Falkland Yard at 05.25. Indeed, at the time of my trip, only four Ayr drivers had the 'route knowledge' necessary to work this train. Regulations demand that drivers have to work regularly over a route, otherwise their 'knowledge' elapses and they have to re-apply to learn the route under instruction before being passed to work over it again.

Glenn's game plan was to get away before five if possible, and we were at the exit to the depot at four-thirty, metaphorically pawing the ground in impatience to be off. "Hello Paisley, this is 0Z53 ready for Falkland Yard," spoke Glenn into his mobile, and within seconds we'd got the go ahead to accelerate out on to the main line through Newton-on-Ayr station. John Skilling was waiting for us, just about to finish his night shift this time. He remembered me from my previous visit, but there was no time for even the smallest of talk; Glenn's sense of hurry was infectious.

Dawn was breaking over a sullen sea; Arran invisible behind a curtain of cloud. Re-numbered 7Z53 with our payload, we got away just before five which, according to Glenn's calculations, should get us past the periphery of Glasgow before the commuter traffic got into full swing. We had twenty-nine hoppers in tow, 1,286 tonnes in total; mostly unhooded HAAs but some canopied HBAs as well. Much to Glenn's chagrin we were subject to a 45mph maximum speed limit on account of those open-topped wagons. Apparently a woman, standing blithely on some platform, had been covered in coal dust by a passing train. A bit of a fuss had ensued and, as a consequence, coal trains with unhooded wagons had had their speed reduced by twenty-five per cent. How unreasonable can passengers get? Any self-respecting railway enthusiast would relish being covered in a thousand particles of the black stuff.

Glenn acknowledges the problem but reckons it's easily solved. "Yes, on a nice dry day there's a big black cloud behind us, like a swarm of insects, but quite honestly it's blown off after the first ten miles. But when it's wet you won't get any blow-off at all. And it doesn't matter how wet it is. When it gets to the power station they inject it into the furnaces by force. What we ought to do is erect gantries at a few key locations - Falkland, Carlisle, Mossend - to spray water on the coal when its dry." Sorted! Or should that be 'done and dusted'?"

This corner of North Ayrshire is a fertile stamping ground for English Welsh & Scottish: aircraft fuel comes into Prestwick from Grangemouth; pharmaceuticals go to Roche at Dalry; china clay to Caledonian Paper at Irvine; and of course there's imported coal from Hunterston. We ran through Troon's elegant timber station on a curve and passed the infrastructure sidings at Barassie. My father would have been at home in this land of golf links. Ponies with coats on were standing disconsolately in muddy fields on the outskirts of Irvine, another of the terminally ill towns which The Proclaimers sang about in *Letter from America*. Glenn's story of a lineside school which the pupils were in the habit of setting on fire only served to confirm one's first impressions of a town on the edge of disintegration. He pointed out a housing estate to me: "I would'na go in there - they eat people!" I saw no reason to suppose he was exaggerating for dramatic effect.

Beyond Kilwinning, where we had been joined by the line from Largs and Hunterston, we ran through the pretty valley of the River Garnock. Glenn was telling me that his father had been a driver and that he had been away when Glenn and his twin brother, also a present day driver at Ayr, were born. "He got a bit of a shock when he got to the ward and saw two cots beside my mum's bed. She'd been watching *The Glenn Miller Story* when she went into labour. He asked her what she was going to call us. 'Glenn and Miller,' she said, looking at me.

'Aye, but what aboot the ither?' he asked her.

'Are ye deef o' something - this wain's Glenn and that wain's Miller!'

After I'd stopped laughing, somewhere beyond Lochwinnoch,

Glenn added, with a sense of timing that would have done credit to Francie and Josie. "Aye, I'm glad I came oot first!"

At Paisley it was my turn to indulge in family roots. What with my dulcet Sassenach tones I realised it was difficult for Glenn to believe that I'd been born here, but somewhere in the safe at home, there's a dog-eared certificate to prove it. With time to kill following my aborted trip to Methil, I'd made a brief pilgrimage to Paisley Canal station where, according to family legend, my Aunt Isa had kick-started my addiction to railways by pushing me there in my pram along the cobbled thoroughfares from Espedair Street. As we went through Gilmour Street, another handsome station - partly ascribed to the same architect, James Miller, as Troon - I showed Glenn the bowling club where my Uncle George had played, leaving me to lean happily for hours on the trackside fence and watch a procession of Riddles, Fairburn and Stanier tanks steam by on Clyde Coast trains.

A grey Class 56 came by with what Glenn took to be empties, returning from Longannet to Hunterston; a Motherwell man at the regulator. A degree of rivalry exists between depots. Mostly it appears to be friendly, but there are instances, I'd begun to sense on my travels, where the men of one depot would resent another working into what they regarded as their patch. After years of absence, lodging turns were making something of a comeback. Now, for example, a driver from Yorkshire might work into Ayr, stay overnight in a hotel, then work deeper into Scotland before returning home; covering turns which Ayr men regarded, rightly or wrongly, as their province. I report this at face value, and not to get involved with politics, but I think it goes without saying that a railway operator's traction crews are a key resource and that only happy hens lay eggs.

Glenn tried to point out Ibrox to me. I misread his intent. "Do you follow Rangers?" I asked.

"You'd nae see me in that pigsty!" came the resounding reply. By which I divined that I was talking to a Celtic fan.

So far we'd had a clear run. We approached Glasgow, passing on to the Clydesdale line by way of Shields and Terminus junctions. Then, briefly, we ran along the West Coast Main Line past Polmadie depot before taking what Glenn called 'The R&C', the Rutherglen

and Coatbridge line at Rutherglen East Junction. "This was goods only until recently," Glenn explained. "The track's in good condition but we're limited to thirty while the passenger trains can go at fifty." We passed British Steel's Clydebridge works, no longer rail connected; crossed the Clyde, little more than a modest watercourse this far upstream; and ran by shot-blasted tennements to Carmyle, the first of a series of re-opened stations. At Mount Vernon the stench of coal gas invaded the cab. "It's the methane escaping from the landfill site," said Glenn, and I took his word for it.

Through the cab window I could see that we were tackling a steep gradient but Glenn was happy with 56088's performance. "We've got a guid engine. We're doing thirty-five, a lot of locos would only get up to thirty here." At Bargeddie a pair of Metro-Cammell 101s in the orange and black livery of Strathclyde PTE bounced by heading downhill; rush hour was getting underway. We breasted the summit, Glenn shut off and coasted down to Langloan Junction where we got our first red light of the morning. Glenn put it down to a passenger train blocking the main line at Coatbridge Central. I could tell that the next half hour would be critical if we were to get beyond Glasgow's dense suburban network unscathed.

Glenn was just about to go and ring the signalman when the light changed to yellow and we were able to proceed round the tight curve to Coatbridge. I caught a glimpse of Summerleas Heritage Park where the sort of Glasgow I'd grown up vaguely familiar with was being preserved in aspic. I wondered fleetingly if the same could be done for me.

At Gartsherrie South, we took the Cumbernauld line, breathing a sigh of relief that we were beginning to pull clear of Glasgow's tentacles. But then it seemed as though the gods would mock us, for at Garnqueen North Junction we got a 'feather' indicating us into the loop. "I don't like the look of this," said Glenn ruefully, fearing we were about to be sidelined. But it was just the signalman 'testing his points' and we went straight back on to the main line. Sadly, as far as I was concerned, the Caledonian Railway signal boxes along this part of our route were in the process of being replaced by a new power box at Cowlairs.

"Glenn was happy with 56088's performance. We've got a guid engine. We're doing thirty-five, a lot of locos would only get up to thirty here."

Cumbernauld brings to mind Bill Forsyth's *Gregory's Girl* and, less entertainingly, shuddering visions of brown envelopes bearing tax demands. Yet the railway's progress through the new town's housing estates is surprisingly rural and largely confined to deep bosky cuttings. Glenn was summarising his railway career, which commenced in 1985. Always at Ayr, he'd graduated to secondman status within four years, working with drivers on Ayr's prestigious InterCity rosters to Stranraer and Carlisle with the boat trains on Class 47s; which, like all the drivers I'd met so far, he couldn't speak too highly of. Likewise Glenn had chosen freight over passenger when privatisation loomed. Multiple units, be they diesel or electric, were anathema, "buses on rails".

As we whizzed through Cumbernauld station itself, Glenn pointed out a nearby Chinese takeaway. How did I know that sooner or later the talk would turn to food? Glenn, it transpired, was known to fellow traction staff as 'the kebab kid'. I didn't think it politic to delve too closely into the reason for this, but I did learn of the unsurpassed steak pies of Leven, and the quality of the fish suppers in Cowdenbeath. It began to rain, a fine drizzle, or what the Scots would call a 'smirr'. Glenn would have preferred it to increase in intensity: "Light rain sticks to the track and makes it greasy and slippery. Heavy rain washes itself off."

Even today, post Beeching, the geography of railways in the vicinity of Falkirk can bewilder strangers. We were running along the old Caledonian Railway's Buchanan Street-Stirling main line upon which Gresley's streamliners had enjoyed an unlikely Indian Summer in the mid-Sixties. Presently we passed beneath the rival North British line connecting Queen Street with Waverley. We were in the neighbourhood of the Roman's Antonine Wall and running parallel with the Forth & Clyde Canal; history had left its imprint on the landscape. At Carmuirs West Junction the main line veered north towards Larbert, Stirling and Perth whilst we passed on to former North British territory. A Class 60 with the good Scots name of *Alexander Fleming* came by with a tanker train which Glenn guessed would be bound for Prestwick.

I was enjoying this extended ride on a Fifty-six. They are noisier than Sixties. To converse we had to shout. By the end of the day I had a sore throat. Glenn had warned me they were 'lively' engines. "Well sprung," he'd said; at least that's what it had sounded like over the din. No. 88 took the points like a showjumper, yet always sure-footedly enough to land back on the same track. We'd gone through Falkirk Grahamston and Polmont when, just after seven o'clock, Glenn drew my attention to a high chimney jutting over the cooling towers and refinery pipework of Grangemouth. "There's Longannet," he laughed, "four or five miles as the crow flies, but we're still two hours away!"

Fife lay across the Forth like a foreign country. It seemed inconceivable that we could get there by train at all. On the outskirts of Linlithgow we passed the junction for the line to Bo'ness, now operated as a preserved railway. My friend, Geoffrey Evison - a big-hearted man, both physically and mentally - had been working as a volunteer ticket collector on the line the previous week. We also crossed the Avon Viaduct, which flings twenty-six arches across the eponymous river, one of several notable structures enjoying listed status on this length of railway. Even in Scotland I was not safe from canals. I pointed out the Union Canal to Glenn as it ran alongside us at a slightly higher level, so that its surface was obscured from view. "I'd always thought that was an old railway," he admitted, so I told him about the forthcoming Millennium Wheel and what a landmark it would become on his trans-Scottish journeys.

56088 rocked and rolled its way over the pointwork at Winchburgh Junction and Glenn pointed out a lineside dwelling where: "the old fella usually gives us a wave." It reminded me of John Betjeman's poem *Great Central Railway* and the bit about the diesel driver's friend at Hucknall South, who waved from a front-room window as he hooted round the bend. Sir John would have loved these goods train journeys. His poetry and prose inspired the teenage me towards a deep loathing for the excesses of road traffic and the damage done to the fabric of Britain's topography. Not only would he have enjoyed the ride and the company, he would have endorsed the rationale of carrying goods by rail.

By Dalmeny it was raining more aggressively. It was half past seven and an Edinburgh-bound Sprinter in Scotrail's new colours of predominently purple and green had deposited a small army

"Fife lay across the Forth like a foreign country. It seemed inconceivable that we could get there by train at all."

A Virgin CrossCountry train on the building site otherwise known as the Forth Bridge

of workers who were trudging towards the Forth Bridge. Superlatives are irrelevant in the face of such a structure. One might as well evince awe at Niagara or Everest or Bells of Shotts steak pies. As railway bridges go, only Brunel's Royal Albert Bridge across the Tamar can hold a flickering candle to it. Yet, strangely, whilst nine out of ten people could name the designer of the latter, I'd like to bet that only one in ten could tell you who was chiefly responsible for the Forth Bridge; and I'm certainly not going to give you a clue. Currently, after a period of scandalous neglect - when even the proverbially perennial painting teams had gone part time - the bridge is benefiting from a five year programme of refurbishment. From the cab's front window it resembled a building site. The deck was filled with builders' debris which reminded me forcibly of the chaos endemic at home when we had the central heating installed. At least I profited from the 20mph speed limit imposed on freight trains, being given a bit more time to take in the stupendous views. A southbound Virgin train loomed out of the rain as Glenn pointed out the oil tanker berth far below on our right and the old battery on Inch Garvie. A quick sweep inland revealed the naval base at Rosyth and the Firth elbowing its way inland towards the refineries of Grangemouth.

Then, after 2,766 cantilevered yards of railway flight, we came back down to earth, taking the contrast one step further by quickly burrowing underground at North Queensferry Tunnel. For Glenn, this was going to be a decisive moment. "Either they'll send us round the Fife Circle or we'll be routed via Dunfermline and have to run round at Townhill." Not until they've rounded the curve at Inverkeithing can drivers tell from the signals which way they'll be going and, whichever way the signalman has decided, the driver of a loaded coal train has his work cut out to launch his heavy train into a tight curve and stiffish gradient: climaxing at 1 in 89 on the direct Dunfermline route and 1 in 94 coastwise through Dalgety. This time, on the signalman's whim apparently, we were signalled round the Fife Circle, and I was glad, not only because it lengthened an already hugely enjoyable cab ride, but also because I'd get to add a few more Scottish football grounds to my collection.

An antiquated, Scottish-built, Pressed Steel Class 117 multiple

unit chattered past on a rush hour commuter train as we reached the top of the climb at Dalgety Bay. Then it was downhill through Aberdour and on to the coast through Burntisland, where Agricola landed his legions in the first century AD. I made a mental note to return and photograph the lattice-weave viaduct in its dockland setting where a sizeable coastal vessel was berthed as we squealed round the curve. Glenn was regaling me with the description of a railway trip he'd made in New Jersey where he'd been impressed by the provision of a chilled water dispenser in the cab. "And if it's not filled," he added pointedly, "the driver is in his rights to declare the locomotive a 'failure'." On the same subject he thought I ought to drop a gentle hint to EWS that, these days, a microwave would be a whole lot more useful in the cab than the old fashioned hotplates currently provided. The tacit insinuation being that drivers of locomotives thus fitted would be gastronomically self-sufficient. There you are then, Glenn, don't forget the cheque!

There was a big trackside works at Burntisland whose function we couldn't decipher, but it looked as though the volume was there for rail transport to become involved. As the line clung to the coast I was rewarded with sweeping views of the Firth, Edinburgh and Arthur's Seat, the Pentland Hills and Bass Rock. By Pettycur Bay, Glenn drew my attention to a line of houses with their 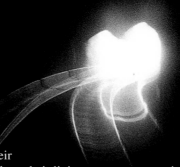 backs to the railway. "See how their living rooms are upstairs so that they can look over the watter?" At Kinghorn we encountered the 'Irish Tunnel', apparently so called because of the pronounced kink in the middle, as though digging had commenced simultaneously from both ends and not so much met in the middle as been given a glancing blow.

I got a grandstand view, so to speak, of Raith Rovers' ground as we ran into Kirkaldy. I had to interrupt Glenn, who was waxing enthusiastically over his hobby of model soldier collecting and war games, a pastime he takes seriously enough to visit the

> "Either they'll send us round the Fife Circle or we'll be routed via Dunfermline and have to run round at Townhill."

The kinky 'Irish Tunnel' at Kinghorn

prestigious 'Sheffield Triples' annually. See-sawing with the gradients, we climbed to Dysart, bade adieu to the coast, and descended through yellow fields of rape scarred, here and there, by scrapyards. Fife is one of those post-industrially flawed regions which appeal to my perverse aesthetic values; not so much a case of beauty being in the eye of the beholder, as being in the eye of the gasholder. Bucketing downhill past abandoned coal 'bings' I glanced at the speedometer, amazed to find that we were dutifully within our ceiling of forty-five miles an hour.

We left the main line to Dundee and Aberdeen at Thornton South Junction. My original itinerary to Methil would have continued for another mile or so along the main line as far as Thornton North and thence along a remaining stub of the East of Fife Railway which once ran romantically around the coast through the likes of Largo, Pittenweem, Anstruther, Crail and St Andrews. Scenically, let alone socially, few Scottish closures have resulted in greater loss. A fixture in my 'all-time fantasy train rides', the *Fife Coast Express* once used cast-me-down luxury carriages from the pre-war *Silver Jubilee* on its nightly two and three-quarter hour amble from Glasgow Queen Street to St Andrews. But I digress, an occupational hazard where travel writers are concerned; all too easily are we beguiled by byways and branchlines. I left us traversing the sombre periphery of Thornton Yard. No true railwayman, professional or otherwise, could draw satisfaction from seeing such a vast installation reduced to an outpost engulfed by acres of sapling-seeded ballast. In 1958 the editor of *Trains Illustrated* wrote - ironically, in hindsight - of the principal reason behind the siting of a new "wonder yard" at Thornton being the shift of importance in coal-producing from the west to the east (sic) of Scotland. Back then there were twenty-eight deep mines in the vicinity of Thornton and Cowdenbeath, now a branch leads from the yard's remaining sidings to Westfield opencast loading pad, the only local source of coal for Longannet. Thornton was notable in being the first British marshalling yard to use radar and closed circuit television to monitor shunting. There was even talk, forty years ago, of introducing unmanned, radio-controlled shunting locomotives - "days of future past" as the Moody Blues might have put it.

His eye, consciously or subconsciously forever on the clock, Glenn telephoned Doncaster to double check our booked arrival at Longannet and was told 08.50. "Aye, but that's by way of Townhill with a runround!" he said: "And I would'na be saeprised if the schedule had'na been woorked oot on Class 6 timings." In other words, with the train permitted to run up to speeds of sixty miles an hour. Traversing the Fife Circle, the distance from Inverkeithing to Longannet is in the order of forty-five miles as opposed to nineteen via Townhill; though time is naturally saved by avoiding the need to run round.

Some decidedly rough, wooden-sleepered sections of track encouraged 56088 to show off like an energetic eight year old. At one point I was hurled across the cab, almost landing in Glenn's lap. It must have crossed the mind of the driver of the 150 Sprinter, which passed in the opposite direction at that moment, that EWS staff are a close-knit bunch of lads. When I'd put a respectable distance between us, Glenn didn't know whether to be amused or concerned. "They'll be relaying this in the summer," he said diplomatically. We were deep in the old Fifeshire coal belt now, an equivocally ambivalent landscape of 'grey toons' and 'green braes'. In the old days Fife miners would have gone on strike at the notion of coal being brought in from Ayrshire, and rioted if it hailed from abroad.

At Cowdenbeath I added another lineside football ground to my collection. These Scottish club names make spontaneous poetry. A relatively modest Third Division club with a ground capacity of five thousand, Cowdenbeath's glory days were at the outset of the Great War when they were twice winners of the old Second Division. The team may be a pale shadow now, but I bet the mutton pies still taste good. We passed under the M90, which slices Fife in half, and came upon the loops at Townhill. A series of 'double yellows' had made Glenn jumpy. Something had been in front of us from Cowdenbeath. He had hoped it would be an Edinburgh-bound passenger train but now feared a worse scenario. "I think it's a coal train. It'll have jumped the queue at Longannet. It's like a pack o' cards there. You can draw an ace or a deuce. You can get away in forty-five minutes or spend two and a half hours waiting to unload!"

We rumbled down through Dunfermline on a 1 in 74 descent overlooked by substantial stone built properties. We got glimpses of the abbey and the football ground; rival religions. At Charlestown Junction we shuddered across the down line onto the Kincardine branch, a North British byway which once connected with Alloa and Stirling, and which may well do so again if voiced proposals come to fruition. The branch struck me as a mirror image of Killoch. The same bucolic mix of single track and encroaching vegetation. We came to the delightfully named Elbowend Junction, where a branch of the branch goes off to a Ministry of Defence site on the banks of the Forth. Glenn had never seen anything go down there, but the rails looked suspiciously burnished; perhaps the traffic is so secret that it goes undercover of darkness. Anyway, the junction signal showed red, confirming Glenn's worst suspicions that another coal train had beaten us to it. A battery chicken farm stood close to the line, and while we waited for the signal to change I told Glenn about the free-range hens we keep at home. So free, in fact, that they'd recently bitten the ends off all our neighbour's sweetpeas. This led to a lively discussion on the relative methods of making an omelette. "Mine always come oot too runny," sighed Glenn. "The wife says I put tae much milk in."

"Milk? I don't put milk in mine," I countered, "just a splash of Filippo Berio virgin oil and the eggs themselves; though I crack them first of course."

How sad can you get, two grown men and a coal train, trundling along a branchline, in the Ancient Kingdom of Fife, debating cooking recipes. That branchline grew prettier and prettier, climaxing with the traverse of Culross, its pantiled roofs and Dutch gables a throwback to the 17th century and direct trade with the Low Countries.

At fifteen miles an hour we made stately progress along the seaweed-exposed shoreline of low tide. Inland there were saltings and reedbeds. A few days later I returned here and sat on the shore for an hour or two photographing a procession of passing coal trains with only seabirds and the sound of saltwater oozing out of the sands for company.

It was just coming up to nine when we entered the power station precincts. The coal trains are worked round in a circle, 'Merry Go Round' style, to discharge their cargoes. The 56s are equipped with slow speed control which enables them to run at a measured half mile an hour through the automatic hoppers. I found it faintly amusing that such a beefy, butch locomotive could be so delicately handled. It was like finding out that the Scottish rugby pack attend flower-arranging classes.

There was another train in front of us, already running through the hoppers to discharge its load. We were on a parallel track and could, theoretically, have unloaded simultaneously, but for the fact that there was only one EWS staff member, George Brownlie, and one Scottish Power employee, on shift to oversee the manoeuvre. So Glenn drew our locomotive up to the signal guarding the entrance to the hoppers and scuttled off to make himself a coffee. I wandered around taking photographs. The light wasn't great but it lent a certain sense of drama to the surroundings. A pale pink weighbill on the solebar of the leading wagon in our consist caught my eye. Curiosity got the better of me. I unclipped the perspex wallet from its holder and opened out the advice note within. My jaw dropped. It wasn't Ayrshire coal at all. It had been imported through Hunterston. Scotland was driving and warming and lighting itself with Australian coal!

Empties returning from Longannet along the Firth of Forth

steeling the marches

"One by one the great steel works and their blast furnaces have been ethnically cleansed from the landscape, reduced by circumstances to rolling mills or, even worse, retail parks."

IT had been a funny old week in Wales, as Max Boyce might have put it. I should know, I'd been staying there. It was the middle of April, yet one day the children were building sandcastles, the next snowmen. I could have got even longer odds on Wales beating England at rugby. But they had, with a Scott Gibbs try and Neil Jenkins conversion on the stroke of injury time, which dominoed my beloved Scotland to the top of the last Five Nations Championship. England had trudged from Wembley's pitch visibly crestfallen 'Tae Think Again'.

I had come down from the frozen wastes of Carmarthen by passenger train, journeying alongside the sluggish, slate grey estuary of the Tywi. Beyond Llanelli I'd been invaded by two women and their broods, garrulously speaking Welsh in such a way as to emphasise the gulf between two neighbouring, yet foreign, countries and their cultures. I was in this 'other' country to experience the steel carrying activities of English Welsh & Scottish, and I was due to travel the length of Wales from Port Talbot in the south to Shotton in the north.

Just as with its old ally coal, steel's relationship with rail has undergone a post-industrial sea change. One by one the great steel works and their blast furnaces have been ethnically cleansed from the landscape, reduced by circumstances to rolling mills or, even worse, retail parks. And whereas, in the past, the likes of Round Oak, Bilston, Shotton, Corby, Ravenscraig, Shelton and Workington made their steel on site, it is only in

Llanwern Steel Works

Middlesbrough, Scunthorpe, Sheffield and South Wales that steel is manufactured in Britain now. Consequently, whilst the railways have lost most of their traditional short haul steel - and associated raw materials - traffics, new long distance flows have emerged profitably to carry coil and slab between the four major steel making plants which remain and the outlying works where the raw product is finished and enhanced to meet the needs of the market place. One of the busiest and most regular of these traffics runs by way of the sublimely scenic Marches Line from the steel works at Port Talbot and Llanwern, near Newport, and British Steel's Shotton Works on the north bank of the River Dee between Chester and Flint.

Roger Moss, Standards Inspector of Margam Depot, had arranged to meet me at Port Talbot Parkway. He'd said I'd know him by his fluorescent EWS jacket. I said I'd have cameras hanging all over me. In the event we would have found each other blindfold, being the only two people left on the station in the wake of the Paddington express. People are rarely how you picture them over the telephone. I had imagined someone squat, dark and Gareth Davies-like. Roger was thin and greying with a wispy beard. He spoke with the indigenous, singsong lilt of The Valleys, descended, genetically I suppose, from all those Male Voice Choirs.

Margam Depot lies a four mile hike down the line, so Roger had purloined the staff minibus and its driver, Gwyn, who was something of a local history expert, old enough to remember when the massive steel works' site was a wilderness of sand dunes. Opposites obviously attract in the relationship between industry and nature hereabouts. The narrow plain may be industrialised and bisected by the railway and the motorway, but the hinterland of hills stretches back to a horizon of conifer plantations harbouring ancient earthworks, whilst Margam Sands are firm and wide and conducive to surfing. Gwyn pointed out the *Gormenghast*-like ruins of Margam Abbey, then went on to emphasise the peculiar juxtapositions in local land use by telling me that a new deep coal mine was earmarked for sinking soon on the adjoining hillside. Obviously good news for South Wales' other significant commodity in the EWS portfolio, coal.

It would have been a tall order to find Margam Depot without the help of Roger and Gwyn. Looking back now, even with an Ordnance Survey 'Landranger' map on my knee, it's difficult to trace the exact route we took, but it must have been close to the remains of the lost town of Kenfig, a thriving community a millennium ago, but a victim of the sea's remorseless tidal action. I don't know what kind of author Roger had built me up to be. Judging by the warmth of my welcome I was obviously up there with Michael Palin and Bill Bryson. On a whistle-stop tour I appeared to shake hands with everyone at the depot. I met: Phil Musslewhite, the Train Crew Manager, in a rush to meet a Transatlantic VIP; Phil Jones, a senior engineer; Dai Bowen, a driver who immediately informed me that he had starred in a video called *Hot & Heavy* - though before I leapt to the wrong conclusion he was at pains to point out that it wasn't a porno flick so much as a rail buff orientated film about the steel run up to Dee Marsh; and Keith Target, a young man who'd sadly lost a certain amount of hearing in one ear and, as a result, was confined to moving locomotives around the depot, even though his doctor had said that his one good ear

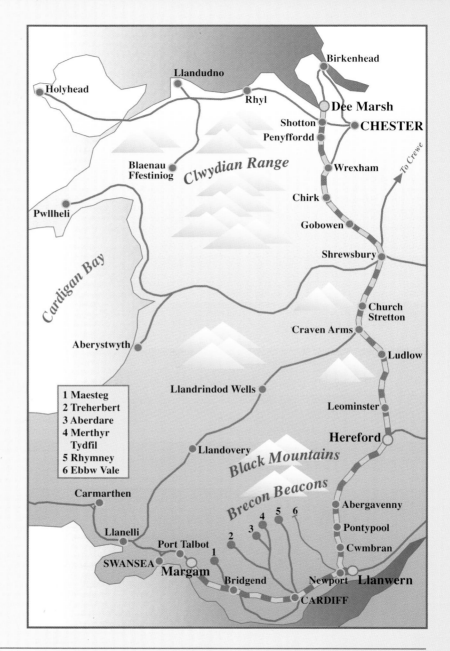

gave him the aural ability of most people, it wasn't enough for Railtrack's stringent hearing test.

Finally Roger introduced me to Ivor Wynne, the driver who was booked to take us as far as Hereford, his home town. Ivor won't mind me writing that, by EWS standards, he was a driver of age and experience. All these young dudes I'd been mixing with were good company and enthusiastic and professional in their way, but I welcomed the chance to rub shoulders with a man who had been coming up with the goods since the heyday of post war steam traction. He had started as a cleaner on Hereford shed in 1952 (when I was just a wee thing in towelling nappies) which gave him a certain cachet in my eyes.

Margam's motive power depot is younger than both of us. It was purpose built in the mid Sixties to cater for the advent of dieselisation in South Wales. It replaced a steam shed called Duffryn Yard where Roger had begun his own railway career as a proverbial engine cleaner. Margam was a modest comma between the mighty full stops of Landore (Swansea) and Canton (Cardiff), mythic engine sheds revered by generations of enthusiasts awed by the motive power on their respective books.

Now EWS locomotives range the country seeking employment. No doubt this simplifies planning for Control at Doncaster but, as Phil Jones pointed out, it clouds the issue of maintenance. Margam services around thirty locomotives a day, a sizeable task for twelve engineers. Warming to his theme, Phil had told me how it's increasingly difficult to get to the root of a malfunctioning locomotive's problems, now that a depot no longer knows the background of any given engine. "We used to know exactly what we were dealing with," he told me, "We had records of each locomotive's service history. Now they come in here from goodness knows where and we have to start from scratch with them." We'd been interrupted by two engineers with an urgent enquiry to be dealt with, and I left Phil sounding like a general practitioner trying to analyse a previously unknown patient's problems without

Roger Moss and Ivor Wynne

any medical records.

We were due away at ten-fifty and had about a quarter of a mile's walk to the departure road at Margam Moors. The sun had come out to gild the snowy hillsides and there was an invigorating tang in the air. Ivor was telling me that he had signed on his shift at Hereford that morning just after six, and that, if all went according to plan, he'd be off the engine and heading home by twenty past three. We kicked our heels for ten minutes, waiting for our train to emerge from the yard. A clutch of passing trains emphasised how busy this stretch of main line can be. A Class 66 thrummed by on its way back from Llanwern steel works, where it had gone with imported coal shipped in - probably from Canada according to Roger - via Port Talbot docks. A shower sent us scurrying under a nearby overbridge, but soon our train hoved into sight and we trudged along sleepers made slippery by the rain to meet it. Secretly, for the sake of variety, I had hoped that this might be my first encounter with a Class 66. They share the Dee Marsh run with Class 60s and 56s, but on this occasion I was thwarted by the appearance of 60071 *Dorothy Garrod* at the front of the train. I comforted myself with the thought that the Sixty-sixes would soon become so ubiquitous that any sense of novelty would have worn off. Whilst, in any case, I was pretty certain of finding one at the front of my next train I was due to journey on, the Safeway containers from Mossend to Inverness.

It would be difficult to imagine a name more Welsh sounding than Dai Llewellyn, but that was the outgoing driver's name. We had a quick word with him. He told Ivor that there were no obvious problems with *Dorothy* and bid us a good trip. We got aboard and waited for signal PT 333 to give us the road. Roger gave me

New Thrall BYAs

a copy of the train list. We were 6M86 with a consist of six wagons totalling 614 tonnes. A Paddington bound High Speed Train shot past and we followed it out on to the main line. Roger pointed out the site of Margam's hump yard, a victim of British Rail's intransigence when it came to wagonload traffic.

Initially we faced a climb up Stormy Bank through Pyle. In steam days, Roger said, there would have been banking engines on offer at Margam Moors to assist the heaviest trains. 60071 made light work of the incline. With an authorised maximum load of 2,030 tonnes we had a featherweight in tow. Ivor said that the Port Talbot to Llanwern trains of imported ore loaded up to three and a half thousand tonnes and went over the top at ten miles an hour. Llanwern works is so hungry for ore that it eats up the contents of seven trains a day. Roger told me that the ore comes into Port Talbot docks from as far away as Australia and Africa. Some of it is in powder form, some in pellets, and that it gets blended at the docks before being loaded on to some fairly ancient, well twenty-five year old, wagons. A couple of former National Power owned Class 59s, transferred from their previous Yorkshire haunts, handle most of this flow.

It was to be a day of switchback gradients. We bowled downhill into Bridgend, crossed Ogmore River and passed the Vale of Glamorgan line, which leads to Aberthaw Power Station, recipient of coal from a number of loading points in The Valleys, notably Tower Colliery, currently - pending the sinking of Margam pit - the only deep mine in the region. Roger spoke proudly of Tower pit, how it had been bought out by the workers when management had slated it for closure. Now it was making a profit and EWS was carrying two full trains of coal a day from it along the Aberdare branch. It was heartening to hear of freight's toehold on the Valley lines. They were one area of former heavy industry that I was regrettably unfamiliar with. I wished I'd explored them in the Sixties instead of standing on Cardiff General station taking down engine numbers. Yet now, when I could easily have picked over their remnants, I was reluctant to do so, put off by fears of being too late to enjoy them in their *How Green Was My Valley* pomp.

The Vale of Glamorgan line runs down to the coast through

Barry and apart from its freight-carrying role often proves a useful diversionary route for passenger traffic when engineering work blocks the main line. For our part, we turned inland, passing Pencoed, where Ivor said the steel trains are sometimes looped to let a passenger train overtake. An old Great Western signal box controlled a road crossing here. The sunshine had grown in intensity. Gorse bloomed radiantly yellow in the snow-dusted cuttings - a Christmas card scene down-loaded into Spring. We breasted another summit at Llanharan and went down through Llantrisant (or "Flan-Thrithant", as Roger put it) winding our way through the pretty Ely Valley towards Cardiff. Roger was explaining the maintenance routines undergone by locomotives as they passed through Margam. How there would be daily top-ups of fuel and water, weekly checks, and an eight weekly A Exam which sounded like a pretty thorough going over. Good maintenance is vital if motive power is to have a high availability rating.

The new Millennium Stadium gleamed metallically in the sunshine as we rumbled into Cardiff. It was difficult not to think of it as Arms Park and, in Roger's estimation, it would inevitably revert to that name, officially or otherwise, through force of public opinion - sooner or later. We had already passed the more modest Ninian Park, where Cardiff City were looking a good bet for promotion, and Cardiff Canton, a major maintenance depot for English Welsh & Scottish. You name it, virtually every type of diesel locomotive currently operated by EWS was 'on shed'. A sad row of Class 47s looked as though they would never turn a wheel again - the Sixty-sixes were already making inroads at the expense of older designs.

We ran through the station and, almost subconsciously, I found myself thinking of a day I'd spent here in the mid Sixties, when I had logged over two hundred engine numbers and, even more spectacularly, downed sixteen cups of vending machine oxtail soup, with no noticeable after-effects; not of a physical nature anyway. Roger pointed out the Cardiff Bay redevelopment of the docks, but I was miles away, still mentally reproaching myself for not making more of my boyhood visits to Cardiff: for not riding the trolleybuses; for not exploring the docks, where I might have bumped into Shirley Bassey in Tiger Bay; and for making

"The sunshine had grown in intensity. Gorse bloomed radiantly yellow in the snow dusted cuttings - a Christmas card scene down-loaded into Spring."

"a long tunnel led into Newport station and a thumping noise from the rear suggested that one of our wagons had a 'flat', or slightly misshapen wheel,"

futile pilgrimages to the steam necropolis that was Barry Docks.

Passing the container depot at Pengam, a cornucopia of brightly-coloured boxes, being swung through the air with magnificent ease by high gantries and cranes, we left Cardiff behind and emerged into a billiard table landscape edging the Bristol Channel. I encouraged Roger to reminisce. Like Ivor, he also hailed from the steam era, having joined the railway in 1961. Within a couple of years he was a passed fireman transferred to London's legendary Old Oak Common motive power depot. Still a teenager, he found accommodation in the neighbouring railway hostel, a self-contained world with its own canteen, laundry, mess room, and Staff Association club. He worked on Castles, Halls and Granges to Didcot, Severn Tunnel junction, Banbury and all points west. "I enjoyed working with steam, but it was hard work and dirty," he added wryly. So 'hard and dirty' that he had recently put himself forward for a refresher course on the Severn Valley Railway which would lead to him acting as an Inspector on steam excursions in South Wales. Like they say - steam gets in the blood.

The main line had burgeoned into four tracks east of Cardiff. Unusually, according to Ivor, we were on the up main, whereas freight is normally confined to the relief lines, the southernmost pair. On the outskirts of Newport a Class 37 was waiting to come off the Ebbw Vale branch with stone from Machen quarry destined for export through Cardiff Tidal Dock. Machen is a Railtrack approved source of track ballast. There is metals traffic to and from Ebbw Vale as well - mainly tinplate, but also some cold rolled coil - and this steeply-graded branch is a favoured haunt for enthusiasts who want to see - or more pertinently, hear - diesels working flat out.

A long tunnel led into Newport station and a thumping noise from the rear suggested that one of our wagons had a 'flat', or slightly misshapen wheel, though not severe enough, Roger judged, to halt us in our tracks. At Alexandra Dock Junction a degree of misunderstanding had arisen in the cab. "That's AD Junction," Roger had said as we passed a cat's cradle of lines spiralling out in a number of directions. Still coming to terms with Welsh names, I'd asked him to spell it for me. "J.U.N.C..."

"No, no, I meant A.D!" I protested, unsure who was the perpetrator, and who the victim, of the joke. Newport is no joke when it comes to the serious business of trainspotting. Mid-morning, midweek the platform ends are filled with male spectators. "They're there all day and night," said Ivor. I could empathise with their enthusiasm. The monotony of High Speed Trains and Sprinters and Pacers apart, Newport is possibly unparalleled in the frequency of its freight services and variety of locomotives on view. Statistically, there are said to be a hundred and fifty goods trains a day passing through the town.

Roger drew my attention to the EWS office at the east end of the station before we launched out over the River Usk, its muddy banks glistening in the sun. At Maindee, on Newport's eastern outskirts, there's a triangular junction providing access to the Hereford line from both directions. We continued for a mile or two further on to the entrance to Llanwern Steel Works. Here we were held at a signal for quarter of an hour, presumably while the relevant reception road was cleared for us. A Class 60, appropriately named *Tower Colliery*, came by, then 66066 - a bingo-caller's number if ever there was one - with coal empties returning from the steelworks. Next, on the down fast, the anomaly of an EWS owned engine, 37414 *Cathays C&W Works* painted in British Rail's old Regional Railways two-tone blue and on hire to Wales & West hauling a Weymouth-Bristol-Cardiff passenger train.

A steel train, made up largely of the new Thrall wagons built in York for English Welsh & Scottish, emerged from the works behind a Class 56, then we got a yellow light permitting us to proceed. Ivor drove steadily in while Roger explained the layout of the three mile long complex: how the western end is largely devoted to the automated unloading of coal and iron ore; whilst the easternmost end contains rows of siding space for incoming and outgoing steel trains. An additional traffic is slag waste from the blast furnaces currently being taken by rail to Cardiff Docks for use in the construction of the Cardiff Bay barrage.

There's a 15mph speed limit imposed on the lines within the works - "Quite high speed for an internal railway," said Roger. Incoming and outgoing trains are required to draw to a halt at a series of Stop boards and to telephone for further instructions. We progressed from board to board with Ivor using his mobile phone to keep in touch with the shunting cabin. "Hello, it's 6M86 at number three stop board, can I come down?"

Through a mask of silver birch, separating us from the main line, I glimpsed a lonely church, remote amongst fields of pasture. No greater dichotomy than the steelworks with its flaring chimneys could have manifested itself. On all these journeys I'd carried with me a clutch of relevant 'one inch' Ordnance Survey maps - needing no less than seven for this particular outing. Technically way out of date, they were nevertheless a boon for identifying topographical features, long lost industries and, of course, railways ripped up ages ago. Perplexingly my 1953 vintage Map 155 of Bristol & Newport (Cloth, Six shillings and Sixpence Net) showed no signs of Llanwern Steelworks. Later I learnt from Rex North, EWS General Manager Metals, that the works had been commissioned in 1962.

We were in the yard for about three quarters of an hour. Ivor had to reverse our original six wagons on to the rear of another eight vehicles destined for Dee Marsh, then run round the whole consist so that 60071 faced west at the head of the train. Roger meanwhile filled a flask so that we could have some coffee on the way and I took some snapshots of the steelworks silhouetted against the shimmering light of the Bristol Channel. Llanwern comes under the same management as Port Talbot and in effect the output of the two plants is combined. Between them they have a capacity to manufacture six million tonnes of steel a year.

Shunted and sorted and ready to go, we left at half past one. The train was made up of four different types of wagon. There were three of the new, EWS maroon liveried, sliding-roofed Thrall-Europa wagons designated BYA; three JSA covered coil carriers owned by British Steel; two KIA vehicles of similar design hired from Tiphook, a wagon leasing company; and six BLA bogie wagons which can carry up to five coils per vehicle in cradles. Still coded 6M86, for this is regarded as a through train between Margam and Dee Marsh, we totalled 1433 tonnes and were 714ft long. Retracing our steps back to the main line, we passed a train being loaded with slag by fork-lift road vehicles and a train unloading coal, both in the hands of Class 56 locomotives. At the throat of the yard a Class 59 had been

Backing down on to a BYA in Llanwern yard

detached from its train while its iron ore wagons were discharged. Roger told me that these trains are fitted with rotary couplings to enable each wagon to be emptied by being turned through 360 degrees without the need to separate it from its neighbours.

I was really looking forward to the next stage of the journey over the Marches Line through Hereford to Shrewsbury. It enjoys the reputation of being scenically ravishing, and I was to be treated to' the best seat in the house', a pleasure denied to mere mortals since the demise of the sort of diesel multiple units which offered passengers a view over the driver's shoulder. We went round the Maindee curve and got a red light at the North Junction, just to enable a Wales & West Class 158 Sprinter to get in front

"There's a
railway culture, a
comradeship,"
Roger continued:
"We're united by
the need to move,
to travel about."

of us. "You can see how driving is increasingly a battle of wits," said Roger. "Ivor here has to contend with signalmen, yard staff, and Doncaster Control as well as concentrating on driving his train." Ivor nodded in agreement. "It can be a real obstacle course," he added with a Gallic shrug. Yet I sensed it was a challenge he enjoyed and invariably surmounted. "But you wouldn't swap your rails for the road, and your locomotive for a lorry," I replied.

"Perish the thought," Ivor laughed, "we're all good companions on the railway; it's a brotherhood."

"There's a railway culture, a comradeship," Roger continued, "we are united by the need to move, to travel about. We wouldn't want to be stuck in one place would we Ivor?"

We crossed the Usk and headed northwards into hill country. All trace of the snow had gone. It was as though we had stolen a march on Spring. Roger and Ivor continued to discuss the pros and cons of railway employment. "Of course there's a high divorce rate, a lot of women can't get used to the unusual hours," Roger told me. "And historically we weren't rewarded financially; though the wages are very good now." In common with many low pay industries, it transpired, there had been an overtime culture on the railway; extra working hours were welcomed as a way of supplementing income. Now, I'd sensed on my journeys, overtime was almost anathema. Shifts were tailor-made to schedules and only unforeseen circumstances led to late working. "It was difficult to arrange social functions," added Ivor. "You could say you'd take the wife to the cinema, but you couldn't say for certain that you'd be back in time. If I needed to go somewhere particular I would ask for a day off in lieu."

"The railways have been losing drivers," said Roger, "because the younger ones couldn't come to terms with the uncertainty of their shifts. As a company we've got to get the diagrams right to attract them back."

All this had brought us to Cwmbran, where a southbound Sprinter was pausing to pick up passengers. We continued past a couple of rail linked factories. A glassworks where rusty sidings betrayed a dearth of rail traffic and, in contrast, a stainless steel outpost of Avesta to whom wagons are tripped in from Sheffield via Alexandra Dock Junction. I would hardly have noticed

Pontypool Road station if Ivor hadn't voiced memories of it in its heyday. Now it's a bare island platform with a bus shelter. Once there were acres of sidings and bay platforms for branch line trains to Monmouth and Neath. During the Great War, quality Welsh 'steam coal' for the boilers of the Home Fleet berthed in Scapa Flow was routed this way. At least we were part of that tradition of moving Welsh goods northwards over the Marches Line.

All this encouraged in Ivor a mood of remembrance of things past. Proust would have been proud of him. He had signed on as a cleaner at Hereford engine shed in 1956 and worked diligently enough to become a 'passed' cleaner within six months. Modestly he maintained: "All you had to do was pass some simple exams, they were that short of firemen." He became a regular on the Gloucester-Hereford line which played hopscotch delightfully with the River Wye and skirted the Forest of Dean. Another long abandoned route he became familiar with was through Three Cocks to Brecon, along which he remembered working lengthy troop trains of soldiers bound for manoeuvres on the Beacons. From what I could gather, apart from short spells away, he'd spent most of his career based at Hereford, which is still the home to seventeen EWS drivers outbased from Newport. A soft-spoken man with the rosy complexion of a Herefordshire cider apple, he could only mumble, "a bit of gardening." when I asked him what he did with his spare time. Roger, in contrast, has three energetic labrador dogs to contend with at home, and - like all domesticated males - when he's not taking his wife around the supermarket enjoys a bit of hillwalking.

The line ahead was see-sawing characteristically. We were breasting summits at barely twenty-five miles an hour, but bucketing down the following slope at close on our sixty limit. Semaphore signals welcomed us at Abergavenny, lower quadrant designs of Great Western parentage whose arms drop to forty-five degrees when they are at go, and resume to horizontal when you cannot pass them. Indeed this whole line is something of a museum piece in signalling circles. Post-Beeching it was almost abandoned and subsequent investment has not necessarily kept pace with the route's revival. Abergavenny signalbox is quaintly built of timber. I've read somewhere that it monitors a hot box detector which

I've read somewhere that it monitors a hot box detector which checks the axles of northbound trains to make sure that none of them are overheating. A dozen miles separate Abergavenny from the next signalbox at Pontrilas. This is the longest block section on the route. But although the line as a whole has an air of the past about it, rationalisation has taken place down the years - once there were over forty signalboxes between Newport and Shrewsbury, whereas today there are but fourteen.

Traditionally, the stiffest, and in steam days most toilsome, climb on the line is the one facing northbound trains between Abergavenny and the summit at Llanvihangel. It begins as a brute of a 1 in 82, easing euphemistically to 1 in 95. In steam days they provided bankers, but diesel traction is expected to take it in its stride. At least there is time now to take in the scenery, with Sugar Loaf rising to 1955ft on our left and Ysgyryd Fawr a more modest 1596ft to our right. We couldn't have been blessed with a better day. Half of me wanted to be out in the bracken watching *Dorothy* growling up the line. Class 60 cabs are so well insulated that we were barely aware of the massive Mirrlees engine thundering a few yards behind us. We went over the top at 22mph. "I don't think this one's as strong as most Sixties," Ivor said ruefully, "I'd normally expect to get up here at about thirty with a load like this. But it's a steep pull up here," he grinned, "no doubt about that!"

Most boundaries have a tendency to blur, and though Pontrilas sounds decidedly Welsh it lies just over the border in England. There's a feel good factor to freight here since a siding, disused for decades, was recommissioned to accept timber wagons whose contents are destined for the nearby premises of Pontrilas Timber. This company had been a customer of British Rail until the dismembering of the Speedlink wagonload network in the early Nineties. They would receive quantities of Scottish wood transhipped from rail to road at Hereford. English Welsh & Scottish has contrived to bring about a small revolution in the amount of timber carried by rail and Pontrilas now receives five deliveries a week via the Enterprise network from a variety of sawmills in the north of England and Scotland. We were to see another destination for timber trains, at Chirk, later in the journey.

I was getting a lecture on the driver's vigilance device as we went past Tram Inn. There had been a station here, typically miles from anywhere, and though long closed the signal box remained in use. On all my cab rides I'd grown used to the frequent beeping of the SSF. Basically, if the driver hasn't done anything for a minute, it will beep and he has to press a button to cancel it or the brakes will automatically come on. Actually it doesn't go that often, because rarely a minute passes without a driver notching the power control, or applying the brake. Simultaneously the AWS sounded at the approach to a yellow signal and Ivor had to cancel that too or else the train would have been brought to a halt. Arm and legs flailing, he looked like a man coming to terms with the rudiments of the Hokey Cokey.

Hereford station looked as handsome as it always does. The first time I ever came here was on a Hymek-hauled local from Malvern on a July evening; a sunkissed ride through the highly strung hopyards beyond Ledbury. We drew up at the face of the northbound platform to exchange drivers. Ivor brought us to a stand bang on time. "I'll tell 'Basher' what a wonderful asset you are to his team in Hereford!" said Roger by way of a parting shot. An EWS colleague of Roger's, Nick Edwards, was on the platform and we were quickly introduced. Roger told him he would spending the night at the Queen's Hotel in Chester; and, as Nick was staying in Crewe, they agreed to meet up for a lemonade or two. All this bonhomie somewhat spoilt the entrance of Ken Goodman into the cab. A year or two younger than Ivor, he must have been rehearsing his lines, for within minutes I'd learnt that he'd begun work at Kidderminster *on the 2nd June* 1956. "What time of day would that have been, Ken?" I asked. A year later he moved to Hereford and had been there ever since.

Getting away from Hereford, past Shelwick Junction and the now singled, but still sinuously beautiful, line to Malvern, Ken needed little encouragement to mine a rich vein of railway memories. We heard about the Hereford-Dowlais ICI run; rostered, because of weight restrictions, for nothing more substantial than a Pannier tank. How they would leave the shed with the bunker filled to the roof with coal and get back - if they were lucky - with a few lumps on the floor. How white ice would form on the outer skin of the tank wagons on account of the chlorine inside.

Ken Goodwin of Hereford

How he worked the Clee Hill Quarry branch from Ludlow and would get sent, by the old stagers, in a wagon up the rack & pinion incline to collect their cider from a pub at the top.

We went through Moreton-on-Lugg (that lovely, north-south flowing tributary of the Wye) where some overgrown, barely visible sidings are all that remain of a once busy exchange yard which connected with an extensive military depot. Isolated in riverside meadows nearby stood the spired church of Marden. Fleetingly, I wondered if the presumably paltry congregation managed to squeeze their hymns between the roar of the Sabbath's passing steel trains, of which two each way are scheduled; a figure underlining the constant appetite that Shotton has for coil and slab. The river licked lazily around the base of a wooded hillside as the up and down lines briefly followed different alignments, our own up line running noticeably higher than its neighbour. Then we were plunged into Dinmore Tunnel, each line contained in a separate bore.

Ken could remember the Bromyard 'Auto' from Leominster, a one carriage push & pull affair peculiar in that, in push mode, he would work solo on the footplate while his driver sat in a driving position provided at the far end of the carriage and communicate - not unlike in maritime circles - with his fireman by a system of coded bells. It seemed amazing that one man's working life could span such metamorphoses in machinery. But then, I began work when printing type was made up of individual metal characters and now I'm tapping this story out on a computer, so none of us are exactly immune to the march of progress.

Woofferton jogged more memories for Ken. This time of the Cleobury Mortimer & Ditton Priors military line whose locomotives were fitted with spark-arresting cowls on their chimneys. One stray hot coal and whoosh, half Shropshire would have been blown to smithereens. This reminded me of my father's only journey by goods train. In 1941 he'd hitched a lift from Tomatin in the guards van of a southbound goods train, not thinking to ask, until he deposited in Perth, what the train had been carrying. "Mines!" laughed the guard, somewhat demonically: "Four tae each wagon, you ken."

We passed Ludlow at ten to four. Jackie and I once sat in a Ludlow tearoom opposite an elderly couple consuming cakes in silence until the man asked portentously: "I wonder what's happened to England?" With baited breath we waited for him to expound a theory of cultural, economic and moral decline, only for him to continue: "They were forty-eight for five at lunch."

The racecourse lies lineside a couple of miles north of the town. A Class 60, running light engine, came past us down the line. "That's the afternoon Dee Marsh-Margam steel empties," Ken told us. "They mustn't have had anything ready to come back." At Craven Arms we saw the single track coming in from the celebrated Heart of Wales line, a route even more renowned for its scenery than ours. Roger surprised me by saying that EWS was going to use the Heart of Wales over the May Bank Holiday, as a diversionary route for the steel trains, because the Marches Line would be closed for engineering work. Margam drivers would be used as far as Llandrindod Wells, and Hereford drivers north of there. I half wished I had been making the journey then, but it would be churlish to seek any more enjoyment than I had already derived from making the journey on the regular route.

Just north of Craven Arms Ken pointed out the boundary between the old Western and Midland regions of British Railways, though the Shrewsbury & Hereford line itself had been owned jointly by the GWR and LMS companies. We were also crossing the border of Railtrack telephone zones, and Ken had to redial from 065 to 040. All along the line he'd kept up a running commentary on the signalling, but I hadn't taken too much notice until we reached Marsh Brook, where the colour light distant showed yellow and the following home semaphore was horizontal. It transpired that the signalman had a message for us. He leant out of his cabin waving a red flag. We drew forward and he told us to look out for sheep on the track. "Eight miles and forty-five

Top: Marsh Brook's signalman comes to tell us about the sheep
Above: The sheep!

> "With such dispiriting talk we almost forgot the sheep, but came upon them, four large lambs gorging themselves on the greener grass of the forbidden side of Railtrack's fencing,"

Opposite: **Stokesay Castle near Craven Arms**

chains up the line," he informed us jovially. Where, but on the railway, would you measure in chains in 1999? And before you ask, there are eighty of them to the mile - in other words, exactly the length of a cricket wicket!

Leaving Marsh Brook on an upward gradient of 1 in 112 60071 took some time to get into its stride. In Ken's opinion, this was a characteristic of the type. We encountered the hills once again, clustered round Church Stretton like bodyguards. Various summits of the Long Mynd lay to our left and Caer Caradoc to our right. It was all very pretty but Ken and Roger were somehow discussing suicides. Part of Roger's remit is to visit the site of 'fatalities' as the powers that be euphemistically put it. "I dread it," he admitted. "Especially if they're mangled." Ken talked of a driver he knew who'd decapitated an acquaintance. "The man saw him coming, put his head on the line, then looked towards him as the locomotive came close, and he knew immediately who it was!"

With such dispiriting talk we almost forgot the sheep, but came upon them, four large lambs gorging themselves on the greener grass of the forbidden side of Railtrack's fencing, by an accommodation crossing and a cream-washed cottage in the vicinity of Dorrington. It was not our business to chivvy them back into the field, presumably the farmer would be contacted as soon as possible. The Wrekin came into view ahead and we ran downhill into Shrewsbury past Bayston Hill Quarry whose stone had been tried, Ken said, as a ballast in the past but had proved insufficiently durable.

Even towns as nice as Shrewsbury surround themselves with retail parks nowadays. We passed various drive-ins with household names, and though I hadn't eaten anything at all for six hours, my mouth refused to water at the sight of them. At Sutton Bridge junction, where the line from Mid-Wales comes in, Ken pointed out an old shunting signal and told me how the Midland men would call it a 'Tommy Dodd' whilst Western men would refer to it as a 'dummy'. I reflected that it would take much more than privatisation and a forthcoming millennium to erase the old rivalries and cultures of both the original railway companies and British Railways' regions.

I've extolled the virtues of a number of railway authors and heroes throughout this book, but one hitherto unmentioned is Canon Roger Lloyd, one of many churchmen with an amateur interest in railways. Many hackneyed analogies have been made between railways and religion and I don't intend to add to them here, but I always admired Roger Lloyd's literary style. He was a sort of Neville Cardus of trains and produced a trio of classic collections of railway essays published by George Allen & Unwin in the early Fifties. I mention him now because Shrewsbury was one of his favourite stations for, as he put it, "sauntering" on. He valued its "variety", its mock Tudor architecture and its setting above the River Severn. The last two elements of Shrewsbury's attractiveness remain intact, but variety is a thing of the past. Trainwatchers now exist on a staple diet of Sprinters, only one through Virgin train a day to London remains locomotive hauled apart from passing freight trains, and it's a long time since the York-Swansea mail paused here in the small hours.

There's a fifteen miles an hour speed restriction through the station and Ken got us seamlessly down on the dot. A 'D' in the 'theatre', or indicator box, told us that we were signalled on to the down line. This was followed by a 'W', indicating that we were to be routed on to the old Western Region main line to Chester. Earlier in the day, when the talk had turned, inevitably, to food, Roger and Ken had recommended the pies in a butcher's shop in Shrewsbury called Thom's but we were so engrossed in Ken's vivid description of a runaway train which demolished Cotton Hill signalbox in the Sixties that we forgot to look for the butcher. "I was up there that morning, and the signalman told me how he'd decided to go and move his car round, so he could get quickly off shift. The next minute there was an ear-splitting bang and his box was in pieces!"

It's a steep climb out of Shrewsbury on the old Great Western main line to Chester and Birkenhead - 1 in a 100 to start with. A bit of a byway now, with a bi-hourly passenger service, the track's rickety in places, and you get the distinct impression that British Rail probably had intentions to single it, because the down line (which somewhat confusingly we were now running on) seems decidedly inferior to the up.

The evening was turning out to be every bit as beautiful as the day. There was a golden quality to the light which lit up the old, high-chimneyed station house at Rednal. We passed two sources of traffic for EWS: a small oil depot at Whittington which is served by trains from Thameshaven; and, something of a rarity now, a domestic coal terminal at Gobowen, served on an occasional basis from Warrington. I'd told Roger to look out for the canal aqueduct at Chirk. All this was new territory to him, Hereford being the usual limit of his involvement. Chirk mirrors Marple in the close juxtaposition of lofty canal and railway bridges. In both cases you seem to come upon the respective structures at the last minute as the land falls dramatically away. At Chirk it's the River Ceiriog which is spanned. We had a second or two to look down on the parallel aqueduct, before we were gobbled up into a cutting and the canal vanished into a tunnel. More significantly, we were back in Wales for the first time since Pontrilas.

In common with Pontrilas, Chirk is another increasingly lucrative location for railborne timber. Kronospan has a massive plant here served by a daily train from Warrington which brings in Scottish timber in large tonnages. Cadburys also has a rail-connected plant here. British Rail must have treated it shabbily because it hasn't been used for years. Surely the time is ripe for a revival! Ken had recently taken up golf and was keen to point out each passing course. I asked him what his handicap was, half hoping that he'd pick up my feed and say 'the day job', or 'the missus', but he missed his cue and said something instead about not having filled in enough cards yet.

An even more imposing viaduct took us across the River Dee and gave us a distant glimpse of Telford's Pontcysyllte Aqueduct, which carries what has become known as the Llangollen Canal across the same deep valley. Ken told us about a driver of his acquaintance who suffered from vertigo and whose habit it is to duck down and hold his head in his hands whenever he crossed this Dee (or Cefn) Viaduct. Bearing in mind that it's 148 feet high, with nineteen arches totalling 510 yards in length, who can blame him?

At Ruabon we entered a former coal mining area. Spoil tips, trying to grow grass, like hair transplants, with mixed success, lined the track. My old map proved as useful an interpreter of the past as I had expected it to be. One abandoned colliery, at Bersham, retained its headgear, as eloquently symbolic of generations of miners' toil and suffering as a war memorial. Wrexham's dense network of railway lines has all but evaporated. Ken spoke of Croes Newydd, a big motive power depot, and Brymbo, an important ironworks, and how trains used to queue up back at Shrewsbury to wait their turn to gain access to Wrexham.

We were about to enter upon the last leg of our journey along the length of Wales. The main line - if that's not something of an exaggeration in terms nowadays - continues to Chester. We were to branch off on to a former outpost of the Great Central Railway (and subsequently LNER) built to extract maximum revenue from a busy industrial area between Wrexham and the Dee Estuary. First, though, we had to wait for one of the line's hourly passenger services to get ahead of us. We marked time by the handsomely restored station within sight and smell of the famous lager brewery. Weaker men might have been broken by the aroma of yeast and hops. We gritted our teeth and changed the subject. About a quarter of an hour passed and then a Class 153 single unit Sprinter rumbled by on its shuttle service to Bidston on the Wirral. "We'll have to wait until it's cleared the block section at Penyffordd," explained Ken. "That'll be another twenty minutes."

The next stage of the journey proved particularly 'branchline' in character. It was the sort of line you'd have expected Beeching to have strangled without so much as a squeal. For us there was a line speed maximum of twenty-five, reduced to fifteen in places. We plodded up hill under Hope Mountain, past faraway stations with strange sounding names. "Round here they say that you 'live in Hope and die in Caergwrle'," laughed Ken. We went beneath a sequence of flat-decked overbridges and through pigeon-haunted cuttings. A little Pacer unit bounced by us southbound. Some of the track was still supported on wooden sleepers, which contrasted bumpily with the sections that had been relaid on steel or concrete sleepers. This was another line which looked as though someone had once earmarked it for the economies of singling.

Castle Cement has a plant at Penyffordd which receives two

Miners' 'memorial': the rusty headgear of Bersham Colliery near Wrexham

or three deliveries of coal a week by rail. It operates its own diminutive shunting engine (or 'pilot' as Ken put it) which stood in its headshunt like a mechanical factotum awaiting the next visitor. Beyond Buckley we crossed the line's summit and began our descent, like an airliner, to the Dee estuary. "The wagons would be pushing us now if we were up to the two thousand tonne limit," announced Ken. "But I must say the brakes on these wagons are very good - disc aren't they Roger?"

Roger concurred, and for a minute or two they talked, somewhat unnervingly in the circumstances, of brakes seizing, and trains running down banks out of control, and how drivers in The Valleys make mental notes of where they should leap out if things take a turn for the worse. "It's coming back that's the problem here," added Ken. "It's 1 in 53 up from Dee Marsh up Shotton Bank. I got stuck up there with a Class 56 in the rain once and had to call for another engine to give me a push from the rear. I've been stuck with a Class 60 there too, but managed to get away again."

Wheels squealing round a tight curve, we came to Hawarden, Michael Owen territory, and a grand vista opened up ahead of the Dee heading out to sea with the Mersey basin and Liverpool beyond. It really did feel as if we were coming in to land at an airport. I expected Railtrack to break the silence and tell us the runway was clear. Instead we ran through Shotton High Level and crossed Hawarden Swing Bridge (opened ceremoniously by Gladstone in 1889). It doesn't swing anymore - hasn't done for years, there being no shipping on the upper reaches of the Dee now - but it still has a certain presence. A disturbing, or should I say unsettling pattern was beginning to emerge on these goods train journeys. Almost without exception, each destination had resonated with a potent 'edge of the world' feel. The sort of places where ancient map-makers would have drawn an elegant line and written 'here be dragons'. It sounds fanciful and contrived I know, but it felt real to me none the less. Just look at the places I'd ended up so far and try to present a coherent argument against my senses: Workington, Penzance, Scunthorpe, Purfleet, Gravesend; need I go on? Or perhaps all railway yards are like this. We will see how I get on from here ...

Dee Marsh Junction signalbox gleamed in its well kept cream

and green paintwork. There were potted plants on the window sills and bags of nuts for the birds under the eaves. We pulled into the headshunt at six thirty-five, five minutes down on schedule. Ken opened his cab window and shouted, "Hi Bryn" down to the shunter who'd come to see us into the yard. "It's a good place to run in to," Ken confided to Roger and I, "you know it's more or less flat." Bryn waved and we reversed steadily back into the yard. "The weight pulls you," Ken explained. His diagram stated that he was to return from Dee Marsh at 19.50 hours with train 6V80. I hadn't realised that the return workings often convey scrap metal for recycling at Port Talbot or Llanwern, or finished, metallically-coated coil which EWS moves to ports for export or to other businesses within the UK. On this occasion Ken had several JXA wagons in his consist, box/tanker hybrids favoured for returning offcuts in covered conditions. The rest of the return train was made up of empty cradles. Ken was disappointed to see that the loaded scrap wagons were positioned at the rear of his train. Gradients, he'd told us, were more easily tackled with the bulk of the weight in wagons coupled immediately behind the locomotive.

Though due out at ten to eight, English Welsh & Scottish has no objection to their drivers departing early given a suitable path by Railtrack, and Ken was hoping for a quick turnround. Roger and I were going to walk back down the line to Shotton station. We were barely half way before a roar at our backs heralded Ken's departure. He'd saved half an hour and we could only hope, for his sake, that he got a clear run back to Hereford which, if he kept this far ahead, he'd reach before ten. He waved regally from his cab. It had been a great day. Great scenery, great company; exemplary timekeeping. All I had to do now was find my way back to Cardigan Bay.

The approach to Dee Marsh

nightride to inverness

IT was a pretty auspicious day to be travelling in Scotland. Parliament had just reconvened after a hiatus of two hundred and ninety two years. I hoped one of its first initiatives would be to transfer a good proportion of freight from road to rail. The Scottish Office Development Department had already grant-aided Safeway and English Welsh & Scottish towards the railing of refrigerated containers nightly from Glasgow to Inverness.

I say Glasgow in the broadest sense. The yard they leave at 2am, six days a week, is at Mossend, which is nearer Motherwell, if your geography's up to it. It's a crack train, running through the 'wee sma oors' at up to seventy-five miles an hour. A sublime example of all that rail can offer, and those of us who are fully paid up members of the 'rail is right'

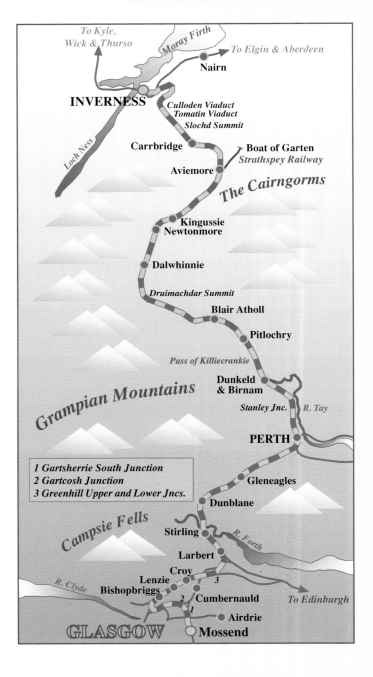

society, can only hope that the logistics managers of other blue chip companies sit up and take notice.

Mossend isn't hard to find if you've spent twenty years writing guide books. Your days are numbered, I thought, overtaking lorry after lorry on the spray-bound M74. I fantasised about queues of lorry drivers exchanging their Fodens for General Motors 66s in much the same way as bargees had been forced to swap their vessels for lorries in the Fifties and Sixties. And nothing I saw at Mossend contradicted my rose-coloured predictions. For standing there, tail to tail, stood two perfect examples of a brave new world of road/rail co-operation. Facing south: a Rail express systems Class 47 at the head of a 'piggyback' train of Parcelforce trailers - facing north: a Class 66 with my own train of Safeway containers; London and Inverness, here we come.

I was acquiring a railwayman's immunity to the tyranny of the clock. My body was beginning to achieve a certain imperviousness to the demands of day and night which had so taken their toll on the callow traveller from Teesport to Workington. Likewise my bladder could go seemingly days and days, and endless cups of railway tea, without needing to be emptied. These days I visited the loo as infrequently as an EWS locomotive visits its home depot.

Sandy Barclay was the man I had to meet, a Standards Inspector from Millerhill, Edinburgh. He arrived by taxi as I was locking my car. We walked over to the Eurocentral Rail Terminal where Safeway's specially built, refrigerated railway containers are transferred by giant Italian-built cranes from lorry trailers to the French-built flatbed railway wagons: talk about the Global Village; and a Canadian locomotive to boot.

More, perhaps, than any other traffic flow I had so far sampled - with the obvious exception of the Cornish Postal - the Safeway job is one where timing is crucial. Fortunately the supermarket chain's warehouse is located nearby at Bellshill, so the journey by road to Mossend is short and unlikely to be subject to delay. By the time Sandy and I arrived the containers had already been transferred from road to rail. Nevertheless, the staff involved kindly waited with patience and courtesy while I set up my tripod and exposed a few frames of the train waiting departure under the glare of floodlights.

"Nothing I saw at Mossend contradicted my rose-coloured predictions. For standing there, tail to tail, stood two perfect examples of a brave new world of rail/road co-operation."

"Andy Clarke, an Inverness man, is our driver," Sandy told me, but as we shook hands I was surprised by the complete absence of Scots in his voice. Moments later I was even more taken aback to learn that he hailed from Burton-on-Trent, my home town as well! Thereafter we might have spent the whole night in parochial gossipmongering, but there was work to be done, and many moonlit miles to cover.

'Moonlit' is actually a bit of artistic licence. The rain which had accompanied me all the way up the M74 showed no inclination to turn in for the night. If you are heading northwards out of the secure compound of the Eurocentral Terminal, you have to proceed to the end of the headshunt and set back to gain access to the main line. We didn't hang about. Andy went through this complicated procedure while Sandy and I stowed our baggage in the roomy cab. Two thirds of the way through my programme of freight journeys, I was finally united with a Class 66 - number '60' in the sequence - and both Sandy and Andy (whose names, when combined, sounded uncomfortably like a Scottish variety duo from the days of *The White Heather Club*) had positive things to say on this Canadian locomotive's behalf. Though for Sandy there was a caveat: "They're good," he insisted, "but not as good as a Deltic!"

Andy, and the other seven drivers at EWS's northernmost signing-on point, were already familiar with the new class's characteristics, and although Andy had reservations on the design's tendency to vibrate and bounce, he was finding them both reliable and freewheeling. "They can run away with you if you're not careful, especially with a train as light as this."

'This' consisted of three articulated bogie flats; in other words, six wagons. On this occasion four of them were loaded with a single refrigerated container equipped with individual generators to power the controlled temperatures within. By coincidence I had just read an article by Hamilton Ellis in *Trains Illustrated* (November 1961) about carrying Birds Eye frozen peas by rail in three and a half ton insulated containers which looked positively antediluvian by modern standards. Blocks of dry ice were used to keep the contents refrigerated; three 25lb blocks were said to be effective up to twenty-four hours. These days we are a mite more sophisticated in our techniques - each

of these new Safeway railway containers holds up to 27.5 tonnes of ambient goods - but an awful amount of frozen food (peas, fish, ice-cream, chicken) was lost to road in the rationalisations of the Sixties and Seventies. Ellis made tantalising reference in his article to "fish specials in Lent". We've come a long way since then, and most of it, regrettably backwards.

Mossend is one of EWS's busiest freight centres and it witnesses arrivals and departures around the clock. Much of the traffic is European in nature, a large proportion being whisky for export and imported wine. Cars and coal, timber and steel are other commodities associated with the modern Mossend, but it is with EWS's 'Enterprise' network of services that the yard is perhaps principally concerned now. Enterprise is the English Welsh & Scottish riposte to British Rail's belief that only bulk trains carrying one commodity could be made to pay. Basically it consists of a network of direct overnight services linking strategically located centres at which trains are broken up into smaller units and 'tripped' to their destination, be it a private siding or a distribution centre for a wider area. Mossend, for example, despatches and receives Enterprise trunk services to and from London, Birmingham, South Wales and other parts of Scotland, whilst feeder services link it with Ayr, Oban, Grangemouth, Longannet and various other local depots.

We left Mossend twenty minutes early and took the Cowlairs line at Coatbridge. Andy had worked 66060 light engine down from Inverness the previous evening. Travelling through the night, one is apt to become confused as to what to call the days. When did Wednesday 'night' become Thursday 'morning'? Technically at midnight of course, but it was difficult not to think of this being Wednesday still, not having seen one's bed in the interim. On arrival at Inverness, the four containers we were carrying would be transhipped on to waiting lorries and sped to Safeway supermarkets in Keith, Buckie, Nairn and Inverness itself. The previous day's containers are worked back on a lunchtime Enterprise from Inverness to Mossend powered by a different locomotive. Where possible, the containers are utilised to convey Highland produce southwards for onwards distribution to Safeway supermarkets in other parts of the country.

Sandy and I were intending to work our own way back on

Sandy and Andy, fresh from
The White Heather Club

the earliest southbound passenger if everything went according to plan. It *had* to go to plan, of course - Safeway were relying on that. It is one matter - though no less alien to EWS intentions - to let scheduling slip with coal or steel or car parts, but evidence of unreliability would soon scupper customer confidence where perishables are concerned.

Good timekeeping, therefore, is of the essence for 4H44, and we were soon in our stride, past Gartcosh Junction where Lesley Harradine, the canny Scots lass unfortunate enough to be my personal finance adviser, would be sleeping soundly, always assuming she hadn't been flipping through my case notes before she went to bed. Curiously, though booked to travel over the old Caledonian line via Cumbernauld to Larbert, Andy told me that in his experience the train frequently takes the route we were following on former North British Railway metals to Springburn and Cowlairs. It suited me, having previously covered the Cumbernauld route with Glen Elvin on the coal run from Ayr to Longannet.

Compared with most of my other cab rides, we seemed to be hurtling along. Being in the Sixty-six was like travelling in an Audi when you'd hitherto been used to a Bedford van. "Did you know," Sandy asked us, "that by now there are more examples of Class 66 in use than Class 60s or 56s or 58s?" It was a sobering question, however rhetorical. In the midst of a bloody revolution there is no time to count the dead, and already some of these relatively young machines were being withdrawn or put in store.

Working from Inverness, Andy currently only drives classes 66, 47 and 37 on a regular basis. In addition to the Inverness-Mossend Enterprise workings, he also has route knowledge northwards to Wick and Thurso and west to Kyle of Lochalsh; the Inverness-Aberdeen line being presently the preserve of Aberdeen drivers. One of his most interesting duties is the *Royal Scotsman* charter train, a sumptuous hotel on wheels which has a specially designated Class 37 allocated to haul it painted in a dark plum colour to match the luxurious carriages.

Rapidly we reached the outskirts of Glasgow, passing ranks of Sprinters stabled overnight in the bay platforms at Springburn. Anyone with an ounce of enthusiasm for industrial archaeology will recognise this Glasgow suburb as a historic centre of railway engineering. A certain amount of activity remains and it was here that the Deltic *Royal Scots Grey* was refurbished for main line use in 1998. Sandy had been involved in testing the locomotive and, as he'd already hinted to me, it had made a big impression on him. "Those Napier engines are like stereos," he told us. "They make the hairs stand up at the back of your neck."

Ah, those Deltic days. I used to fall asleep to the sound of them roaring out of York on their way north. We all had our favourites, *Meld* was mine and she has gone to that great engine shed in the sky. When you stood on a platform beside one the earth moved under your feet, quite literally, such was the vibration from twin Napiers, an engine design, I think I'm right in saying, originally intended for maritime use - aircraft carriers one imagines.

A Deltic once hauled me out of Queen Street up the bank to Cowlairs and here I was again, a generation later, aboard a locomotive imported from Canada. Another casualty of progress was Eastfield motive power depot, a charismatic concern in its dieselised heyday, in the habit of adorning the sides of its locomotives with the image of a Highland terrier, or 'Scotty' dog. Its pristinely-kept Twenty-sixes and Thirty-Sevens have passed into railway folklore, and now all that's left is an infrastructure yard. All this was passing through my mind as Andy brought us to a halt at a red signal. He wasn't used to delays on this roster so he wasted no time in clambering down on to the trackside ballast and telephoning the signalman. "We'll be here about twenty minutes," he announced lugubriously on his return. "There's a 'possession' on, they didn't expect us yet, that'll teach us to leave early!"

The delay gave me the chance to quiz Andy on his career. He had started at Derby on August 13th 1979 at the age of sixteen - these railwaymen's memories are amazing, I thought to myself. By the mid-Eighties he was a secondman at Birmingham working InterCity electrics to Crewe, Rugby and Preston. But he found himself working fifteen hour shifts, and though "the money was good", his wife, a Teeside girl, was "getting sick of it". So he transferred to Thornaby on December 12th 1989 and enjoyed some "good years there" before "it started going downhill". Latterly he'd fancied a fresh start "perhaps in The Highlands or

"'Those Napier engines are like stereos,' he told us. "They make the hairs stand up at the back of your neck.'"

Semaphore signals at Larbert Junction

the West Country and had duly found himself at Inverness and was enjoying it greatly.

They weren't quite as long as twenty minutes. One of the engineering gang walked up the line and kicked over the portable lamp which had been shining red between the rails. We accelerated like a Rolls Royce up the slight incline to Bishopbriggs (where Dirk Bogarde spent an unhappy part of his childhood and likened the tram lines to sabres gleaming in the sunlight) and along the level to Lenzie. Flashing yellows, distorted by bubbles of rain on the windscreen, heralded Greenhill Upper Junction. Beyond Carmuirs we came under the anachronistic control of semaphore signalling operated from signal boxes of classic Caledonian design. It was like finding a policeman on point duty at a motorway interchange.

The sense of speed was extraordinary. In the winking of an eye we were through Larbert, past Bannockburn - still of much resonance to the Scots' psyche some six centuries after the battle - and approaching the outskirts of Stirling, where we got a yellow, followed by a red. "It's unusual this," mulled Andy, unused to having this particular train halted in its tracks. A phone call revealed that another engineering occupation had been taking place, but that it was just about to end. All these gangs beavering away in the darkness emphasised just how much maintenance work Railtrack and its contractors get through each night. I had never seen Stirling station in daylight, my only rides along this route hitherto having been made comatose on the Inverness sleeper. I was impressed by its size and the large number of platforms. Later I learnt that its flamboyant styling was the work of James Miller whose work at Troon and Paisley I'd encountered on my coal run. Sandy pointed out a rare survivor, a lower quadrant signal on a lattice post at the southern end of the station and, nearby, Stirling 'Middle' signal box.

It was two-fifty as we pulled away from Stirling and crossed the River Forth, and it was time for Sandy to dig deep into his railway memories. His pedigree is impeccable; his father and both grandfathers having worked for fifty years on the railway. To that hundred and fifty years of experience and tradition Sandy adds his own twenty-five year stint, having started on the bottom rung as a junior railman at Edinburgh Waverley in 1974.

Whilst his father had been a sleeping car attendant, Sandy's career went off at a different tangent. After a period as a parcels clerk, he worked as a guard on goods trains from Edinburgh Millerhill to the likes of Dundee, Perth, Carlisle and Newcastle, recalling for Andy and me night rides in the jerky jolty guards vans of partially fitted freights, doing his best to keep warm with a bag of coal to fuel the stove. Some drivers gave consideration to the comfort of their guards, others were indifferent. "There were a few things you could do to make sure you got a smoother ride," Sandy hinted, but wouldn't be drawn further on this tantalising remark. In 1982 he'd decided to join the 'footplate fraternity' and progressed along lines I was by now well versed in to the status of Traction Inspector. He'd had spells at Thornton, Eastfield, Waverley and Millerhill. But it was his recollections of the parcels department and the sorting of Sunday newspapers on a Saturday night which intrigued me. The railways, historically entwined with the newspaper trade, lost that traffic in the wake of the Wapping dispute and I couldn't help feeling it might make a potentially lucrative target for EWS to regain.

We went through Dunblane, redolent of inexplicable tragedy now, but once, more happily, the gateway to a gorgeous railway route through Callander, Killin Junction and Crianlarich to Oban. Ravishing, it must have been, to journey Obanwards along the osprey-haunted shores of Loch Lubnaig and under the western flank of Ben Vorlich. But few railway routes survive on tourism alone, and it was always a geographically unsustainable way of getting from Glasgow to the West Coast. Post Beeching, it made economic (though not necessarily poetic or romantic) sense to divert Oban traffic away from Buchanan Street (and the circuitous route via Stirling) to Queen Street and the West Highland by way of Crianlarich. The Callander & Oban was tabled for closure on 1st November 1965 but didn't even last that long. Three days in advance, a landslide in Glen Ogle closed the link, precipitously in more than one sense, causing inconvenience to a funeral party bound for South Uist who had to be ferried by road from Balquhidder.

Through Strathalan we ran to Gleneagles where, thirty years earlier, I had endured a family holiday in the prestigious railway-owned hotel and patiently plodded round the King's Course with my father, attempting to do justice to its majestic greens and fairways; though to his disappointment, no doubt, it was wasted on me. A hopeless hapless golfer, I was more in my element trundling to Perth behind a North British Type 2, a diesel design as incompetent as my golf, which the Scottish Region couldn't consign to the scrapyard quickly enough. Now, the enthusiast fraternity is so nostalgic for the lost class that a group has proposed rebuilding a working replica from scratch; whilst even more ironically, I quite enjoy the occasional round on my father's local course at Moffat.

The hills on the horizon were discreetly backlit by the lights of Perth. We exchanged Strathallan for Strathearn. The river wound phosphorescently beside the railway to Hilton Junction. "Welcome to Perth-on-Sea," said Sandy. I laughed politely, suspecting a subtle joke. "It's true," he insisted. "Coasters come up the Tay to load timber." I liked the sound of that. If justice isn't done to our railway system in the carriage of freight, then neither does enough go by water, tidal or otherwise.

A big modern signalbox presided over a tangle of lines. It was three-fifteen. Some somnolent Sprinters snored beneath the handsome station's high stone walls, elegant ironwork and flamboyant fenestration. Aesthetically, Perth deserves better than its current passenger diet of Sprinter units peppered by the occasional high speed train. To be fulfilled, its long platforms need elongated locomotive-hauled trains. On the Dundee platforms there are murals featuring giants of the past - Stanier and Gresley Pacifics - and one pines for them. Farther back in railway history, Perth was where the Caledonian gave way to the Highland, and still, aboard our *fin de siecle* diesel, with its state-of-the-art container train, there fell upon us a tangible sense of negotiating a border post. These days there is little in the way of regular freight activity for EWS at Perth, other than the occasional consignment of bottled water, but it is a busy centre for the amassing of infrastructure equipment and there is a wagon repair depot too.

Sandy was telling me all this as we left the Fair Maid's city behind and soon reached Stanley Junction and the Highland Railway proper. East from here, the Caledonian Railway used to thread its way through Strathmore - the 'big valley' - to Coupar Angus, Forfar and Kinnaber Junction, formerly the main line to Aberdeen via the West Coast, and scene of the fabled Railway Races of the 1880s. Now it is a junction in name only, pointwork being restricted to a sole turnout singling the line northwards. The days of Gresley streamliners, enjoying an unforeseen twilight along here in the mid Sixties, seem awfully long ago.

Topographically hazy hereabouts, I assumed we had seen the last of the Tay as it curved eastwards into the darkness at Stanley, but it was soon back beside us on the approach to Dunkeld & Birnam. "You know your Shakespeare?" asked Sandy rhetorically. I nodded, knowing enough about 'the Scottish play' to be well aware that it was considered bad luck in thespian circles to mention *Macbeth*. Hazily, I rifled through box files of my memory bank to A Level studies and the threat of Birnam Wood moving to Dunsinane. But it was almost impossible to remember the plot thirty years on; after all I'd had enough trouble remembering it when I sat the exam.

We plunged into Kingswood Tunnel, one of only three on the Highland main line. 66060's powerful headlight lit up the unlined interior, making it resemble a fairy grotto or a fairground ghost train ride. There was a spectral element about this journey anyway, racing through conifer plantations, menacingly black against the side of the single line, and I was brought to mind of some music by Sibelius called *Nightride and Sunrise*. Certainly the muscular, rhythmic music of the Finnish genius would have provided a suitable soundtrack to our progress had we been working on a film rather than a book.

I emerged from my reveries on hearing Sandy and Andy talking about "The Pipes". Naturally I assumed they were discussing Scotland's indigenous music, but I should have known better. To present day Scots railwaymen, 'the pipes' is an occasional traffic of tubes conveyed between Hartlepool and Georgemas Junction, near Wick, in connection with the oil trade.

Running through the loop at Dunkeld, we came upon the second signal box kept open especially for us and caught an agreeable glimpse of a female form silhouetted against the interior lights of the cabin. "It's the girl," said Sandy with a degree of satisfaction. "Do you know her?" he asked Andy. "A lovely girl that," he mulled, almost to himself, as though he were some lonely lighthouse keeper and she a passing mermaid.

"A big modern signalbox presided over a tangle of lines. It was three-fifteen. Some somnolent Sprinters snored beneath the handsome station's high stone walls, elegant ironwork and flamboyant fenestration."

Dunkeld signal cabin, George
Holyhead at the frame
(everything but *the* girl)

We crossed the Tay at Dalguise by way of a turreted and castellated bridge which could easily have served on the coach road to some wealthy Highland landowner's baronial pile. We began to sense a hint of daylight in the skies ahead. An owl swooped across the track in front of us, close enough to be caught in our headlight momentarily. The darkness and the narrow confines of the line combined to accentuate our speed. Cheering, we symbolically overtook a Safeway lorry on the adjoining A9. I had noticed on the side of the containers, wording to the effect 'Project supported by the Scottish Office Development Department'. David Hodgson, EWS Marketing Manager, Consumer Goods explained that Safeway had been awarded a grant towards the cost of acquiring ten refrigeration units for use on the Mossend-Inverness service. At the time of my journey the contract between Safeway and EWS was three months into its three year span. David saw this particular flow as part of what he termed "a developing relationship" between the two companies.

It was still too dark to see if there was any sign of Ballinluig station and the former former branch line to Aberfeldy. In *Double Headed,* David St John Thomas described 'bunking' the branch in 1963. "We were the only passengers on the single coach hauled by a two-year-old express-size diesel locomotive; the guard stood by our side in the corridor relating local history and pointing to the Tay's most famous fishing reaches." I hoped fervently that my journey wouldn't seem so quaint thirty years from now.

We could have done with an accordion for the next bit. Sandy looked like the sort of guy who might be a dab hand at traditional Scots music. I had this soundtrack running in my head, something from the Battlefield Band, Boys of the Lough or Blackeyed Biddy. Whether or not he's a musician, Sandy's a mountaineer with eighty or ninety Munroes under his belt. That weekend he planned to plant his tent in Glencoe and spend a day or two on the mountain tops and a night or two in the nearest bar.

Beyond Pitlochry, we entered the Pass of Killiecrankie, where viaduct and tunnel seem an organic part of the dramatic scenery. To the west lay "Tummel and Loch

Rannoch" and the *Road to the Isles* and I thought of my step-grandfather's shellac seventy-eight of Sir Harry Lauder's rendition of that famous walking song. The signalman waved to us at Blair Atholl as we passed through the unlit station and commenced the climb to Druimuachdar Summit (1,484 feet above sea level), several miles being as steep as 1 in 70, but 66060 handled the 313 tonnes behind us as easily as if it was slicing the top off a Clootie Dumpling.

We moved on to double track as far as Dalwhinnie. The sky to the east grew eggshell-coloured, lineside sheep became identifiable pale blobs, banks of mist lay like silk scarves on the bare shoulders of the mountains. "You wouldn't know we were climbing," Andy remarked, indirectly praising the locomotive, and again I sensed that the 66s were beginning to win drivers over.

"You can just make out the Sow of Atholl and the Boar of Badenoch," Sandy said as we neared the summit and crossed the boundary between Tayside and Highland Region, or what I remembered more fondly, from a pastel-shaded map in my school atlas, as Perthshire and Inverness-shire. Andy waxed lyrical about the landscape. "Every time you come along here it's different. The sky, the sun, the hills; it never gets routine. It was snowing coming down. You get stags on the track staring you out."

Breasting the summit, we ran down to Dalwhinnie past Balsporran crossing, where Sandy told us to look out for a platelayer's cottage he had once thought of buying. I looked at my watch, it was 4.15am and decidedly dawn had broken. Snow fences could be seen beside the track. We had the River Truim for company now and, as we slowed for Dalwhinnie station, Sandy got us to look back up Loch Ericht where *The Dambusters* was filmed.

Dalwhinnie is notable for its distillery which, according to Sandy, "produces a fine single malt". Not being a whisky drinker I had to take him at his word, but the whitewashed distillery was undeniably pretty and I thought it would provide a picturesque backdrop for a photograph of the Safeway train. The line singled again beyond Dalwhinnie. We traversed Glen Truim in fine style. Sandy said we should look out for the 'Sleeping Lady' and the 'Resting Man' but reckoned that the cloud cover was too low. One of General Wade's 18th century military roads, built to get government troops quickly to the scene of Jacobite uprisings, accompanied us on one side of the line, the modern A9 on the other. South of Newtonmore, the Truim made its confluence with the Spey, and the latter would seldom be out of sight all the way to Aviemore. Sandy spoke highly of the shinty team at Newtonmore, summarising the sport as "hockey for men - all blood and guts!".

By way of preparation for this trip, I'd read H.A.Vallance's classic *The Highland Railway* which I'd picked up for a song secondhand in Carnforth. It portrays a stylish, individualistic railway company characterised by lengthy single track routes and a fierce pride in its operations. Arguably its finest hour came with the First World War when, with the Grand Fleet established at Scapa Flow in the Orkneys, the Highland main line became an umbilical link of exceptional significance. Huge increases in freight traffic occured, straining to breaking point the company's meagre rolling stock resources. A Naval Special ran daily in each direction between Euston and Thurso, the seven hundred plus miles being covered in around twenty-two hours. Sleeping compartments were provided for officers, other ranks had to cram as best they could into day stock. Certain compartments were reserved for the use of prisoners - deserters, malcontents and malingerers. But Valence's eminently readable book also evokes vivid pictures of the Highland Railway's main adversary - the weather. On December 17th 1880 a train was buried to a depth of sixty feet on Dava Moor. Its passengers escaped, but livestock travelling at the rear of the train in cattle wagons were too frightened to be herded from the trucks and suffocated to death. We had seen evidence of snow fences on the way up and they still have a part to play. The Highland fine-tuned their positioning, erecting them where experience indicated the deepest drifts would amass; sometimes three abreast.

But of all the stories in the book, the one which intrigued me most related to the theft of the Highland Railway company's steamship *Ferret*, a 347 ton vessel built in 1872, primarily to work between Strome Ferry, Portree and Stornaway. In October 1880 it was chartered privately by someone claiming to be a relative of the First Lord of the Admiralty and sailed from the Clyde for the Mediterranean. Last seen at Gibraltar on November 11th, thereafter nothing further was heard of the vessel until some wreckage bearing its name was washed on to the Spanish coast. Not unnaturally it was assumed to have foundered with all hands lost. That might have been the end of the story had not a remarkably similar ship named *India* arrived in Melbourne a few months later and offered for sale. To cut a convoluted story short, this was the *Ferret* in disguise and the hirer with Naval connections turned out to be a notorious swindler.

Barely two or three miles separate the stations of Newtonmore and Kingussie. Only the latter has a passing loop and signal box. "The distant's bound to be on," guessed Andy. He was right, but we weren't delayed, the only occupant of the unstaffed station was a rabbit nibbling grass on the down platform. The line crossed a bog-like expanse of low ground beside the Spey as it neared Loch Insh. Apparently the railway builders laid their track over a raft of sheep's bladders. "It's a wonder they never rot away," said Andy: "they never seem to have to replace them!" Rather fortuitous, that - one can imagine Railtrack having a spot of bother sourcing sheep's bladders in this day and age.

We bowled along the banks of Loch Insh. Pockets of mist hovered over the landscape as if it was waking from a cinematic dream sequence. The line was level and we were coasting over welded track, an uncanny silence hung over the cab. We ran through corridors of silver birch past clearings with log cabins for holiday hire. I wondered if this early morning train woke the occupants each morning or whether it glided noiselessly through their slumbers. "There's Aviemore's distant," Andy announced, and we slowly rumbled through the elegant timber station, recently refurbished to stunning effect. From here the original, circuitous route to the north headed along Strathspey to reach Inverness via Forres and Nairn. When the direct line opened in 1898 it shaved twenty-six miles off the journey. Aviemore station dates from this improvement, though the substantial, stone-built engine shed is of 1863 vintage, the date of the opening of the line from Forres. Nowadays the shed is occupied by the preserved locomotive stock of the Strathspey Railway which presently runs as far as Boat of Garten, but which is being extended to Grantown-on-Spey. Stabled outside the shed, however, we saw an EWS engine, 37428, the one specially allocated to the *Royal Scotsman*. Apparently the luxury train regularly sleeps over at Boat of Garten, hauled there by steam while the EWS locomotive waits at Aviemore to be reunited with its train the next morning.

When the direct line was built it added a second summit to the Highland line at Slochd. From Aviemore it's more or less uphill all the way, and steep at that. Initially, in contrast, the surrounding countryside is flat scrubland and lochans. But that's a false impression, there's a lot of forestry too, which had the effect of heightening and emphasising the railway's bond with nature; something that a road seldom aspires to. We cut a swathe through rocky cuttings that I imagined reverberating long afterwards to the sound of our passing .

"Not a bad morning is it," Sandy ventured.

"No, it's nice," echoed Andy.

They should have known better!

I was surprised to hear - Pitlochry and Aviemore excepted - that the stations between Perth and Inverness are unstaffed. They didn't appear to be suffering as a result. Mass vandalism obviously doesn't reach this far north. Carrbridge is a nice timber structure of gabled wings flanking an awning supported by cast iron columns. In England it would probably have been demolished

and replaced by a bus shelter. The surrounding landscape began to take on a wilder aspect. I looked forward to seeing the whole of the line in daylight on the way back by passenger train; always assuming Sandy and I could get window seats, some Sprinter units seemingly being designed on the highest egalitarian principals, denying *everyone* a decent view.

On the way up to Slochd we ran over a carcass between the rails. "Looks like a dead wolf," said Sandy.

"Are there still wolves in the wild in Scotland?" I wondered aloud, thinking that I'd heard recently on the radio of plans to reintroduce them. Perhaps this poor creature had been by way of a trial. There's a loop at Slochd, 1,315ft above sea level. We emerged from the cover of forestry plantations to its bare summit. A pair of deer skipped insouciantly across the track in front of us. This whole wilderness thing was invigorating, even from the shrink-wrapped, air-tight fug of the cab. Secretly I wanted to stop and re-enact *Brigadoon* on the slopes of Carn nam Bain-tighearna. But I didn't think EWS, let alone Safeway, would approve.

We swooped down the 1 in 60 to Tomatin where my father had inadvertently boarded a munitions train in the war. It was becoming decidedly dreich and darker, as though the day was ending not beginning. Sandy and Andy had obviously angered the weather gods with their blithe talk of a nice day. Andy was prompted to remember a nightmarish run in blanket fog from Gloucester to Derby on a coal train back in the mid Eighties. "Jeez, I thought the journey would never end. They put me inside at Abbotswood and I couldn't even see the main line!" Sandy was more phlegmatic, joking: "It's because we're getting further away from the Equator. We're nearer to Norway than London."

"It even looks like Norway," I responded morosely.

Culloden flings disappointment in the face of most Scots and romantics at heart. Here on the 16th April 1746 'bad signs had been multiplying throughout the morning' and 'a visible damp and dejection spread among the Highland troops'. Nothing much seemed to have changed, meteorologically at least. The twenty-eight arch viaduct spanned a cotton wool world of cloud and mist. The River Nairn, allegedly below, remained invisible. It was five fifteen and raining more determinedly.

Quarter of an hour later we were in Inverness. Andy was

"A pair of deer skipped insouciantly across the track in front of us. This whole wilderness thing was invigorating, even from the shrink-wrapped, air-tight fug of the cab. Secretly I wanted to stop and re-enact *Brigadoon* on the slopes of Carn nam Bain-tighearna."

The southbound Caledonian Sleeper crosses the River Findhorn, at Tomatin, hauled by an EWS Class 47 on lease to ScotRail

pointing out local sights of interest as we crossed over the Aberdeen line and slowed for the centre. Rail freight in the area was buoyant, he told us, there being Enterprise links with Mossend, Aberdeen and the Far North where a refrigeration firm called Norfrost had established a depot at Georgemas Junction. Cement and bottled water are other commodities currently carried by rail; the latter in the shape of Lovat Pride, brought by road from Beauly and railed to distribution centres at Blackburn, Daventry, Dagenham and Bridgwater. Our own wagons were destined for the old Harbour Branch which had been built to carry munitions for the Grand Fleet in the Great War. Latterly it has been a truncated siding, last used by a coal merchant, but expressly for the Safeway traffic it has been recommissioned for use by Highland Haulage, the road carriers responsible for onward delivery of the refrigerated containers.

Andy had to change the points himself to gain access to the Harbour Branch. We proceeded round the Rose Street Curve. It was a tight fit to squeeze into the siding. If, as is hoped, Safeway takes up the option of increasing the number of containers carried, the siding will need to be lengthened, probably by slewing it across the yard.

Four lorries were parked in the yard. There was no sign of their drivers, but then, after all, we were early, the contract stipulating that we should be in by 06.15. Andy shut down the locomotive and secured the train. We walked back along the Harbour Branch in an ungainly fashion from sleeper to sleeper, parting company at a level crossing on Rose Street; Andy making his way back to EWS's office in the freight yard, Sandy and I covered the shorter distance to the station. Andy, who lives in Strathpeffer, told us he'd be in bed by seven and hopefully sleep through 'til three in the afternoon. He was due back in Inverness by seven-thirty to repeat the whole exercise. Sandy and I ensconced ourselves aboard the 06.35 Sprinter to Edinburgh; he would travel all the way, I would change for Glasgow at Perth and somehow find my way back to the wilds of Mossend. We made ourselves comfortable and looked forward to a reprise of the northbound journey. Sandy was asleep by Aviemore, I lasted to Kingussie - just about where daylight had come in!

Dawn unloading at Inverness

steam over the settle & carlisle

DAYS afterwards I still had grime and soot on my skin, but I didn't want it to go. Like a lover's perfume left on clothing, it was precious to me. You see, I had been mixing with gods. Men who had driven and fired *The Caledonian* and the *Midday Scot,* or worked Peppercorn Pacifics over The Waverley. Life, as I said when they dragged me screaming from the footplate of *Canadian Pacific* at Carlisle, would all be downhill after this.

That English Welsh & Scottish, with its ambitious, mould-breaking outlook on rail freight, should be involved in the operation of steam locomotives at all merits explanation. It was,

after all, way back in 1968 when British Rail formally abandoned steam propulsion, in some cases consigning to the scrap heap capital equipment which might reasonably have been expected to depreciate over another twenty or thirty years of useful life; a folly compounded uncomfortably soon afterwards by the withdrawal of numerous examples of the diesel locomotives ordered to replace them. The same image-makers responsible for getting rid of steam so precipitately, then insisted that the few survivors would never run again on British Rail metals. A blanket ban on steam remained in place for several years until it slowly dawned on the nationalised railway that there was money to be

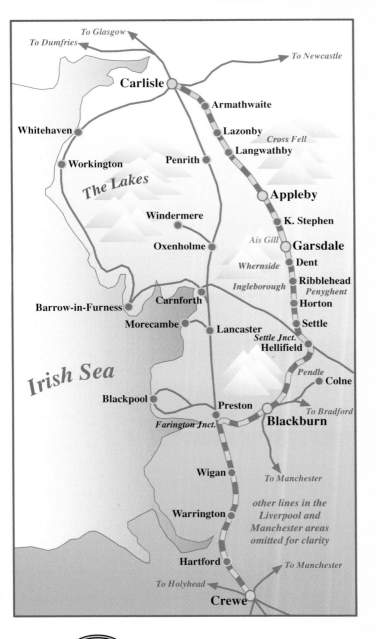

made - and more importantly perhaps, goodwill to be fostered - by operating steam excursions on selected lines. For the next twenty-five years, steam became a regular sight in many parts of the country, re-establishing itself on routes like the West Highland and the Settle & Carlisle as a bona fide tourist attraction. On privatisation, the operation of such activities - which required small pools of trained men at strategically located depots - came under the umbrella of Rail express systems, a predominantly parcels-orientated business which EWS eventually acquired as part of its freight carrying portfolio. In the name of competition, one or two other operators have access to run steam trains over Railtrack routes, but the overwhelming majority of steam hauled charter trains are currently crewed by EWS driving staff.

I recall asking Andy Lickfold, my mentor at EWS headquarters in Islington, if it would be feasible to include a steam trip in my itinerary, and only half convincing him that the request came simply out of a desire to cover *all* his company's activities and nothing to do with the fulfilment of boyhood fantasies of engine driving. In fact I *almost* convinced myself that there would be nothing special about this trip, that I would treat it as methodically as any of the other journeys, and that the thought of eight hours in the close company of an express passenger locomotive would mean no more to me than catching the number ten bus into town.

Almost? Who was I kidding! My insouciance lasted barely five seconds before I was bowled over by the big blue locomotive basking in the early sunlight of a late May morning on a siding in the Heritage Centre at Crewe. Basking? Purring more like. Loitering with intent to assault and batter the 'Long Drag', a.k.a. the Settle & Carlisle. Around it several acolytes were attending to this monster: tightening bolts, lubricating valves, burnishing its nameplates with Brasso and filling the tender with water and coal. I chatted to Bob Meanley of the Birmingham Railway Museum where *Canadian Pacific* is based. He was part of a team of six enthusiastic 'minders' - including the locomotive's owner, Andrew Naish - who were attending to its needs prior to the run to Carlisle with an excursion chartered by Past Time Rail of Lichfield, which was on its way to Crewe (behind an electric locomotive) from Finsbury Park on the northern outskirts of London.

The team went about its work systematically, not letting panic creep in, even when Andrew Naish received a call on his mobile to the effect that the lorry of Polish coal, which should have been nearing Crewe, was still in Bromsgrove. Happily the Heritage Centre had stocks of its own and a JCB Loadall was soon busily conveying five tons of it into the tender. "Will that be enough to get us to Carlisle?" I asked Nick Smith, an EWS driver from Toton depot, who looked too young to have remembered the real thing. "My parents tell me I saw Black Fives at Blackpool when I was three," he laughed. And as we all know, this business of steam is so contagious that fleeting encounters with steam and ozone are more than enough to account for a lifetime's passion. Bob Meanley put it altogether more fundamentally, reckoning that a fascination with things mechanical is generic in the male of the species.

We were due 'off shed' at 09.42. The team had been preparing the locomotive since six o'clock. It was coming nicely to the boil. Like a good journalist, I had done some homework

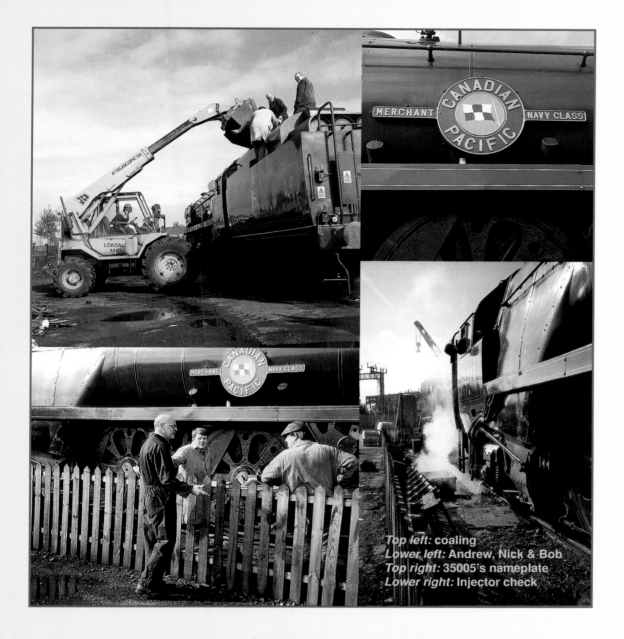

Top left: coaling
Lower left: Andrew, Nick & Bob
Top right: 35005's nameplate
Lower right: Injector check

on my subject. 35005 *Canadian Pacific* belongs to the Merchant Navy class, a Southern Railway design dating from 1941. It was the work of a Chief Mechanical Engineer called Oliver Bulleid. Railway historians tend to fall into two camps over his contribution to steam locomotive design: some lauding him as a farsighted last defender of steam; others as an eccentric left high and dry by the tide of progress, a theory substantiated, though not proven, by his twilight days spent in Ireland experimenting with peat-burning engines. His Merchant Navy design - so called because the thirty engines in the class were named after shipping lines - were ground-breakingly streamlined, though not in a Gresley or Stanier sense for speed, but to reduce the need for maintenance. Like all avant-garde works they were before their time and misunderstood. In the Fifties British Railways set about rebuilding them along more conventional principles of design. It was like forcing Boy George to wear a suit. They went into Eastleigh Works in one shape and came out in another - not so much a nose job, more a sex change. Bulleid's admirers were horrified, his critics vindicated. A good proportion of rebuilt Merchant Navys saw out the Southern Region's 'Waterloo Sunset' of steam in 1967. 35028 *Clan Line* was sold into preservation, the rest went to the breakers' yards of South Wales, many to Dai Woodham's at Barry from whence, miraculously, virtually all re-emerged phoenix-like to enjoy a life in preservation.

I came upon another of *Canadian Pacific's* devotees going round the valve gear with a long spouted oil can. He was Dave Thompson, an ex-BR fireman from Toton near Nottingham who'd been so fond of steam that he'd left the railway when diesels took over and gone to work for British Steel at Stanton. Later he'd become another sort of fireman altogether, not the sort that nurtures them but the sort that puts them out. But you have to retire from active service in the fire brigade at the age of fifty-five, so he'd gone back full circle to his first love, and now worked on the Great Central Railway at Loughborough. You can learn someone's life story walking round a locomotive with an oiling can, and I could have gleaned more, for Dave had a grimy notebook with him appertaining to his days at Toton, but we were signalled out of the yard and it was time to go.

On their main line travels, preserved steam locomotives usually tow a support coach behind them, to carry their team and any light equipment deemed useful on the trip. A diesel had shunted our chocolate and cream Mark 1, brake corridor second on to the tender and, supervised by a Railtrack official, we made our way out of the Heritage Centre and on to the main line.

We were lucky that 35005's tender is roomier than most. It was designed for a team of two, of course, but on this occasion Bob Meanley was representing the support team and I was being accompanied by Standards Inspector Pete Davies of EWS Warrington, so everyone was on pretty intimate terms. Bob took up position on the tender plate, Pete ushered me on to the fireman's wooden tip-up seat and generally busied himself helping the crew.

Word had reached us that the excursion was "twenty-five late" at Lichfield. Charter trains are the bane of control's life. They seldom slot neatly into timetabled paths and are prone to what are euphemistically known as 'operational difficulties'. Often operators only receive timing details from Railtrack days before their departure date, leaving a late rush of postings to customers incredulous that they know they're booked on to Flight XWZ to Malaga months in advance but cannot ascertain the departure time of a rail excursion to Skegness a week ahead. The fact that five different bodies were directly involved in *Canadian Pacific's* jaunt to Carlisle underlines the complexity of the rail charter business and explains its fickle nature. It's not a business for the faint-hearted, let alone the financially astute. Operators are in it for love not money. My publishing business sells our *Settle & Carlisle Souvenir* guidebook to a number of charter companies and we can sense how difficult it is for them to make ends meet. In the last twelve months two of our customers have gone out of business, another is paying in instalments for stock it bought a year ago, and a third told us recently that he was sorely tempted to give up and go back to being a dustman. It costs on average over ten thousand pounds to hire a ten coach train with six hundred seats in it, so there are a lot of tickets to be sold before you are into a profit. Beyond the tour organiser there is rolling stock to be hired, a suitably charismatic locomotive to be found and paid for, and contacts to be made with EWS and

Ray tells Pete a thing or two

Railtrack. Yes, running a charter train is about as simple as landing a man on the moon, only you're more likely to run late. There are moments, however, when it is all worth it. Like when you see the huge grins of the people who have turned out to see this behemoth from a lost age going through its paces.

Pete had warned me, with tinderbox dry Scouse humour, that the driver was "straight from the history books". As he introduced us I saw his point. With his greaseproof cap, blue serge engine-driver's jacket, and a red and white spotted neckerchief adorning his throat, Ray Hutton looked as though he'd just come back from filming *Brief Encounter.* I looked quickly out on to the platform to see if Celia Johnson had got the smut out of her eye yet. It was difficult to believe that, most days of the week, Ray was to be found driving diesels and electrics. Altogether more of the present was Eddy Williamson, a gangling, softly-spoken fireman whose age I guessed at being somewhere in that blurred region between the late forties and early fifties.

I had a few minutes to quiz Ray and Eddy as to their respective careers. Not, however, before Ray had satisfied himself as to my background and motives. Thereafter his gruff demeanour evaporated like a wisp of steam and I learnt that he'd begun as an engine cleaner at Crewe North shed on 21st April 1952 and subsequently worked through the links at both the North (express passenger) and South (goods) sheds with a two year gap for National Service. It had taken him thirteen years to achieve the status of 'passed fireman' and another five to become a fully fledged driver. Statistics which eloquently say more about the plethora of footplate crew and the hierarchical staff structure than any lack of aptitude or application on Ray's part.

Eddy prepares to tackle the coal dust

Eddy joined the railway in 1964. The Leek-born son of a signalman at Bosley on the old 'Knotty' line from North Rode to Uttoxeter, it had taken him twenty-one years to become a driver. Based throughout his career at Crewe, his work nowadays for EWS was concerned mostly with Royal Mail workings. Ray and Eddy belong to a pool of five drivers and two firemen passed for steam work at Crewe. They would be taking 35005 to Blackburn where Carlisle men would take over. Another regular steam run for the men from Crewe is along the North Wales Coast route to Holyhead.

A certain amount of derogatory, but good-hearted banter echoed around the confines of the cab. "Every time I'm out with this man disaster overtakes us," said Pete of Ray. "Last time we went to Holyhead he dropped his camera out of the cab and had his cap blown off!"

"Did a lot of caps get blown off?" I asked, having wondered idly for years if enginemen were issued with hat pins to retain their headgear in seventy mile an hour slipstreams or whether they just relied on the adhesive properties of Brylcream.

"All the time," laughed Pete. "You'd see platelayers wearing them, cheeky blighters!"

Pete's own career commenced at Speke Junction on the outskirts of Liverpool on 30th April 1957. At last I discovered why all these railwaymen have perfect recall where dates are concerned. Apparently your seniority related to the date you actually started, so you were entitled to pull rank on anyone who'd joined even a day later than you. Pete passed as a fireman in 1964 but became 'redundant'. Displaced is a better way of putting it. In those days you didn't become redundant in the strictest sense of the term, rather you were displaced, meaning that there was no work for you at that particular depot and that you had to apply for a vacancy elsewhere. Pete's change of location couldn't have been more spectacular. He swapped Speke's sooty freight depot for Camden, London, soon finding himself firing crack trains like The Caledonian and becoming familiar with the footplates of the pride of the line; locomotives like the 'Duchesses', 'Big Scots', and 'Britannias'.

"When you worked The Caledonian - Euston to Carlisle - you were presented with a scroll. There was also a slot on the side of the cab where little wooden plaques bearing the driver's and fireman's names were dropped in," said Pete.

"Yes," butted in Ray. "I. Thrashem and I. Burstem!" Not to be outdone, Ray recalled for me his heyday working the Midday Scot from Crewe to Glasgow and the Night Sleeper as far north as Perth.

Meanwhile, our excursion arrived behind EWS electric locomotive 86210, an engine normally confined to parcels and postal work. It would make its way, light engine, over Shap and wait for us at Carlisle. We backed down on to a long rake of 'blood & custard' coloured excursion carriages, an authentic early Fifties match for Canadian Pacific's blue livery, though, to be pedantic, 35005 had never worn this colour subsequent to being rebuilt.

"Keep an eye out Eddy."

"A good three coaches yet Ray." We had some difficulty matching the buckeye couplings on what was a slight curve, but we persevered and soon made a good connection.

I had not been prepared for the intensity of our welcome. Footballers, film stars and chat show hosts with failing ratings would kill for the adoration we received. Pete busied himself with the injector, a crucial component which literally 'injects' water from the tender into the boiler. As someone pointed out, we could run out of coal with impunity, if not embarrassment, but if we ran out of water we'd be putting the big bang theory to the test. The capacious Merchant Navy tenders take six thousand gallons of water. It sounds a lot, but these are thirsty engines and, despite having filled to the brim, we were booked to top up twice - at Blackburn and Garsdale - to ensure safe arrival at Carlisle.

Eddy was rhythmically shovelling coal into the firebox to maintain sufficient heat to keep the boiler pressure at 240lbs per square inch. "We have to bring it to the boil just nicely," explained Pete. "Too much heat and we'll waste it. Not enough and we'll be off to a sluggish start." I was reminded of our old Rayburn, a law unto itself at the best of times and heavily reliant on the direction of the wind. If we didn't judge it right the food was either served at midnight or incinerated.

Satisfied for the moment that the fire was sufficiently hot, Eddy picked up a galvanised bucket, embossed with the initials BR, and started scrubbing the wooden floor of the footplate. "It's not just good housekeeping," he explained. "I'm doing this to keep down the coal dust."

"Later on we'll use the hose," added Pete. "But under the electric wires we have to be careful not to cause a short."

Suddenly Ray, who had been basking in the adoration of platform admirers, jerked to attention, wound the reverser (even more rapidly than I prided myself in winding sluice gear on the River Nene) and tugged at the cable in the roof controlling the whistle. A mellifluous call reverberated around the cast iron canopies of the station - somewhere between the bass hoot of the Midland and the high treble shriek of the Great Western - and at 10.56, almost half an hour late, we were off.

Puff, puff, puff - I can't avoid the cliche - there just isn't any other way to describe the gathering intensity of our departure. There were smuts everywhere - I was lucky to be optically challenged and wearing spectacles. Eddy drew my attention across the cab to see his family waving us off from the car park; well four of his six sons anyway, and their mother looking remarkably serene in the circumstances. We lurched over the complex

pointwork of the station's throat, gathering momentum. By the time we'd left the last of Crewe's pigeon lofts, football pitches and cabbage patches astern we were up to forty miles an hour and I was mentally negotiating terms with the din and the vibration.

Through the forward facing spectacle plate, shaped like an inverted rhomboid, I had a surprisingly good view ahead along the gun barrel of a boiler. I glanced across at Ray who looked like a latter-day Casey Jones. One has a mental image of the driver's hand being glued to the regulator arm, but as I was to see throughout the journey, the reverser plays an even more significant role in controlling the speed and power output of the locomotive.

We gobbled up the miles like Billy Bunter on a midnight feast. On some routes Railtrack lets steam run up to seventy-five miles an hour, but on this occasion we had a ceiling of sixty which Ray kept to assiduously. I caught cameo glimpses of rural Cheshire roaring by. Lush fields of Friesian cows, a woman walking down a lane with a shopping basket, half-timbered houses ancient enough to have been old when steam made its first tentative steps along here over a hundred and fifty years ago. Each wayside station was thronged with bystanders and cameramen. At Hartford a fellow in a tweed jacket and flannel trousers with a pronounced side parting and thick-rimmed glasses looked like a lost link with the first, Ian Allan inspired, post-war generation of trainspotters. Perhaps he was, there's every possibility he was occupying his own time loop.

Then there was a sudden change of atmosphere in the cab, a new focus of attention and alertness. Rapidly Ray shut off steam and applied the brakes. At length we shuddered steadily to a halt. Invisible from my side of the cab, Ray had seen a signal at danger. We came to a standstill - half a mile later! - by a lineside photographer whose day must have been made by the incident. His face was suffused with pleasure; he was beaming like a small boy who'd just discovered an amiable wild beast at the bottom of his garden. There was a momentary lull, a second or two of something approaching silence. The view ahead lay

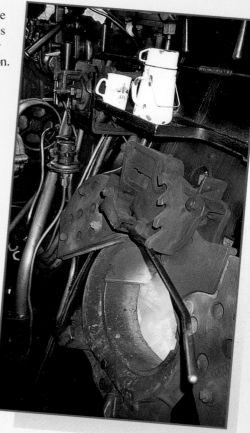

Ray's billycan simmering above the firebox

enveloped in clouds of steam. Presently it evaporated to show that the signal had turned to green. Eddy raised his eyebrows. "Just the signalman being slow," he explained. Then it was one-two-three, one-two-three, one-two-three again, in a distant echo of my mother's futile attempts to teach me to waltz. Oliver Bulleid had worked with Sir Nigel Gresley at Doncaster and retained his superior's preference for three cylinder propulsion. On the Midland and Western, Stanier and Collett built engines that ran through the landscape in common time.

Joseph Locke's magnificent, twenty-arch viaduct carried us across the Weaver Navigation at Dutton. Twenty years ago I'd sailed beneath it on the last of the ICI 'Brunner' barges fondly imagining that I was 'seeing life' then, but here I was, both literally and symbolically, on an altogether higher plane of existence. The line to Liverpool veered left and we dashed through Preston Brook. *Canadian Pacific* seemed to be laying more smoke trails over the countryside than the cooling towers of Fiddler's Ferry power station crouched on the horizon to the west. A big box girder bridge hurled us over the Manchester Ship Canal and into Warrington's industrial landscape of soap factories, chemical plants and marshalling yards. Whistle blowing, we passed EWS's Arpley Yard, Pete's home base, a busy centre for both coal and Enterprise traffic.

There must have been a hundred men on Bank Quay station, all clutching cameras, all seeking the quintessential shot. Eddy took a turn shovelling as we gathered speed past the massive Royal Mail Terminal where Ray and Eddy were more normally to be found at work on postal trains. Then we reached out into a brief rural interlude separating Warrington from Wigan. A car paralleled us briefly on a lonely road, its driver gesticulating to children in the back to look at the steam train. At a riding stable, activity was reverently suspended to watch us pass. Ray used the whistle liberally, a clarion call: we are the Cocks of the North; we are the circus come to town; we are all your yesterdays evaporating in smoke rings across the sad pubescent pastures which lie in wait at the end of childhood. Eddy finished his stint of firing and stood

Dave Thompson does a spot of oiling at Blackburn

back in the glow of his handiwork. The pressure gauge flickered around 240lbs, outside on top of the boiler the safety valves were blowing off. Pete placed an avuncular arm around my shoulder and appeared to be asking me if I was enjoying the ride. I couldn't shape an answer. Already deafened, now I was mute as well.

I know Wigan well from my boating days. By Abram I watched the Leeds & Liverpool Canal sidle in from Leigh, its banks raised high to combat mining subsidence. At Springs Branch, where Jimmy Eccles had worked as a youthful engine cleaner, there were sad rows of withdrawn EWS diesels being 'cannibalised' for spares before being broken up. It was 11.42 when we pounded through Wigan North Western and passed the garishly painted gable end of Uncle Joe's Mint Ball factory. The line climbs from here at 1 in 104 to Boar's Head. Pete, his forehead glistening in the sauna-like atmosphere of the footplate, shouted in my ear again, gesticulating dramatically to make himself understood. "It's about pride and heart and satisfaction." That Scousers wear their hearts on their proverbials is common enough currency, but this was a guy manifestly enjoying his work with a passion one could only admire and envy.

A series of 'yellows' forced Ray to ease the regulator back and adjust the 'cut off' on the outskirts of Preston. In any case our route would take us away from the electrified West Coast Main Line at Farington Junction, at which point we would turn east towards Blackburn and The Pennines. Bob was working his passage with a spot of firing as we curved sharply away from the main line. I looked back down the cream and red train, a diminishing perspective of craning heads and hand-held microphones. Lostock Hall motive power depot stood hereabouts, one of the final bastions of steam in 1968. Many of the greying, balding, weight accumulating fifty-somethings travelling on the train, or spectating from the lineside, would have been twenty-somethings then, making pilgrimages to Lostock Hall, Rose Grove (near Burnley) and Carnforth. They were faced with imminent loss, like watching a loved one die. They foresaw a life bereft of the animate machinery closest to their heart. Put yourself in their shoes - Doc Martens before they became fashionable. Imagine being an angler faced with the extinction of fish, or a rambler discovering that all public rights of way were to be closed by decree. Now you can grasp how these men - and of course they were overwhelmingly *men* - felt. Little wonder they follow in such enthusiastic droves wherever and whenever these beasts are let out of captivity.

Such hunger for steam explains the patience of bystanders, still looking up the line for us, still straining to hear a distant whistle in the woods, long after we were scheduled to pass. Half an hour is of no consequence to the railway photographer. He will wait half a day if necessary. We climbed through Pleasington to Cherry Tree. Whole villages, or so it seemed, had come down to see us. In a cutting of rhododendron bushes, four men stood shoulder to shoulder, like a barber shop quartet, to see us go by. I could swear I heard their sweet harmonies carrying downwind as they disappeared from view. "Dinah, how could anything be finer, in the State of Carolina ..."

The summit won, Ray shut off steam, and we ran past the baleful backs of terrace housing into Blackburn. By Mill Hill we came to a stand at another signal. There was a moment of comparative calm. I looked out across the moorland tops to Darwen's Jubilee Tower. Ray opened the regulator. The driving wheels slipped. For a moment we were like an Olympic sprinter running on the spot. Men poured out of a lineside foundry to see our pyrotechnic display. Steadying, 35005 found its feet and we drew forward into Blackburn's half demolished station. "Did you enjoy that?" asked Pete as, a trifle reluctantly I thought, he left the footplate. "It beats sex, beer and football," I replied, "though not necessarily in that order."

    *   *   *

A road tanker had brought fresh supplies of water but there was a slight hitch - we had a bayonet connection, it had a screw. I thought of A level English and E.M. Forster, if it would "only connect!" Luckily Nick located a handy hydrant and refilled the tender to the brim. The new crew familiarised themselves with the locomotive's foibles, not that there were many, by common consent *Canadian Pacific* was an excellent engine. Bob had boasted earlier of its recent exploits on the climb to Whiteball south of Taunton where some sort of power output record had

The tanker which wouldn't connect!

been achieved. My minder for the second leg was Gordon Hodgson, accompanied on the footplate by driver Brian Grierson and fireman Steve Chipperfield. Gordon was the eldest of the three. I didn't get much opportunity to delve into his railway background on account of the pervading cacophony on our ride over the Settle & Carlisle, but I did learn that he had worked on the Waverley line, across the bonny watersheds of the border hills between Carlisle and Edinburgh, and that was enough to elevate him to hero status in my eyes.

It was just after one when we left Blackburn, climbing steeply away from Daiseyfield Junction overlooked by old textile mills and tight-knit streets of terrace housing defying gravity on precipitous hillsides. Before passenger trains were reintroduced to Clitheroe in 1994, the old Lancashire & Yorkshire route between Blackburn and Hellifield was virtually disused. Excepting the occasional diversion from the West Coast Main Line, the Sundays only 'Dalesrail' services, and a thrice weekly train of imported coal which journeys up to Hellifield to run round before reversing into the cement factory siding at Horrocksford, this is still the case beyond Clitheroe. Rusty rails brought home this lack of use, as did a series of speed restrictions and a tendency for trackside vegetation to encroach upon the permanent way: cow parsley in the cuttings, and grass sprouting through the ballast. "Don't lean out too far", warned Gordon, "or the hawthorn will have you!"

"But I did learn that he had worked on the Waverley line, across the bonny watersheds of the border hills between Carlisle and Edinburgh, and that was enough to elevate him to hero status in my eyes."

Our run through the Ribble Valley under the rheumy-eyed gaze of cloud-topped Pendle was a world away in character from the WCML. I'd read of rough footplate rides, but hitherto *Canadian Pacific* had been more comfortable than one or two of the diesels I'd been on. Now I could see that a locomotive could only ride as well as the condition of the track would allow. It might also have had something to do with the fact that I had swapped sides with Bob and was now standing on the tender behind the driver. Nevertheless, it was a scenically satisfying journey up the valley past fields freshly cut for silage and bends in the river where dry-fly fishermen stood ruminantly knee-deep in waders. More significantly there was a hint of sunshine up by Penyghent after a good deal of cloud cover in Lancashire. I was relieved because Keith (the disappearing cameraman) and Gloria were stationed at Ribblehead to record our passing, and earlier in the morning he'd rung from Settle to tell me there was blanket fog up there.

I watched the fresh crew at work. Brian wore goggles and reminded me of Burt Lancaster in *The Train,* looking every bit the racy Gallic driver. Both Brian and Gordon spoke with the musical lilt of Carlisle folk, which to the uninitiated sounds more Geordie than Cumbrian. Steve, by some way the youngest of the trio, was an Essex boy. He had worked in a council architect's department in Chelmsford before becoming disenchanted and joining the railway on the serendipity of a newspaper advertisement. He had worked at Stratford in East London for a while, then moved to Shenfield, but was forced to find a vacancy elsewhere when that depot closed. Carlisle suited him, and his partner was able to find work there too, so here he was on a sooty, cacophonous footplate, bucketing through the Yorkshire Dales, a far cry from municipal blueprints in Chelmsford.

"You look too young to even remember steam," I shouted. "How did you get to be here?"

Gordon and Brian

"My neighbour's a steam buff and he goaded me that I might be able to drive diesels, but I'd never manage steam. It was a red rag to a bull, so I put my name down to train on steam and here I am."

And obviously relishing it, I thought, watching him hurl some big lumps of coal into the firebox by hand.

We lurched round the curve into Hellifield, our whistle echoed sonorously through the ornate cast iron canopies of this handsomely restored country junction. We didn't stop here, as planned, so as to catch up on the schedule. The number of spectators hitherto paled into insignificance compared with the crowds here. In one lineside field a rank of perhaps twenty cameramen stood abreast; so close that I could imagine their shutters being released by a sort of domino effect. This relationship between trains and photography deserves investigation. Only women and children seem content to watch a train go by, men have to have a photograph of it, as if involved in some subconscious throwback to the hunting instinct.

A yellow light slowed us to Settle Junction. The sun had popped out. I watched an angler walk across a field towards the river followed by a herd of inquisitive cattle. The Ribble ran close enough for me to smell the musky banks of butterbur. I saw another fisherman arch back and cast

A breather for Steve

Smoke trails over the Eden Valley – *Canadian Pacific* climbs to Ais Gill overlooked by Wild Boar Fell

his line into the dark recesses of an inviting pool. Gordon took the regulator while Steve and Brian began shovelling in unison. Now we were on the Settle & Carlisle proper - the 'Long Drag' - facing a dozen miles of sheer climbing at 1 in 100 to Blea Moor.

Brian and Steve pivoted back and forth like a well-oiled piece of machinery, a sort of human extension of the locomotive itself. I had begun to notice how tactile steam footplatemen were, as if, of necessity, touch replaced sound as a means of communication. The Ribble grew rockier. There was another posse of photographers at Stainforth. We stormed through Horton-in-Ribblesdale at forty-four miles an hour. Bob reached into a compartment in the side of the tender and extracted a large grappling iron and proceeded to rake down more coal from the back of the tender for the others to fling on the hungry fire. Selside brought more onlookers, their cars parked bumper to bumper along the verges of the B6479. Not contributing in any other way, I did my bit by returning waves to the hordes.

Half past two saw us reach Ribblehead in perfect sunshine, a rare occurrence given the quixotic climate of The Dales. The moorlands surrounding the colossal, twenty-four arch viaduct were filled with people. I caught a reassuring glimpse of Keith and Gloria and their golden retriever perfectly positioned at the north end of the bridge. We steamed on beneath Ingleborough and Whernside and past the lonely signal box at Blea Moor. I had been through Blea Moor Tunnel a couple of times in the cabs of diesel locomotives, but to negotiate it on the footplate of a steam engine was an incredible experience. Steve had shut the fire doors and switched on a couple of pale lights in the roof of the cab. The tunnel's portal loomed, gaped and gobbled us up. I knew now how Jonah felt inside the whale. I clung to the tender for dear life, envisaging a swift fall into the yawning darkness. If indeed we were inside a whale, then it seemed to be masticating us slowly and deliberately, such was the shake, rattle and roll accompanying our progress. Tunnels don't frighten me. I have spent enough hours in those of the canal variety without being reduced to a gibbering wreck. But the incredible din, the swaying motion and my ghostly compatriots moving in shadow plays within the pallid lights of the injector glasses created a sort of macabre tableau wherein time was suspended until further notice

and reality expunged.

The speedometer showed sixty as we emerged from the tunnel and thundered over Dent Head Viaduct. Brian inspected the fire, probing a long shovel into its gaping jaw like a dentist checking for cavities. He looked over to Gordon and grinned, obviously satisfied with what he saw. Arten Gill is my favourite Settle & Carlisle viaduct. Unimpeded by double-glazing - indeed, glazing of any sort - I was able to look down on Dentdale like a hawk borne up on some friendly thermal. I saw the Sportsman's Inn and salivated at the thought of a cool pint of Dent Bitter.

Dent station - famous for being the highest on a main line in England, though one could argue pedantically that the Settle & Carlisle is no longer a *main* line - was predictably busy with spectators. Beyond it, and the overbridge which carries the old 'coal road' over from Garsdale, we plunged into a belt of conifers leading to Rise Hill Tunnel. Brian looked at his wristwatch and announced: "We're early!" Omitting the Hellifield stop had allowed us to leapfrog the schedule. We took on water at Garsdale from another hydrant. In the line's heyday there had been water troughs here enabling express trains to slake their thirst without stopping. In the warm sunshine passengers spilt out on to the platform and elbowed each other - firmly but politely, as only the English can - to get a photograph of the engine.

We left, a couple of minutes ahead of our booked departure time of 15.09, for a thirty-five minute run to Appleby where we would take another breather. There was still some climbing to be done as far as the line's famously windswept summit at Ais Gill. From my vantage point back on the fireman's seat I could see the very apex point itself and the elliptical rail commencing its descent into the valley of the Eden. I looked over towards Mallerstang Edge and then down to Outhwaite where I had once waited among the tall, swaying grasses of the graveyard to photograph a train passing beneath Wild Boar Fell.

As we approached Birkett Tunnel a Class 60 locomotive emerged from the cutting hauling a train of southbound coal hoppers. Ten years ago it was inconceivable that the Settle & Carlisle - saved from closure by the seat of its pants - would ever be considered a through freight route again. Yet it has become a key link for English Welsh & Scottish, who now have more trains

Firing stint for Steve

operating over the line than any other company. So much traffic passes over it now that the signal boxes are kept open throughout the night to provide sufficient capacity. Unfortunately, the infrastructure, maintained for a number of years to standards commensurate with the operation of light-weight Sprinters, has not coped well with handling frequent heavy goods trains. There have been landslips, derailments and a general deterioration in the fabric of the route, resulting in freight trains being subjected to a blanket 30mph speed restriction over much of the 'up' (or southbound) track with sections where even slower speeds are compulsory; restrictions which play havoc with pathing requirements.

At Smardale I craned my neck to see the old North Eastern viaduct up its wooded gorge to the west. What a line that would have been to travel over, with its massive, cast-iron viaducts carrying it across the grain of the North Pennines from Darlington via Barnard Castle and Kirkby Stephen to Tebay and Penrith. The track ahead was now virtually a green carpet. It looked pretty, as though *Canadian Pacific* was travelling over one of the old green roads across the fells, but I doubted if a civil engineer would see its sorry state in such a romantic light. We penetrated Helm Tunnel - with the date of the line's construction in 1873 embossed above its portal - and crossed the River Eden at Ormside on the way down into Appleby.

It was still a beautiful afternoon, warm enough to smell the creosoted fencing along the lengthy platform. The passengers detrained, stretched their collective limbs, or visited the Friends of the Settle & Carlisle Line's souvenir shop, but mostly gathered again at the platform end to worship the locomotive. One or two lucky ones were invited up on to the footplate. A child had his photograph taken in the driver's seat. Lacking only a ukulele, I leaned against a lampost, soaking up the atmosphere, commanding a misleading sense of authority in my EWS high visibility vest. I got into a highly technical conversation with a man from Milton Keynes about the Pacific's performance. Brian came over to lend moral support, cutting a swathe through the fawning throng. "What's it like to be a film star?" I asked. A serious young man in a Merchant Navy Class sweatshirt with a soft Scots accent

Class 60, Birkett

"So much traffic passes over it now that the signal boxes are kept open throughout the night to provide sufficient capacity."

"'What would you rather have, Gordon, a Duchess or a B1?'
'Oh a B1,' laughed Gordon, rising to the bait."

Gordon takes the regulator

told me proudly that Brian held the 'Blue Riband' for reaching Ais Gill from a dead start at Appleby in sixteen minutes with *Duchess of Hamilton*, a Stanier Pacific belonging to the National Railway Museum. Gordon, apparently, trailed him by six seconds, but currently held three prestigious steam records of his own: the fastest runs from Carlisle to Beattock and from Carlisle to Shap, and the highest and longest continuous output (2,900hp) for nine miles; all with the A2 Pacific *Blue Peter*.

We returned to the footplate where Brian kept up the friendly rivalry, voicing his opinion that LMS designs could outdo those of the LNER any day.

"What would you rather have, Gordon, a Duchess or a B1?"

"Oh a B1," laughed Gordon, rising to the bait.

"That's cos he's a sad bastard!" joined in Steve.

"Give me a Black Five any time," added Dave Thompson, who had replaced Bob in the cab for the run down to Carlisle. I would have thrown my engine-driver's hat into the ring with a Peppercorn A1 had not the safety valves blasted off at that very moment; probably saving me from some ignominious 'so what do you know about it' stares.

I was looking forward to the run down the Eden Valley, with its quasi-Scots scenery and proliferation of viaducts, tunnels and wayside stations; the latter built to a standard 'Derby' gothic design which had spread as far as the goods sheds and employees' cottages. Nestling beneath the viaduct at Long Marton I saw sheep being driven down the lane past the railway cottages by an eager border collie. We slowed to thirty over track made unstable by gypsum mining. Gypsum also comes by rail to the works at Kirkby Thore, much of it derived from the de-sulphurisation process at Drax Power Station in Yorkshire.

Gathering speed again through Culgaith, *Canadian Pacific* began to oscillate over indifferent track like a fairground waltzer. It became impossible to make lucid notes. Keying this into the computer I am relying on memory - but what memories! Beyond Little Salkeld - where I'd once been shown over the watermill by its proud miller, beaming through the mask of flour on his work-stained face - we recrossed the Eden, glimpsing the overgrown remains of mineral sidings where anhydrite (a source of sulphur) used to be loaded for consignment to ICI in Widnes. We pounded through Lazonby - with its quaint cattle market and Celtic cross in the lineside churchyard - and steamed into the sunlight and shadow of Baron Wood, the boles of its silver birches glinting almost incandescently beyond high banks of bracken and fern.

Rumbling over Dry Beck Viaduct, Brian called to Steve to look out for the distant signal at Low House. Routine professionalism of course, but just as well, for the signal was against us and Brian made a rapid brake application. The signalman was on his steps with a yellow flag, and crossed to 'up' track to tell us that there had been a 'block failure', but that we were clear to proceed to the next box down the line at Howe's Siding. It was no sinecure restarting the heavy train, in a potentially damp cutting on a tight curve, with a Bulleid Pacific prone to slipping, but Brian handled it masterfully and, sure-footedly, in waltz time, we gathered momentum and got on our way.

In the cutting at Cotehill, dappled with sunlight, a boy in a red teeshirt took our photograph and waved excitedly as we roared beneath his overbridge. We went past Howe's siding like the wind, lurching over the pointwork. Steve shouted in my ear. "They're talking about upping the speed limit to seventy-five - ha bloody ha!"

Beneath the M6 we drifted down to the Border Capital. The footplatemen started chatting, a job well done. Big smiles and pats on the back, like we'd just won the cup or climbed Skiddaw, as opposed to Ais Gill. Suddenly it dawned on me that my magic carpet ride was all about to end.

There was another steam locomotive in the station, a Stanier 8F waiting to return to Hellifield with an out and back excursion. Two steamers under its capacious roof must have rekindled evocative memories of The Citadel in its sooty, smoky heyday for many of the onlookers. We came to a rest in Platform 6, like many an Anglo-Scottish express before us. *Canadian Pacific* would be spending a couple of days at Upperby depot before its return working southwards over the Settle & Carlisle. I shook hands emotionally with Steve and Brian and Gordon and Dave. "Have you seen your face?" they all asked me. I took that to mean the fixed smile and went back to the support coach to get my bags, bumping into Andrew Naish and thanking him profusely for allowing me to ride on his engine. "Have you seen your face?" he said.

Back in the compartment I picked up my gear and glanced in the mirror on the bulkhead beneath the luggage rack, catching the reflection of a stranger; a coalminer by the look of him ...

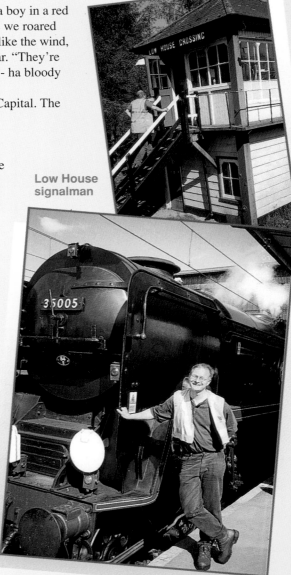

Low House signalman

"Have you seen your face?"
(Gordon Hodgson)

sand for the bottle factory

YOU don't need a bloodhound to follow in the tracks of the sand train. A trail of spillage marks the train's itinerary from Norfolk to South Yorkshire. It's there in the sidings, in the loops that the train waits in for expresses to overtake, at junctions and runround places, an unmistakable manifestation, a cast iron case which would hold up in court; proof that the sand train has passed. Three times a week, all year round, the sand train leaves the bosky, bucolic siding at Middleton Towers to the east of King's Lynn and commences its hundred and fifty mile journey to the glassworks at Barnby Dun on the outskirts of Doncaster. Aficionados might argue that it is not the most spectacular traffic flow in the English Welsh & Scottish portfolio, but it must be one of the most steeped in tradition, and it keeps around five thousand annual lorry movements off the already overcrowded roads of Eastern England, so I thought it was worth investigating.

I left my car at EWS's Peterborough depot. It leases its sooty, cream-brick office from Railtrack. Its history goes back to the dawn of trains, part of it once being a mission to railwaymen. On a mission of my own, I locked the car and grabbed my gear.

"I'd move that back a space," said a voice, "or Railtrack'll have it wheel-clamped!"

It was John Hutton, the Operations Standards Inspector who was going to accompany me on the trip. "So much for post privatisation integration and co-operation," I was thinking as he ushered me into Colin Graham's office. If I'd looked more closely I would have seen that the car park has a demarcation line between EWS spaces and Railtrack's, which pretty much says it all, doesn't it?

Colin Graham is Traffic & Traincrew Manager for Peterborough and Leicester. He had set up the sand train trip for me and kindly offered to drive John and I over to Middleton Towers to save us a tiresome drive at what would be the end of a long day. His help seemed all the more selfless when I discovered that it was his day off, and that when he got back to Peterborough he was due to drive his wife over to Birmingham to take part in a swimming event at the Transplant Games. Furthermore, all this was on the back of a gruelling session of emergency conferences emanating

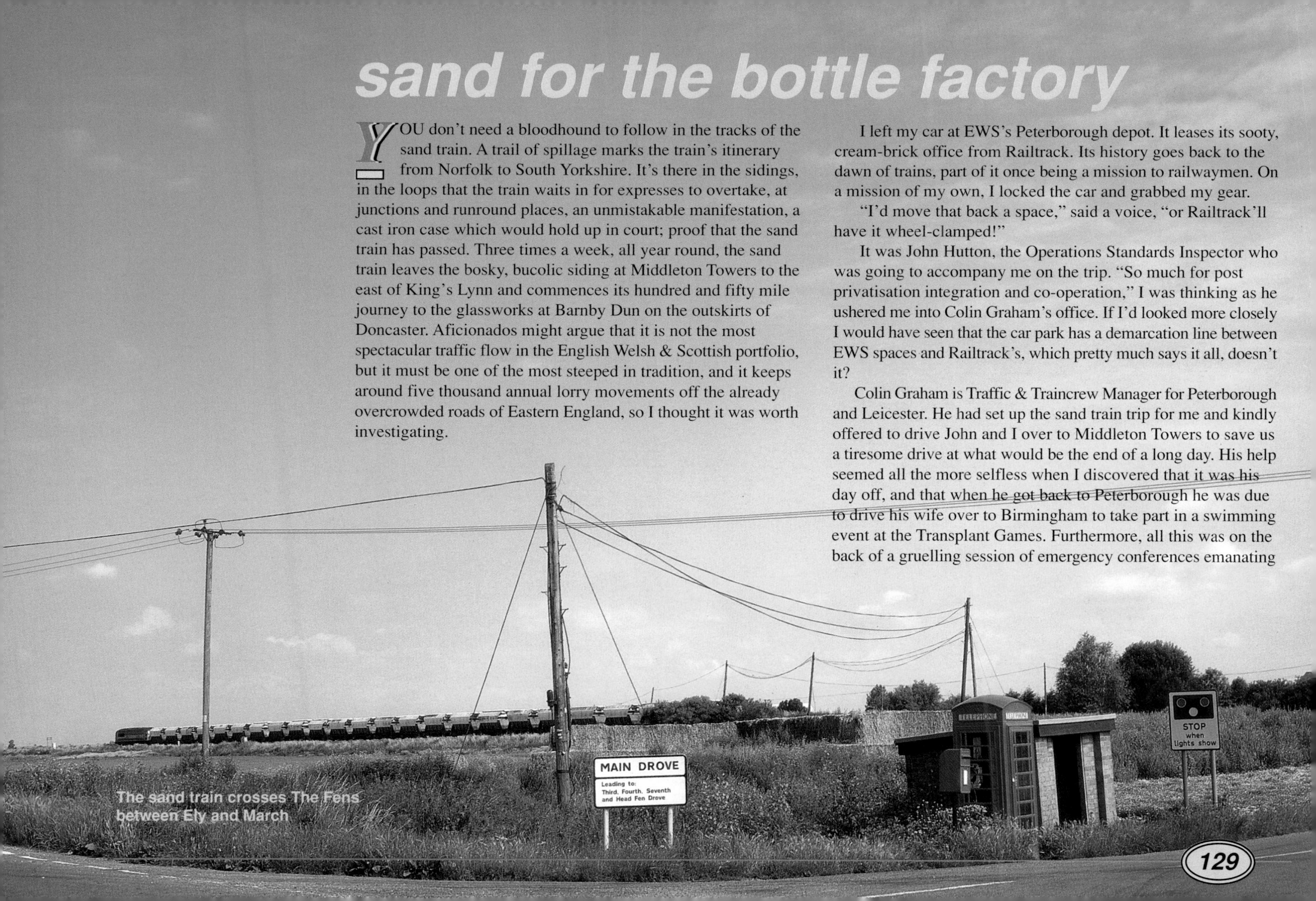

The sand train crosses The Fens between Ely and March

MAIN DROVE

Leading to:
Third, Fourth, Seventh and Head Fen Drove

STOP when lights show

from the Winsford collision on the West Coast Main Line and the need to re-route a good deal of that artery's freight through Peterborough. I could see, though, that Colin thrived on such a challenge.

"I had a work experience lad with me last week. At the end of each day he asked what we'd be doing tomorrow and I'd tell him I'd no idea, which more or less sums the job up perfectly."

Colin hadn't set out to be a railwayman at all. He'd got an engineering apprenticeship in a biscuit machine factory, and was doing nicely until he broke his arm playing football, rendering him useless at a lathe and therefore expendable to the biscuit machine factory's future. I judged their loss the railway's gain. Twenty years on from qualifying as a porter on Peterborough station, he exudes boundless enthusiasm for his work, if not for trains as such.

"I'm not an enthusiast. I couldn't give a damn about railways for their own sake, but I'm passionate about the job."

I saw more and more of that passion as Colin drove John and I across the early morning Fenland landscape. Coming over from Staffordshire it had dawned decidedly murky, but here the sun was punching holes in the cloud and there was a reassuring sheen about the level countryside. Colin and John talked - I listened. They were in resilient mode, speaking optimistically of making inroads back into the business of sugar beet, historically a core traffic in this part of the world before British Rail began shooting itself in its corporate feet. EWS has been particularly successful in capturing the carriage of 'sugar stone', a limestone used in the refining of sugar, and is serving plants in Norwich, Thetford and Ipswich. It is also doing well with timber from Brandon on the Ely-Norwich line, whilst the aggregates traffic between Mountsorrel (near Loughborough) and a number of East

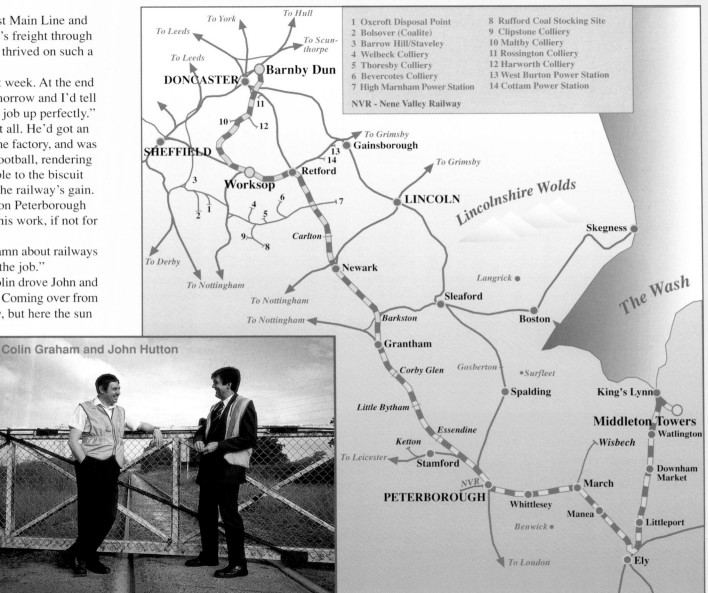

Colin Graham and John Hutton

1 Oxcroft Disposal Point
2 Bolsover (Coalite)
3 Barrow Hill/Staveley
4 Welbeck Colliery
5 Thoresby Colliery
6 Bevercotes Colliery
7 High Marnham Power Station

8 Rufford Coal Stocking Site
9 Clipstone Colliery
10 Maltby Colliery
11 Rossington Colliery
12 Harworth Colliery
13 West Burton Power Station
14 Cottam Power Station

NVR - Nene Valley Railway

Anglian termini is healthy, but there are flies in the proverbial ointment, problems from directions you wouldn't anticipate. In Wisbech, residents adjacent to the rail terminal have complained of being disturbed by shunting, whilst in Lincolnshire local authorities are less than thrilled by Railtrack's suggestions that the Peterborough-Spalding-Sleaford-Doncaster secondary route might be developed as a freight channel to alleviate crowding on the East Coast Main Line. I wondered if the good burghers of Wisbech hadn't noticed a railway yard at the bottom of their gardens when they bought their houses, or if the councillors of Kesteven would prefer their roads filled with yet more lorries. Increasingly on my rail freight travels I was struck by the obstacles rail operators have to negotiate to be able to offer any sort of service at all.

"The number of railway lines lifted round here is unbelievable," said Colin, "and it's all potential lost. We'll invest in new sidings and trackwork if we're reasonably sure of a long term flow, but we have to be professional. One could argue that we perform miracles every time we run a train on time."

I heard too of the railway's retreat from the Port of King's Lynn where a degree of uncertainty as to ownership of the trackwork in the docks resulted in a once significant trade being abandoned.

"You'd be better off with a fleet of lorries," I remarked, tongue in cheek.

"Well, we're already in bed with the road operator Rail Services", Colin replied, "and that's an admission that we can't always get where we'd like to go!"

But at least EWS can still get to Middleton Towers, about three miles out of 'Lynn on the old Great Eastern branchline to Swaffham and Dereham, closed and truncated beyond the sand terminal as long ago as 1968. Nevertheless, a good deal of Great Eastern atmosphere remains tangible in the vicinity of the old station, which retains a timber waiting room with a valanced canopy and a level crossing guarded by a pair of elderly looking gates complete with the sort of circular red warning signs seen only on preserved railways now. The station house has become home to a couple who keep Rottweilers. The dogs greeted the

appearance of John and I on the platform with enthusiasm, probably thinking that we were their breakfast. As Colin drove away a pipe-smoker in a 4x4 lowered his automatic window and quizzed us as to the departure time of the sand train as he intended to photograph it on its way into 'Lynn. He was the first of half a dozen or more lineside photographers who took our picture that day, such is the enthusiasm for rail freight now that passenger trains are so standardised in their styling and formation.

The sand train was still moving slowly through the loading hopper in a tree-lined avenue beyond the old station. The sand comes up from Hepworth's quarry by conveyor belt. Under 'slow speed' control the locomotive, usually a Class 58 or 56, draws the wagons through the hopper guided by a series of marker lights. Three diagonal lights from top left to bottom right tell the driver to move forward; three diagonals in the opposite direction indicate that he should set back; two horizontal reds flanking a central yellow show that the next wagon to be loaded is positioned properly and that the train should stop.

John and I walked towards the locomotive at the far end of the train. "Watch you don't get sand in your shoes," he said in a far off echo of seaside holidays. In fact the siding and its loop looked more like a sequence of sand dunes, so deep was the sand and so high the vegetation growing between the tracks. On the day of my journey there were thirty wagons in the train, though, with ten minutes to go before our booked departure time of 08.26, several were still to be loaded and it looked likely we would be late away. John patiently followed me about as I did some photography, and outlined his railway career. I was fascinated to learn that, his father being a signalman, he had been born in a railway house at Langrick on the old Boston-Lincoln 'Loop Line'. But John didn't follow directly in his father's footsteps.

"When I left school I got a job as a storekeeper at a Vauxhall dealership. After a while they asked me if I wanted to be a junior salesman and I did that for three years. But I was getting a boy's wages for a man's work and I couldn't see any future in it, so I joined the railway and went to the signalling school at Retford."

We must have looked an incongruous pair: John standing dapper in a charcoal suit reliving his railway history for me as I, in tee shirt and jeans, lunged about in the undergrowth experimenting with camera angles.

"My first box was at Surfleet on the old East Lincs, a nice straight road, a block post with a set of gates which meant that there was always some company. We had DMUs, light freight and King's Cross expresses. Then I went to Gosberton on the Joint Line between Spalding and Sleaford but I didn't like that so much. The other signalmen were always 'hanging out their washing' - if you see what I mean - and neither was I happy with the three shift system, so I decided to join the footplate."

The last wagon had been loaded, one of eight filled with wet sand for the glass factory at Worksop. The locomotive, 58044, which went under the romantic name of *Oxcroft Opencast*, had uncoupled, drawn forward, and circumspectly run back over the loop to get to the front of the train. John went on. "I went down to King's Cross, staying at the railway hostel in Ilford. My word it was a big change!" He broke off and grinned at the memory, I surmised, of a Lincolnshire innocent sowing his wild oats in The Smoke. Then we had to take a 'rain check' on the rest of his railway career because it was time to go.

Clambering up into the cab of the first Class 58 I'd encountered on my travels, I was introduced to driver Malcolm 'Mac' Harpley and trainman/guard Chris North. I felt I had to tread carefully with Mac, because he was about to be made redundant. March was closing down as a Train Crew Depot, and the men who didn't want to travel to Peterborough to start and finish their shifts were having to leave the railway. But in his flat cap, and with his Norky accent, he seemed stoically cheerful, and grateful for a happy forty-five years on the railway. Chris was also a March man, but younger, and prepared to move his base, not that he would spend much time at Peterborough, his work taking him far and wide throughout East Anglia in search of trains to shunt and sidings to shunt them in.

It was just coming up to nine when, half an hour late, Chris swung the level crossing gates open in our favour. Mac drew the train forward so that the rear wagon was clear of the road and Chris closed the gates behind us, freeing two or three motorists waiting impatiently for us to pass. We did a brake test before setting off on the short run to King's Lynn where we would have

Main picture: Loading at Middleton Towers
Left: John and 'Mac' **Right:** Chris closes the gates

to reverse. Loping pleasantly along the branchline, like some throwback to the days of pick-up goods, we made our way into 'Lynn. A pheasant strolled nonchalantly across the track in front of us, cow parsley swayed in our slipstream and in the flat fields beside the line cabbages sparkled freshly from the fine spray of irrigation fountains.

I cast my eyes around the cab of the Fifty-eight. Only fifty were ever built, so they are not an exactly widespread design. The first one emerged from BREL's Doncaster Works in 1983. They were conceived in modular form for ease of maintenance and are characterised by a slender engine compartment parenthesised, as it were, by full width cabs at either end. For a number of years they were pretty much confined to working Merry Go Round trains from the East Midlands coalfield to Trent Valley power stations, but since the days of the shadow franchises and the advent of EWS they are to be found further afield, particularly in the South and East. Just as we were coming into King's Lynn some old blue brick abutments - holding back an embankment like bookends - denoted the course of the celebrated Midland & Great Northern Railway's cross country route between the East Midlands and the Norfolk coast. In its heyday it was promoted glamorously as the 'Line to Poppyland'. Its locomotives - some built in the company's own workshops at Melton Constable, the 'Little Crewe' of North Norfolk - were adorned in a distinctive yellow ochre livery. Mourned by hoteliers, potato merchants and railway romantics - but not by railway accountants - it closed unceremoniously in 1959. "The Muddle & Go Nowhere," as Mac pithily put it; but you know by now that it was just my sort of line.

Beating out a rhythm on the short-jointed track, Colin prepared to hand the Middleton Towers staff - a hefty metal cylinder - to the signalman at Kings Lynn Junction. Gripping the handrail, he leaned out over the track just like the Italian Captain trying to save Frank Sinatra at the end of *Von Ryan's Express*. Happily there were no bullets pinging round our heads and the baton change was neatly accomplished. Out of path now, Railtrack made us wait, giving preference to a West Anglia Great Northern electric multiple unit bound for London King's Cross. We ran round in a grass-grown, sand-spattered loop adjacent to the

platform then spent the enforced delay nattering on the track in front of the locomotive. I learnt something of Chris North's background. Fourteen years on the railway, he roams itinerantly throughout the region overseeing shunting movements: Broxbourne, Barham, Brandon, Wisbech and Welwyn, the railway world's his oyster. He felt sad to have lived through March's decline.

"I remember when Whitemoor Yard was the busiest in Europe. They say it was modelled on Bremerhaven. There was a daily procession of coal trains working down from the Midlands and The North to London and East Anglia - three thousand wagons a day! Now they've built a prison on the site, but it could have been retained for Channel Tunnel traffic. I was a guard - I saw the brakevan go ..."

"You saw March go!" interjected Mac laconically.

"I still enjoy my work but there's a lot that needs putting right," Chris continued: "Both ends of the team have something to learn from each other."

A mild mannered, thoughtful man, and obviously no radical or malcontent, I reckoned if he was on *my* team I'd listen good to what he had to say. Then it was Mac's turn: "I started in 1954 at King's Lynn as an engine cleaner on 'Claud Hamiltons' and 'Sweedy Fours'. A pair of 'Sweedys' would take the sand train to Middleton with fifty mineral wagons. When they got there one of the engines would run round to the back of the train to make shunting easier. There was a back entrance off the Joint Line as well. As a fireman I worked to Hunstanton, Dereham, Cambridge and, later on, Liverpool Street. We did bomb trains to the military depots."

"Did you ever work the Royal Train?" I asked him, remembering Sandringham's proximity to King's Lynn.

"No, but I cleaned it," he laughed, "2614 was the 'Royal Claud'. We painted its roof white and its buffers silver. We filled the tender with Welbeck hard coal so it didn't smoke too much. On the Royal link you got a pound extra as a driver and ten bob for firing. The shed was just there," he added, jerking his head over his shoulder towards a wilderness of rosebay willowherb.

Mac left 'Lynn for March in 1960, getting married on Boxing Day and moving house in the process. "When I left, the shift

The sand train waits impatiently for a passenger train to clear the section

foreman, Fred Jackson (who always wore a black and white dickie bow - he was Mayor of King's Lynn) told me March would never close!" So much for soothsayers, so much for steam, so much for the railway town of Fenland.

We got away in the wake of the London passenger train at 10.02. 58044 growled out of town along the single line which looked incongruously important with its overhead catenary. Until we got on to the fast track of the East Coast Main Line we'd be restricted to forty miles an hour maximum on account of the weight borne by the axles of our four wheel wagons. Gently, thus, we plodded across the waving grasslands, crossing shimmering, glassy drainage dykes, passing prosperous farms under a wide, becoming bluer by the minute, sky.

Only once before had I travelled this way, thirty years ago at a time when it was still a double track main line served by 'proper' trains from Liverpool Street hauled by big-nosed, woad-coloured English Electric Type 3 diesels; what we'd now call Class 37. It was winter and it had snowed and I had joined a restaurant car express at Ely. We'd moved across the icy landscape like something out of poem by Pasternak. Decanted in King's Lynn, with little more than half an hour before the train was due to return, I ran all the way to the riverbank to pay homage to the Custom House in the fading light, darkening almost as rapidly as the Great Ouse drained out into The Wash.

I was woken from my winter reveries by the approach to Magdalen Road signal box and Watlington station. The track doubles here and a down electric was waiting for us to clear the section. "A line went through from here to Wisbech and March," Mac recalled. "There were stations at Middle Drove, Smeeth Road and Emneth." The nomenclature of The Fens suits the landscape's horizontal asceticism. No wonder they built such lofty churches. They must have figured they could reach God more easily with a leg-up. I remembered Magdalen Road from Arthur Randell's enjoyable book *Fenland Railwayman*. Working here between the wars in the days when the station was busy enough to warrant three shifts of staff, he recalled the goods yard bursting at the seams with sheep and cattle; the nightly mail train to London; and a porter's platform duties including the loading of milk churns and boxes of eels, the keeping of oil lamps, and the provision of foot warmers.

Blue linseed fields, lumped against the high poppy-covered banks of the Great Ouse's flood channel, led to Downham Market; Mac's old home town. "I used to cycle up to 'Lynn to get to work. You had to complete two hundred and eighty four firing turns to qualify as a fireman. But, living in Downham, I was at a disadvantage compared with the lads who lived in 'Lynn, being outside the calling up area. In the end they used to send me a telegram or get a porter from Downham station to come round for me. This was a busy place then. There were turntables for wagons in the goods yard and horses to do the shunting."

Like Arthur Randell, Mac Harpley might have been remembering life on another planet, light years away. There is no goods yard at Downham Market now; not even, irrationally, a siding into Heygates flour mill. Vanished too, the Stoke Ferry branch, once so busy with sugar beet. Colin Graham's words about EWS not always being able to get where it wanted to go echoed in my head. Beyond Denver Sluice we crossed the Great Ouse. The Fens reminded John of childhood on an uncle's farm in Lincolnshire. Mac was concerned that our late running would have ramifications on the time his shift ended. He was due to start the next day's work at ten past four in the morning and take a stone train to Bishop's Stortford, but unless he could be back at March by ten past four that afternoon, he wouldn't have the mandatory twelve hours rest in between. He was booked to leave us at Worksop and travel back 'on the cushions', though at the rate we were going, it looked doubtful if he'd make it back to March in time. Using his mobile phone, he rang control to ask their advice. They rang back almost immediately to say they'd swapped his duties. Tomorrow he could sign on at 9am as stand-by.

"That's all right then," he laughed. "I can catch up with the rule book."

"Which one Mac?" joked John, knowing Mac's intention to see out his retirement on a preserved railway. "Diesel or steam!"

We'd been back on single track since Downham Market, but at Littleport the line doubled. Mac was telling us about his 60th birthday. He'd been up on the North York Moors Railway and his family had organised a surprise meal on the train after he'd

"It was winter and it had snowed and I had joined the restaurant car express at Ely. We moved across the icy landscape like something out of a poem by Pasternak."

Fenland silhouette

fired *Taw Valley* up the 1 in 40 to Goathland. "I hadn't fired for thirty years, but you don't forget it. In the end I was flicking coal into the far corners of the smokebox like I'd never stopped."

I wondered how many times Mac had passed Ely Cathedral in the course of his work, tens of thousands of times for sure, yet if it was me I don't think I could ever tire of it and I envied him seeing it in all lights and all seasons. Boxing the compass, we were to run round the West Curve, curiously - as John pointed out - bi-directionally signalled, but only passed for working in the 'down', Peterborough direction, so that when the sand train returns empty at the crack of dawn, it has perforce to work into Ely station and reverse.

A signal held us at red while we waited for two Sprinters to pass. Alongside stood the Potter Group's prosperous freight terminal which handles a wide variety of traffic including a daily Enterprise service from Doncaster. Strangely enough we passed this train soon after leaving Ely, though, on this occasion, it was a light locomotive - a Res Class 47 - there obviously being no incoming traffic on the day in question. To find out more about the operation I chatted on the telephone to Vivian Oram, the lady responsible for co-ordinating rail traffic at the Ely depot. I discovered that there was a growing enthusiasm for rail transport, particularly given the overcrowded nature of the region's roads. "Derek Potter's something of a pioneer where rail is concerned," she confided, going on to list a variety of the commodities which make their way through the railhead: paper and seed potatoes from Scotland; chipboard and tinned fruit; seasonal flows connected with the production of sugar beet - molasses, animal feeds and beetroot, which travel up to Elgin for use in Baxters Soup. The company also has a smaller rail-connected depot at Selby in Yorkshire.

Ely had seemed positively Alpine in the context of the Fens, but it was soon behind us as the line to March strode purposefully in a north-westerly direction, interrupted only by frequent level crossings protected, for the most part, by automatic half barriers.

Two big box girder viaducts carried us over the Bedford Rivers and the Hundred Foot Washes which separate them. Mac told us how these flood each winter, bringing back to me a memory of a journey down to Cambridge one February, when it seemed as though the train had suddenly struck out to sea. If I have my history right, the stilt-walking 17th century Fenlanders were a tad reluctant to have their swamps drained. The damp world around them oozed with fish and wildfowl and so what if their feet were webbed and ague rife. No, it was Charles I and the Duke of Bedford who dreamt of profiting from richly alluvial reclaimed lands, and who called in the Dutch expert, Vermuyden, who battled twenty years to tame the marshes. As Vivian Oram said, with reference to the tentative renaissance of rail transport: "Sometimes, you just have to put your toe in the water!"

At Manea we came under the control of semaphore signalling. Mac was telling us he'd been over to the Great Central Railway to see a demonstration of their preserved Travelling Post Office rolling stock and equipment. Whilst there, he'd bumped into an old acquaintance, a Loughborough-built Brush Type 2 diesel locomotive. March had been home to many of these engines, latterly known as Class 31. One of them had been experimentally painted in a golden ochre livery in 1960 to improve visibility for trackworkers and recently the GCR had repainted another preserved example of the class into this striking colour scheme, which Mac likened to - but then again I don't think this is the time or the place to tell you what he likened it too.

Through purple-flowering potato fields we continued to March, arriving in the down goods loop to enable a westbound sprinter to overtake us. On a subsequent photographic follow-up, I chatted to Nick Winn, a congenial signalman at March's immaculately kept South box. He showed me a photograph of the sand train passing his box in the early Eighties with two Class 20s providing the motive power. Naturally he was saddened by March's continuing contraction as a rail centre. "They get so full at Peterborough sometimes and the main line's so busy they can't find paths across it,

Nick Winn,
March South

drivers and firemen. Two mechanical boxes were still in business. We saw the signalman in the East Box pull off his levers in time honoured fashion to set our road, then we moved slowly through the pale shadow of a station, with its distinctive saw tooth canopies, seeing the curves which led to Whitemoor and which still lead - just! - to Wisbech.

"Is that 'dolly' signal still at Whitemoor?" John asked Mac, turning to explain to me that a ground signal had been left behind by the demolition teams, as if it was governing train movements off the now trackless yard. Ghost trains no doubt!

Between March and Whittlesey we traversed more flatlands, glorying - according to the map - in intriguing names like The Turves and Wype Doles. We passed a lonely timber signal box called Three Horse Shoes which once, according to Mac, had overlooked the egress of a light railway that had struck southwards across what are now blue fields of linseed to a place called Benwick, serving sidings with evocative names like Quaker's Drove, West Fen and Burnt House. I had mental images of box vans being loaded with vegetables and fruit, and mineral wagons discharging coal for pumping engines. The Benwick branches of this world ought really to return in a fresh 21st century guise; high tech and automated with modular track sections that can be taken up and relaid in other locations according to demand.

A pretty, dark-haired girl made her way across a field fringed with poppies and waited for us to pass over an occupation crossing. At Whittlesey we went over the Middle Level Navigation just as a narrowboat cruised beneath us. My canal travels had never brought me this far east - there's no profit to be made compiling guidebooks to such esoteric waters - but it goes without saying that I would have welcomed the challenge. Our second cathedral of the day appeared on the horizon, but first we had to negotiate the brick fields, once, but no longer, a significant source of rail freight. Someone had been round the signal boxes with a can of dark green paint - and very fetching Kings Dyke cabin looked too.

As a landmark, Peterborough Cathedral now has a gas-fired power station for competition. The planners may be strict with you when it comes to positioning your garden shed, but ruining

they could be using these sidings here instead of letting them go." We looked out over a disconsolate line of ICI tank wagons which, according to Nick, had been stored in the same siding for over three years.

Chris North left us here whilst Mac reminisced about the goods shed, which had been so busy in his day that the pilot engine was worked twenty-four hours a day by three shifts of

a city's skyline is OK by them. I had journeyed down the River Nene to Peterborough for one of my guidebooks and taken to the city, which feels more like a market town once you reach the centre. Mac showed us where he had shunted in the vanished yard at Stanground, and pointed out the platform edge at what was once Peterborough East, the former LMS station where you could catch trains to Wellingborough, Market Harborough, Rugby and Northampton before Beeching put the boot in. A stretch of the Nene Valley Railway is preserved but, given the quantities of gravel extracted further up the valley, it is a shame that the line did not remain intact at least as far as Wellingborough. British Rail was always in such a confounded hurry to lift disused lines when, in the absence of viable trade at the time, mothballing and minimum maintenance would have been more sensible. When you tire of a piece of furniture you don't drag it out into the garden and hack it to bits, you put it in the loft and, nine times out of ten, the day will come when you want it back again.

We crossed the river and drew level with a Great North Eastern Railway express slowing for the station. It was quarter to twelve and we had clawed back a bit of time. "They are pretty good as a rule, Peterborough and Doncaster," Mac told us. "If they can 'run you' they do." By which I think he meant that the signalmen on the East Coast Main Line are more favourably disposed towards freight than some of their Railtrack colleagues.

"Your car's still there," laughed John, as we passed the depot, and it seemed strange to be passing our point of departure after travelling through such a wide arc to return. In the engine sidings the presence of a Sixty-six, a Fifty-six and two Thirty-sevens surprised John. "Normally there's just the Wisbech engine in at this time of the morning." Then we got a further surprise as a double-headed intermodal train went through on the up line. At first John thought it was one of Freightliner's services, but I pointed out that the locomotives - a Class 47 piloted by a Class 56 - belonged to EWS. Then, as we came level with the last four wagons bearing Parcel Force containers, I realised that it was my old friend, the Mossend-Wembley piggyback train, diverted from its usual route because of the Winsford crash. Wow, I thought to myself, all this experience must be rubbing off when it's *me* who

imparts the information!

The down (northbound) slow line out of Peterborough is shared with the Stamford and Leicester line as far as Helpston Junction. A sign proclaims: "Electric Trains No Access To Stamford," though you couldn't imagine any driver in his right mind attempting to reach Stamford in an electric train *without* an overhead power source. Three miles out, Woodcroft Crossing looks like an escapee from the National Railway Museum, a good old-fashioned level crossing with manually worked wooden gates. Having to contend with two busy parallel routes, the keeper must have his work cut out to find a gap between trains for would-be motorists. A pretty, twin-canopied goods shed has been refurbished for office use at Helpston. The signal box is equally attractive and we got a friendly wave from its incumbent. The Stamford line veered away across the fields. From time to time, John told me, his work takes him to Castle Cement's plant at Ketton which receives coal by rail as required and despatches a daily train of cement to a terminal at King's Cross in London. Cement as a commodity has stayed fairly faithful to rail, and both Castle Cement and Blue Circle are valued customers of EWS. Coincidentally, we were soon passing Tarmac's concrete sleeper manufacturing plant at Tallington, subject of a visit by a daily Infrastructure train.

Now, almost for the first time on our circuitous travels, 58044 had to do some work. We were beginning to climb: 1 in 264 up to Essendine; 1 in 200 through Little Bytham; 1 in 330 to Corby Glen; and then some serious climbing of 1 in 178 up Stoke Bank, the scene, as every schoolboy used to know, of *Mallard's* world breaking 126mph downhill sprint with a test train in 1938. A trackside metalwork image of the streamliner commemorates this prestigious feat, though somehow more plaintive, is the small memorial to be glimpsed on the opposite side of the track back at Essendine where a little post records the foreshortened life of a railway enthusiast called Brian Carter, whom infirmity prevented from enjoying a railway career. Dying in 1950, at the age of 23, his remains were scattered here beside his favourite line.

From time to time a GNER express would whoosh by in one direction or the other; but, for a four track highway, the East Coast

"British Rail was always in such a confounded hurry to lift disused lines when, in the absence of viable trade at the time, mothballing and minimum maintenance would have been more sensible."

above sea level) the line becomes double track and we had to wait for a few minutes for a down express to overtake us before we were allowed out on to the down fast. We ran through Stoke Tunnel and passed from the jurisdiction of Peterborough power box to that of Doncaster. Beyond the tunnel we crossed the Roman's Ermine Street and saw, in the undergrowth, where the High Dyke iron ore branch had once struck southwards to quarries in the vicinity of Stainby.

At Grantham some EWS wagons were being loaded with tin cans and there was a Skegness local in the bay. I had a mental skirmish with the guidebook writer in me not to make mention in my notes of the parish church's soaring spire. Ruskin was apparently 'spellbound' by it and, I think I'm right in saying that it's amongst the top six in terms of height in the country. I suppose, however, that it's for Margaret Thatcher that Grantham is largely recognised now, though earnest students of industrial archaeology and engineering history will associate it more readily with Aveling Barford and Ruston & Hornsby; and quite right too!

I was paying so much attention to the spire that I missed the egress of the Nottingham line, and before I could give it a second glance we were swallowed up by Peascliffe Tunnel. The Barkston triangle, where *Mallard* turned before its record-breaking run, no longer exists, though a loop runs down to the Sleaford line for Skegness trains. The direct line to Allington Junction was still in situ, or at least it looked as though it was, hidden by carpet of grass, but John felt it was rarely used. Able to run up to our maximum speed of sixty now we were on the fast line, we didn't waste much time getting to Newark. I had looked forward to a cab's eye view of the famous flat crossing by which the Nottingham-Lincoln route slices across the main line, especially as Railtrack's 1999 Network Management Statement proposes its replacement by a flyover within a few years. Reconstruction of the Trent Navigation bridge is also planned to permit higher line speeds, but we were doing very nicely thank you, bowling along at sixty on a long section of level track. Bowling, that is, until we were sent into the loop at Carlton-on-Trent for an express to overtake.

While we were waiting to restart, John's pager bleeped with a message that he was required to check the loading arrangements

Top: The sand train passes "The Mallard" pub at Little Bytham
Left: Newark Crossing
Right: Track-workers at Stoke Summit

Main Line seemed unnaturally quiet and bereft of traffic.

Alternately the line ran through biscuit-coloured cuttings or on embankments above a rolling countryside of ruffled cornfields bordered by thick hedgerows broken, here and there, by dark spinneys. A short viaduct took us over the pantiled rooftops of Little Bytham where the local pub is called "The Mallard", in homage to the famous locomotive's feat. At Stoke Summit (345ft

of some infrastructure wagons at March as soon as he got back. Phlegmatically, we rang in to confirm his availability, but got lucky, there was time for it to be done the following morning without causing a delay; I had already sensed he was tired - this being his call out week - and could do with an early night, incidents permitting.

We waited patiently to be overtaken. Some pigs watched us from an adjoining field. Beyond the modern crossing cabin, trees masked a lineside pub. "I could just murder one," said John and we nodded agreement in unison. "It looks like you've been here before, Mac," he added, pointing to a fine residue of sand on the loop line. "Just a few times," Mac responded with heavy irony. This time it wasn't a Class 91 which sped by but an HST looking spritely and purposeful in GNER's dark blue and red livery. Living up to their co-operative reputation, the Doncaster signalmen swung the points and gave us a green in double quick time and Mac opened up quickly, with 58044 growling up the 1 in 200 to Tuxford.

Topographically the East Coast Main Line disappears into a sort of void between Newark and Retford. The countryside seems, on such fleeting acquaintance, characterless and empty. We fell into step with the Great North Road and passed under a remnant of the vainglorious Lancashire Derbyshire & East Coast Railway, retained for coal to reach High Marnham power station on the banks of the Trent. 58044 continued to grumble to itself, the cab bulkhead vibrating in sympathetic resonance with the engine room. Yes, diesels do have character, and this one was muttering under its breath like a teenager ordered to clean their bedroom out.

The crossing cabin at Grove Road has pretty bargeboards. Signal D143 'feathered' us from the down fast on to the slow line, from which we would diverge beyond Retford station round an excruciatingly tight curve leading, via a flyover, to the Worksop line. Wheels squealing in protestation, like something from a piece of modern classical music, we made our way around the curve at a circumspect ten miles an hour. "I got stuck here in the rain not so long ago," said Mac. "Couldn't go back nor forward. So I stopped and let her settle down, then got away. It's not just

a tight curve, you're climbing as well."

We left Retford behind and proceeded along a lengthy straight into a subtly changed landscape; hillier and more wooded, the line traversed shallow cuttings of fern, dog rose, daisy and elderflower. This marked, I supposed the northern fringe of The Dukeries, so we were passing into one of those schizophrenic areas of England where arcady and industry collide: in this instance, half Capability Brown and half Arthur Scargill; though, this being Nottinghamshire, I use the latter name as a simile extremely loosely. The natives were about to change too. "Watch out for those Worksop boys," Mac advised us. "It'll be 'mi flower' this and 'mi flower' that." Actually we became 'mi ducks', but I'd do better to concentrate on railway matters rather than the local patois.

On the edge of a still extensive coalfield, Worksop is an important centre for English Welsh & Scottish. It's a wagon repair, locomotive maintenance, and source of traction crew, point all wrapped up in one. The week after this ride I called in to check the movements of the sand train and bumped into Tony Stocks, who'd travelled with me over the Settle & Carlisle the year before. I'd heard he'd been very poorly, so it was good to see him back in the thick of things. His place of work was an impressive high tech modern building, a far cry from the sooty engine sheds of old; the Barrow Hills of this world where our next traincrew originally hailed from.

Almost before the brakes took hold, Mac was off to catch the first passenger train back to March, albeit with changes at Retford and Peterborough. He was replaced by driver Malc Smith and guard Simon Culverhouse. "Roundhouse men!" as Simon put it, a reference to Barrow Hill's status, until closure in February 1991, as the last working roundhouse where locomotives were stabled under cover in lines radiating from a turntable. Barrow Hill, on the north-eastern outskirts of Chesterfield, is enjoying a new lease of life as a museum, an increasingly popular venue for preserved locomotives; steam, diesel and electric. But our new travelling companions had escaped from the museum, even though we sensed they might have been even happier in it.

Malc had started working at Barrow Hill in 1962 and could thus recall the last years of steam operation: "It was a Midland

"...we were passing into one of those schizophrenic areas of England where arcady and industry collide: in this instance, half Capability Brown and half Arthur Scargill."

Shyness overcomes the winner of Worksop's best decorated shunting pole competition

depot, we had 8Fs, Midland 4s, Austerities and 9Fs. We went as far as Scunthorpe with ironstone; Drakelow and Willington power stations, near Burton-on-Trent, with coal; and Chinley on the Hope Valley line. But it was mostly coalfield work - in those days every depot served a dozen pits." Simon joined the railway in 1979, having turned his back on an electrical engineering course at Salford University. "There was an advert in the *Derbyshire Times* it gave the impression that a guard's pay was £85 a week - I averaged £49!"

The cloying aroma of onion soup from the neighbouring food factory hung like a wet blanket over Worksop Yard. A 350hp diesel shunter - still in British Rail blue - stood waiting to run the tail of our train into Rockware's adjoining glassworks siding. "We'll follow the 'livestock train'," said Simon, and for a moment both John and I wondered if some local initiative by EWS had reintroduced cattle trains to the railway. But no, 'livestock' is a Worksopian euphemism for passenger; an amusing joke laced with irony by the niggling irritation felt by freight crews when passenger trains are given priority.

Leaving eight of our wagons behind, we pulled away from Worksop just before half past two. Malc and Simon set up a running commentary which I could tell John was enjoying as much as me. We listened to litanies of colliery names which, despite privatisation, rationalisation, and the increase of imported coal, still appear numerous in this part of the world. In contrast to my exploration of the Ayrshire coalfield, many of the Nottinghamshire and South Yorkshire pits are still deep mined, but there are opencast operations as well, often, with new technology at their disposal, digging deeper than the old underground workings ever went. Our locomotive's namesake, Oxcroft, cropped up in the conversation, and now I can put a name to a mine I've passed hundreds of times on the M1 south of Junction 30.

I'd only ever travelled over the Sheffield-Retford line once before, in 1974 with an East Midlands Rover ticket stuffed in my back pocket. The train was a lightweight 'Derby' multiple unit bound for Lincoln, but my chief memory is of a woman in a black bra leaning out of an upstairs window on the way into Worksop.

No such excitements manifested themselves on this occasion, though I did keep an eye out just in case. Instead we journeyed parallel with the revitalised Chesterfield Canal, passing through Shireoaks somewhat lugubrious wayside station until, at Barncliffe East Junction, we swung away from the Sheffield line. Simon was proving a 'walking guidebook' after my own heart. "This is the South Yorkshire Joint Line, though, strictly speaking, we're not on that proper until Dinnington."

"It's steep here," Malc added: "and it gets 'interesting' when the rails are wet. There's a fifteen mile an hour limit through the junction, so you don't get a chance to take a run at it. Most of the time we've got a Fifty-eight and they used to have a reputation for slipping, but if you get on top of them to start with you stand a pretty good chance of making it; though once a fortnight, perhaps, in the autumn with leaves on the line as well, someone'll get stuck here."

I liked the "if you get on top of them" bit, as though Class 58 locomotives were some sort of disobedient animal which could be tamed by the right hands. Simon continued. "It's 1 in 70 here nominally, but there's so much subsidence round here that gradients are never the same from one month to the next. In the village where I live there are houses sloping down the hill which used to be on the level. There's a pit at Inkersall where they say you can hear them cutting coal at night under the houses."

No less than five Pre-grouping railway companies dug into their pockets to build the South Yorkshire Joint. It made sense for the Great Northern, Great Central, Midland, North Eastern and Lancashire & Yorkshire railways, in the early years of the twentieth century, to pool their resources to tap the coalfield rather than compete expensively by building their own lines. Their route snaked across the border lands of Notts and South Yorks to minimise the cost of earthworks and maximise the mines it served. Keeping their options open, however, bridgework was built to accept the laying of a second track should traffic warrant. Ironically, this is almost the case now, the line being busier than ever, though frustratingly, the deep and rocky limestone cuttings which characterise several portions of the route were not dug wide enough to automatically accept a second trackbed. In fact the route *is* double tracked as far as Dinnington, beyond which the single line is worked by tokenless block.

It was an entertaining journey over this unusual and characterful line. Suddenly we had left the mining-scarred landscape and pit villages behind and moved out into delightful countryside. A substantial, latticework viaduct carries the line over the picturesque hamlet of Brookhouse under the soaring, flying-buttressed spire of Laughton en le Morthern church. Days later I returned to do some photography, negotiating with an initially dubious farmer's wife to set my tripod up in a field overlooking the viaduct. "Well alright, but there's some nervous bullocks up there and I don't want them getting out." I convinced her that cattle handling was second nature to me (I used to work in the publicity department of an animal feeds firm) but that didn't stop the farmer coming to collect me in his tractor. "I wouldn't mind

The sand train eases its way over Brookhouse Viaduct on the South Yorkshire Joint, overlooked by the spire of Laughton church.

Simon and Malc in the loop at Maltby Colliery

usually, but there's no accounting for those beasts - I wish I hadn't bought them!" They were, it transpired, Charlolais crosses from Ayrshire, purchased for fattening and, unlike most beef stock, whose curiosity would have got the better of them, this lot stood cowering in a corner of the field while I set up my stuff. The farmer, who'd had the land for thirty-five years said he'd "never known the railway line so busy." The fact I'd come to photograph a sand train astonished him: "I thought they all carried *coal*!"

Beyond Brookhouse, we curved through cornfields wounded with blood-red splashes of poppies. John and I had the controversial Judge Pickles' house pointed out to us and, hidden by a belt of trees, Roche Abbey: "One the Great Western didn't get round to using for an engine name," Simon reliably informed us. Not for the first time I was struck by the thought that EWS is sole operator over some of the most scenically ravishing lines in the country, and that, if it wasn't so busy with freight, some lucrative revenue might be made from running excursion traffic on such routes.

A pair of goldcrests fluttered through a limestone cutting ahead of us, but our pastoral idyll was about to be rudely interrupted. "We're coming to 'bomb alley'," chorused Malc and Simon. "They've got 95% unemployment here. They'll chuck anything at us." The trackbed bore this out as we ran, bogie-deep, through Maltby's detritus and scrap. "We should be OK," Malc reassured us: "t'brick-throwers won't be out of school yet mi ducks!"

As well as representing a sinister form of linear coconut shy, Maltby cutting marks the summit of the South Yorks Joint. It was downhill all the way to Doncaster from here on in. Maltby Colliery is one of two deep mines directly linked to the line. Like neigh-

bouring Harworth Colliery, it's essentially a modern pit, characterised by enclosed headgear as opposed to the more traditional exposed wheels. Four or five trains a day call to collect its output but, according to our local guides, its sidings are difficult to enter. "The main line *drops* at 1 in 70 or thereabouts, but the line into the colliery *climbs* at 1 in 35," Simon explained: "And it can be a real struggle to get in with the empties."

We drew to a stand at a semaphore signal beyond Maltby Colliery box to let an up train pass. Simon reckoned it would be coming off the branch from Harworth Colliery and that we'd have a five minute wait before it cleared the section ahead. "Come and see this," he said mysteriously, leading John and me down on to the ballast and into the burgeoning undergrowth at the edge of the permanent way. "Use the toe of your boot in any freight siding and you'll always dig something up. There are some old Lancashire Derbyshire & East Coast chairs on a track panel here." We pushed away weeds, peering intently at the rusty 'chairs' (the iron fittings which hold the rails to the sleepers) and found, not LDEC initials, but those of the South Yorkshire Joint, dated 1907. Ours was the joy of archaeologists uncovering Roman remains - for a moment we were in ferrous communion with a finite past.

Any thoughts of further exploration were terminated by the advent of the up train, a Class 60 with, as Simon had predicted, a string of coal hoppers behind it. "The driver's Dave Warriner," he said as we scrambled into the cab and, with some deft signalwork, got underway again in seconds. Back in pleasant countryside once more, the line pursued a sinuous course before seemingly making up its mind to head more or less north at Tickhill. "The South Yorks Joint lost its passenger trains early," Simon told us. "Buses were already making inroads, and Tickhill & Wadworth, that we're coming up to now, was typical of the line's stations, being miles from their villages."

There were rabbits in the old goods yard, but the platforms were still in situ, though someone had filched the coping stones from the down side, probably for a garden rockery. As we passed under the A1M, Simon perused the TOPS notice. "Three of the wagons are due maintenance," he said aloud. "A private company look after them at Worksop. There were forty originally, but five have succumbed over the years. Graham Farish make an N gauge model of them. We used to work them to a glassworks at Monk Bretton near Pontefract as well, but there was a lot of hassle getting there. People were nicking the track. We only delivered on Wednesdays, so they knew they had from Thursday to Tuesday to do what they liked." Something a tad more substantial than a rockery, one presumes.

Rossington Colliery came into view - of more traditional appearance than Maltby and Harworth. Simon, who I was surprised to learn is a qualified *driver* as well as a guard, had been there the previous day, picking up coal for West Burton power station near Gainsborough. The countryside had acquired a flatness of aspect reminiscent of the Fens. In *Trains Illustrated Annual 1959*, G. Freeman Allen wrote of a trip from Doncaster to Harworth travelling in "an antiquated Great Eastern six-wheel brake van" at the tail of a string of mineral wagons hauled by one of Gresley's O2 2-8-0 heavy freight locomotives. It was from this entertaining and now nostalgic piece that I learnt that, hereabouts, 'carr' means a tract of land reclaimed from marsh. Our route took us over Wadworth Carr and Loversall Carr, then under the M18 to a tangle of lines on the southern outskirts of Doncaster.

Nowadays Doncaster is synonymous with the English Welsh & Scottish Railway's Customer Service Delivery Centre, fulcrum of the company's operations nationwide. We caught glimpses of its steel-clad profile shimmering beyond an orchard grazed by Jersey cows. Only Simon had been inside it, and he likened it to the Stock Exchange, so it's no surprise that the massive, open-plan control area has been dubbed the 'dealing room'. Over three hundred staff work here, twenty-four hours a day, seven days a week, to maximise the carrying potential of EWS' services and to interface professionally with the company's growing customer base. In earlier journeys, the CSDC had come in for a good deal of criticism from EWS staff and customers alike. But, coming towards the end of my travels, six months on, I was heartened by growing acceptance and enthusiasm for the centre.

Just after four o'clock, wheels squealing, rails fluting, we reversed into Rockware's factory. We had skirted the edge of Doncaster Race Course, home of the St Leger

Backing into the glassworks at Barnby Dun

and scene of many an LNER Pacific's equine namesake's victory. We had passed the remnants of Markham Main colliery, one of the Yorkshire pits which never recovered from the Miners' Strike of 1984, and we had learnt that Malc likes cooking with garlic, that Simon likes old buses, and that John's an ace go-kart racer. Me? I just 'get off' on riding freight trains, there being something, obviously, of the American hobo in me. With just two more trips to do, I was beginning to wonder what form cold turkey would take. Would I be found shaking at the edge of freight yards clutching a high visibility vest about me? "Give them a toot Malc," said Simon as we came round the corner to Kirk Sandall Junction past the glasswork's three high chimneys. We crossed the quadruple track Doncaster-Scunthorpe/Goole main line and came to a stand on the up slow in a twilight zone of low-rise factory units and works yards. Simon took his radio to the rear of the train to guide Malc's shunting movements. A Class 66 went by with an Intermodal out of Immingham. A bark of static: "Signal's red, stop there Malc," - pause - "Stop there Malc, he's having something put past us." A single unit Sprinter thrummed by, then we were cleared to re-cross the busy line and enter the glassworks. We had to negotiate a level crossing, its gates operated manually by Simon and a trainee colleague who'd driven over to meet us. Malc and Simon would be marooned here for the best part of four hours, each wagon taking ten minutes to unload. Then they would take the empties back along the SYJ to Worksop. John and I went back 'on the cushions' to Peterborough; catching a local from Kirk Sandall and changing at Doncaster where we treated ourselves to ice cream and orange juice; too tired to even bother making conversation.

Back home I remembered that I'd forgotten to check what Rockware use the sand for. I rang them at Doncaster and was put through to a Peter Finch. "We make bottles and jars, three million of them a day and that train you were on brings in all the sand we need."

So now you know!

THE cars - lucky them - were going to Italy. I was bound - rather less glamorously - for Folkestone. Dollands Moor marshalling yard to be exact, though, strangely enough, I'd been through the Channel Tunnel on Le Shuttle for the first time the very week before, holidaying - en famille - in the French foothills of the Alps. The nearest station was Amberieu, a busy junction between Lyon and Geneva. Making two outings by train, we had been impressed by the frequency - and equally the length - of the goods trains passing through. Furthermore, Amberieu's motive power depot was of classic continental design, still featuring a turntable and a fan of lines into a roundhouse.

Back home, West Midlands Traffic Manager, Martin Horne, had told me that the guys on the gate at Rover's Longbridge plant wouldn't let you through unless you were driving a Rover. I wasn't sure if this was a wind up or not, but to be on the safe side I made sure that I arranged a lift with someone who drove one. Wheeze or not it worked, and at six a.m. I crossed the tracks to the shunter's cabin under the quizzical gaze of Dave Reddington, Resident Chargeman, whose shift was just about to end. He was good enough, however, to give me a whistle-stop tour of the railway set-up at Longbridge, showing me the shunt frame - in reality a Midland Railway signal cabin of some antiquity, a remnant of the days when the line ran through to Halesowen - the North Sidings (EWS property) and the West Yard (Rover Territory).

We were anticipating the imminent arrival of a locomotive from Saltley Depot on the other side of Birmingham; the locomotive which would work my train of Rover vehicles on the first leg of its journey to Brescia in Italy. Automotive traffic, by which I mean the carriage by rail of completed road vehicles and their component parts, is a booming sector of English Welsh & Scottish Railway. Roger Morgan, Automotive Market Manager, outlined various potential flows I might experience, citing the expanding Gefco railhead at Corby, Northants - through which

No 7

66067 EWS

Washwood Heath

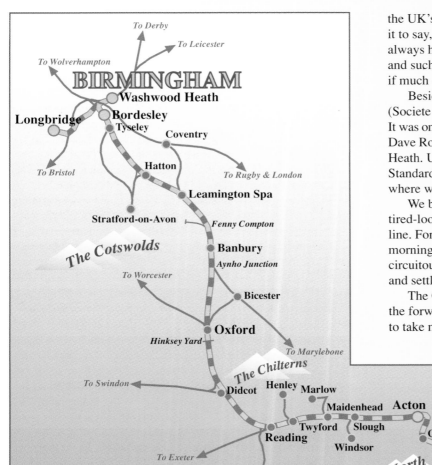

the UK's latest 'near miss' of a recession. This isn't the place to get political, let alone personal. Suffice it to say, the works is still in business and I hope it will continue to be so for a good many years yet. I'd always had a soft spot for the Rover marque. My father ran a series of P4s and P5s throughout the Sixties, and such cars will always be associated with the happiness of family holidays in the West Country, even if much of the time seemed to be spent in traffic jams on the Honiton bypass.

Besides EWS, there's another player involved in the export of Rover Group vehicles, and it is STVA (Societe des Transports de Vehicules Automobiles) who have the contract for distribution on the Continent. It was on to a train of STVA owned wagons that Resident Chargeman, Nigel Lightfoot and Relief Chargeman, Dave Rogers were busily coupling us with a few minutes to go before our 07.00 trip working to Washwood Heath. Up at the sharp end, I was sharing the cab of 66108 with Driver, Gary Masters, and Operations Standards Inspector, Andrew Thomas, who was going to play Boswell to my Johnson as far as Bordesley, where we'd be calling in to collect some of the products of Rover's Solihull works.

We brake tested the four PIA, double-deck wagons in our consist. Longbridge was changing the guard, tired-looking shift workers passing bright-eyed and bushy-tailed colleagues on a footbridge spanning the line. Formalities over, we proceeded slowly to Halesowen Junction to squeeze our way between the morning's burgeoning Cross-city commuter traffic. Just before seven we got a path and headed off on a circuitous tour of Brummagem's bleary-eyed suburbs, taking the Camp Hill avoiding line at King's Norton and settling down for a forty minute hop to Washwood Heath on the northern rim of the city.

The Camp Hill route sees little passenger use, so I journeyed over the line with much interest, enjoying the forward-looking view from 66108's cab. Unfortunately, we were all too busy jabbering away for me to take much in of the passing scene, though I retained a blurred impression of redbrick suburbs.

Andrew's life story was the first to unfold. A native of Crewe, it would have been difficult to avoid a boyhood interest in trains. In his mid thirties now, he has fourteen years of railway experience behind him, from early days as a driver's assistant at Manchester Victoria, to his present position with EWS via Railfreight Distribution and, post privatisation, a short spell with Central Trains. He exuded quiet enthusiasm and determination, admitted that there were areas and issues the company needed to attend to, but maintained - even in the light of Ed Burkhardt's sudden and controversial departure

Citroen and Peugeot cars are imported and Vauxhall, Opel and Peugeot exported - as an example of EWS prowess in this sphere of operations. But I had my heart set on Longbridge, Herbert Austin's original motorcar factory. As yet my freight train travels had ignored the Midlands and I thought it would be good to get at least a 'snapshot' of EWS activities in the area.

Rover's Longbridge plant has been on 'life support' throughout

days before our trip was made - confidence that EWS ambitions could be achieved.

With Gary the talk was less of railways (he'd begun as a goods guard at Bescot, near Walsall, in 1980) and more of "the Blues" and golf. Without much encouragement he would have talked us through every hole of the competition he had played in the day before at Olton, the prestigious Solihull course, but I'm used to listening to my Dad's much embellished golfing tales - the fairways growing more tortuous, the bunkers wider, and the greens more devilish with every hole - so I adroitly turned the conversation towards the unusual wrap-around shape of the portal of Moseley Tunnel and the interesting pediment at its apex. "I've not noticed that before," said Andrew.

"There isn't one at the other end," said Gary.

"I don't suppose we could back up and take another look," said I, tongue in cheek, getting the impression, however, that they thought I was being semi-serious, not yet having route-learned the branchlines of my drollery.

"Er, no um I don't think Railtrack would approve," Gary responded, eyeing Andrew nervously. I read their body language. I can paraphrase it for you thus: "We've got a right one here!"

What with a featherweight 272 tonnes in tow, and a skittish Class 66, we had a breezy, bouncy ride through Balsall Heath. Whatever criticisms one might attach to these Canadian locomotives, poor acceleration isn't one of them. Gary was pretty positive about them: "I'm getting to like these, but they're still a bit noisy."

"One-fifty onwards are being built with extra soundproofing," Andrew responded.

A pair of Direct Rail Services' engines - a Thirty-Seven and a Twenty - thrummed by southbound with an empty flat wagon. Andrew identified the working: "They'll be off to Berkeley for a nuclear flask," he told me. EWS used to have the contract for carrying nuclear waste to Sellafield for reprocessing, and I had planned to include a typical working in my travels before DRS, a BNFL subsidiary, took over the traffic.

A lengthy series of arches carried us past the mosques of Highgate and Sparkbrook to Bordesley, where we were able to look down over the car loading yard at which we would, in the fullness of time, call to attach extra wagons to the train. Then we passed through a cutting in the shadow of St Andrews, Birmingham City's football ground; Gary's team. We shared an admiration for Trevor Francis, who'd enjoyed his best playing days with Birmingham and Nottingham Forest, memorably ghosting in to head the winning goal in the 1980 European Cup Final.

Over canals and under railways, we came to Landor Street Junction, squeezed between a scrapyard and a container depot. Tucked away to the right, on slightly falling ground, stood Saltley Depot, looking businesslike with several lines of stabled locomotives. "It looks busier than usual at this time in the morning," Andrew remarked to Gary, going on to tell me that EWS currently employs sixty-seven drivers at the depot. They are divided into three route-based links colloquially known as Oak, Ash and Elm. Gary's in Oak, which takes him to such divers places as Ironbridge (with coal for the power station), Didcot (with aviation fuel for Langley near Heathrow), Bromsgrove (on the recently reintroduced banking duties on the famous Lickey Incline), and throughout the Birmingham area on local duties like our own automotive working, which he would be driving as far as Bordesley. Gary's shift had started at 03.35 and would end at 12.55 with a taxi back from Bordesley. "That's why I like this link, I can spend all summer playing golf." No wonder he's got his handicap down to seven!

I noticed a couple of Virgin Class 47s 'on shed' and Andrew explained that EWS is under contract for the maintenance of these machines, now a much rarer breed since English Welsh & Scottish had all but eliminated the Railfreight Distribution fleet it inherited. I let slip long ago how much I admired these 'Brush Fours' and I sensed that many professional railwaymen would be missing them in years to come as well.

We snaked over the Derby main line and rumbled past the site of Saltley station towards the yard at Washwood Heath. Heath is a frequent suffix in Birmingham area place names. It promotes images of idyllic open spaces, all bracken and Scots pine, and presumably, pre-industrially, they were. Nowadays, though, in character they are starkly urban, even if this part of Birmingham is being optimistically re-branded as the "Heartlands". Once off the main running lines we came under the control of Washwood

"What with a featherweight 272 tonnes in tow, and a skittish Class 66, we had a breezy, bouncy ride through Balsall Heath."

Bordesley Characters:
Left: Mark Roberts on
the shunting frame
Top centre: Jim Mossley,
Lionel Deeley & Mark
Lower centre: Andrew Thomas
Right: Can Singh

Heath No.1 signal box, a classic Midland Railway timber cabin decidedly due a fresh coat of paint on the outside, though Andrew assured me it was "immaculately kept" within.

Overlooked by the elevated M6 motorway, upon which traffic was still moving - just - in advance of rush hour gridlock, the fan of through sidings at Washwood Heath is, as Andrew put it: "Of eighty per cent automotive and twenty per cent coal usage." A shunter called Mark Roberts welcomed us in. It was seven-forty and there was some shunting to be done before the next part of the journey back to Bordesley. At the time of my visit Washwood Heath was staffed, twenty-four hours a day, by three teams of four - a chargeman and three shunters to each - but Mark was telling us that there were moves afoot to reduce an increasing pattern of twelve hour shifts. "At least the kids might recognise me then." An ex-construction worker, Mark had only been in the railway industry for three years, but he seemed businesslike and enthusiastic and, out of earshot, the other guys referred to him as "a good lad", just

about the highest compliment Brummie males are likely to feel comfortable with expressing about one another. Besides, he is a Villa fan, and there was to be a good deal of football banter for the remainder of our stay in the Second City.

We spent about forty-five minutes at Washwood Heath: running round to the other end of the train, attaching extra wagons and checking brakes. Andrew introduced me to a number of different wagon designs, including the celebrated PJA 'Cartic', an articulated, double-deck veteran of the Sixties still doing the job it was designed to do. Articulated, in this context, means that four wagons are permanently coupled together sharing common, single intermediate axles. In many respects they reminded me of the principle of staircase locks on the canals, whereby chambers are concertina'd together, sharing common top and bottom gates. Of similar design are the PIA 'Autics', but they are coupled in pairs with three axles to each double unit. Cars being a comparatively light load by most railway standards, automotive trains tend to be lengthier than most, yet still within the maximum limits of most Type 4 and above traction.

Mark joined us in the No.1 cab - the more commodious of the two on a Class 66 and fortunately the one which I would be travelling in with various crews all the way to Folkestone. We followed close on the heels of another train taking empties back to Longbridge, as far as the yard's outer Stop Board where we waited until it was clear to proceed on to the main line. Briefly, I took in the urban landscape: purple buddleia waved trackside in the breeze; Saltley's gasholders loomed large ahead; across the main running lines lay a depot equipped for the discharge of stone trains from the Buxton area; beyond stood Alstom's massive rolling stock workshops, previously Metropolitan-Cammell.

Just after half past eight we were passing Saltley again and Andrew was pointing out a reinforced concrete Second World War control bunker which was proving difficult to demolish. "They say a thousand pound bomb bounced off it in the war. We've had a firm of contractors working on it for five weeks now and it's already broken three of their machines." Until quite recently Saltley provided a banking engine for the steep climb to St Andrews. I would frequently encounter one, tucked away in its trailing siding, as my passenger train from the north slowed for the curve into New Street. Throughout the Eighties it was often one of my favourite Class 31s, but they have all disappeared from the Birmingham area now.

Mark couldn't bear to look as we retraced our route past Birmingham City's ground. At Bordesley Junction we crossed what would once have been a significant boundary between the London Midland and Western regions, and the LMS and GWR before them, a sort of mental Iron Curtain of barely forgotten rivalries and uncooperative attitudes. I remember reading a magazine article by R.J.Essery - an ex-Saltley railwayman - as to how the Midland would set up queues of inter-regional freight workings waiting to move on to the Western, just to put them under pressure. Now, however, post privatisation, railway rivalries are differently structured, and the old jealously guarded territories dormant only in the mindscapes of railwaymen of a certain age.

Rationalisation of trackwork had rendered it impractical for us to enter Bordesley Yard directly. Instead, we spent the best part of half an hour trundling up to Tyseley where once again we

decamped to the other cab, ran round the train, and retraced our steps through Small Heath's suburban station to gain access to the automotive sidings at Bordesley. Here Gary was booked to 'jump ship' and spend the rest of his shift at the highly contrasting controls of a Class 08 shunting locomotive. Andrew was leaving us too, having other fish to fry, and for the next leg of the journey I was to be accompanied by Driver Lionel Deeley and Driving Inspector Jim Mossley. They were waiting for us in the shunters' cabin, along with travelling shunter Can Singh.

Nobody had any time to lose. There was a good deal of shunting to be done, and we were already uncomfortably close to the ten o'clock scheduled departure. Hefty penalties for late-running are built into the contract, and everyone concerned is on their metal to avoid incurring them. Gary and I made for the shunting engine, sitting melancholically in its peeling grey paintwork in a corner of the yard. It looked as though Railtrack - who lease Bordesley Yard to EWS - had another potential Lost Gardens of Heligan on its hands. It should get Alan Titchmarsh - or, better still, Charlie Dimmock - down here on a consultancy basis pronto. I imagined that if this had been a Monday morning, Gary would have needed a strong pair of secateurs to get into 08543's cab. Acclimatized to the hi-tech, computerised, cutting edge controls of 66108, the shunter's interior seemed like a throwback to the steam age. In many respects I guess it was; being, essentially, a diesel version of a steam age shunting locomotive, complete with coupling rods linking the six hefty, four foot six diameter, driving wheels. Inside, its original British Railways number, D3707, was still painted on the ceiling. Intrigued, back home, I flipped through old copies of *Trains Illustrated* to uncover its provenance. Hey presto, it was released into traffic in July 1959, being allocated, first off, to the Immingham area then, later, Sheffield.

Gary switched the batteries on, keeping his fingers crossed that the old lady would "fire up" first time of asking. Old lady seemed appropriate, this being the type of engine the Rev. Awdry had when he created the unctuous character of 'Diesel' in the *Thomas the Tank Engine* stories. 08543 didn't so much burst into life as get up, yawn profusely and stretch. "We could do with a set of seat belts," laughed Gary as we lurched into action, swinging

"It looked as though Railtrack - who lease Bordesley Yard to EWS - had another potential Lost Gardens of Heligan on its hands. It should get Alan Titchmarsh - or, better still, Charlie Dimmock - down here on a consultancy basis pronto."

across the rails like a domestic goose waddling in the general direction of a duck pond. Gary perched on the left hand side of the dual-controlled cab. I jammed myself between the door and the rear bulkhead. Alarming or not it was great fun, akin, I imagined, to riding an impetuous, not quite trustworthy horse.

From the portable short wave, Can barked instructions like a referee attending to a scrummage. "Back to Bordesley, back to Bordesley." It took me a while to realise that "Half a 'tic" didn't mean "Hold on a minute", but rather it was the Bordesley way of determining length by equating it to the length of a Cartic wagon. Thus Can would say: "Three and a half 'tics to go, two 'tics to go, three quarters of a 'tic, 'half a 'tic, twenty feet, fifteen feet, five, four, three, two one - stop there!"

Mark joined us in the cab to run up to the other end of the yard, Can rode on the running plate. "Is Can interested in football?" I asked innocently.

"No," guffawed Mark: "He supports West Brom."

Just as each area has its own colloquial term for a lunch break, so too varies the nickname for shunting engines. In Brummiespeak they are 'Jockos'. The Bordesley Jocko lives in the yard from week to week, treating itself to a jaunt to Saltley every ten days or so to refuel its 500 gallon capacity tank. With an average speed limit of fifteen to twenty miles an hour it can be a long trip!

Martin Horne had sent me the train's schedule. Booked to leave Bordesley at 10.40 and reach Dollands Moor - 210 miles away - at 18.13, it continues through the Channel Tunnel the same evening and reaches its Italian destination late the following day. We left an hour late with seventeen wagons in tow, totalling just 764 tonnes; though our length of 1,854 feet would preclude the use, if necessary, of a number of loops en route. Most of the wagons were designated IPA, a French design so lightweight that they have a tendency to bounce off British tracks at speeds in excess of fifty miles per hour. So despite being coded '6', and thus technically permitted to run up to sixty, the fact that these wagons were empty would restrict us until we dropped them off for the Cowley motor works at Oxford.

Jim Mossley and I fought our way through the undergrowth to reach 66108. "We should have brought pith helmets and a machete," he quipped; though without much exaggeration. An MG owner, he was car conscious enough to be able to differentiate between the Rover models loaded on to our train. "We've just picked up some Freelanders and Discoverys from the Solihull plant here, and you'd already brought some 200s, 400s, Minis and MGFs from Longbridge. I expect we'll be adding some new 75s from Cowley as well." Lionel was already comfortably ensconced in the cab when we reached the end of our sub-tropical expedition. At one point I'd recoiled at the sight of what I took to be a boa constrictor, but it was only an old piece of vacuum brake hose. Lionel was tapping into the Q-Tron. "This one was started on the 28th May and its done over eleven thousand since then." Fifteen hundred miles a week I

calculated, as rapidly as my O level Maths (at the second attempt) would permit, almost as much as me since I started work on this book. Lionel had come across one member of the class that had amassed thirty thousand miles in six months. Before we could leave, the 'tapper' had to check the train. "An Irish fellow from Bromford" - whose name no-one seemed to know - he had to examine each wagon, not just to Railtrack standards but for the French, Swiss and Italian railways as well. I'd been vaguely aware of him lurking in odd corners of the yard as we went about our shunting, but I hadn't realised how significant a role he would play.

To reach the main line we had to negotiate Tyseley Through Sidings and, in doing so, pass Birmingham Railway Museum, formerly Tyseley Motive Power Depot, the main Western Region engine shed in the Birmingham area. Lionel had commenced his career here in 1965, at the fag end of steam, preparing locos on shed and working Pannier tanks to Swan Village canal transhipment basin before aspiring to main line work on such famous freight runs as the Banbury-Bilston steelworks iron ore traffic. He must have known *Clun Castle* when it was the last Great Western express passenger steam locomotive in use. Over forty years later we passed it gleaming in the sunshine, all Brunswick green and burnished copper, resting between weekend jaunts to Stratford-on-Avon. Also 'on shed', stood my old friend *Canadian Pacific* back from its holidays on the Settle & Carlisle.

Departing trains face a stiff little incline on to the main line at Tyseley. Lionel told me that the Class 47s, until recently staple motive power for most automotive work, lacked sanding gear and would occasionally come to an embarrassing standstill here. "But they were good engines," he added: "Ideal in the yard."

Once an inbound Sprinter had cleared Tyseley's beautifully restored and typically Great Western station, we got the road, and I noted us passing Acocks Green at noon as opposed to the scheduled time of 10.57. Amazingly, I had already been with the locomotive for six hours, yet, always assuming we no lost no more time, I still had seven hours to go!

Travelling southwards, into a by now fierce sun, I thought about the changes in fortune surrounding the route we were on; originally the Great Western Railway's main line between Paddington, Birmingham and Shrewsbury, the Wirral and Mid-Wales. At first Brunel's broad gauge - albeit with an inner, standard gauge rail incorporated - had stretched this far, whilst throughout the golden age of railways travellers between the first and second cities in the land could mix and match the rival routes with impunity. When, however, in the wake of the Beeching Report, the Euston-New Street service was electrified, the Paddington-Snow Hill line lost its expresses and the bulk of its freight as well. Its quadruple track, built by the GWR with Whitehall, Depression-busting, largesse, reverted to double, and for thirty years, outer-suburban workings to Leamington were virtually the only trains to trundle along

Gary Masters at the antediluvian controls of 08543, Bordesley Yard

its tracks. But privatisation has brought renaissance in its wake. Four operating companies use the line now: Chiltern and Central for passengers; EWS and Freightliner for goods. Once again well-healed Solihull is umbilically linked with London, though it is at Marylebone, not Paddington, that Chiltern Trains' sleak Class 168 units disgorge West Midlanders now. English Welsh & Scottish uses the line to carry - amongst other things - coal (in both directions!), steel, petroleum products and, of course, cars.

At Dorridge, Lionel's home town, we passed an area of new housing occupying the site of sidings where Rover cars used to be loaded, before the development of Bordesley as an automotive distribution point. We left the suburbs behind and ventured out into what the GWR had vigorously promoted as "Leafy Warwickshire". To a certain extent their publicity paid off; and, indeed, a West Midland equivalent of the Stockbroker Belt developed from what, before the railway came, had been a quintessentially pastoral landscape - part of Shakespeare's Forest of Arden. Lapworth was a typical residential railhead. Being close to the junction of the Grand Union and Stratford canals, I'd found it a useful staging post on many of my inland waterway itineraries, but never noticed before how its platforms curved towards their southern end, a characteristic much more obvious from the front end of our train.

Hatton marks the junction of the branch to Stratford-on-Avon. "There was a restaurant room here," remembered Lionel, "which doubled as the village local." On the canal a huge, intimidating flight of locks carry you down to Warwick. On the railway we rolled imperiously down a bank averaging 1 in 100 to the county town, landmarked, in the fast approaching distance, by the high tower of St Mary's parish church. In steam days bankers loitered at the foot of the incline to give succour to heavy, northbound freights. Diesels, naturally, take the bank in their stride and, as if to prove the point, the *Venice Simplon Orient Express* swept into view, with an EWS Class 47 at its head, bound, we guessed without much difficulty, for the fleshpots of Bardstown. Momentarily, I glimpsed the soup course being partaken in gracious Pullman cars, but I wouldn't have traded places for the world. All of a sudden it struck me how difficult it would be, once these goods train journeys were over, to be a mere passenger again.

The Great Western rebuilt its station at Leamington Spa in the Thirties, probably with the 'loose change' of that Government money spent on quadrupling the line north of Lapworth. Very much in the spirit of the times, it features great blocks of white stone and much use of stainless steel. It could easily be mistaken for a cinema or department store. "We're an hour and fifteen late," remarked Lionel lugubriously, "I bet they put us in at Banbury."

I waved to a little girl and her granny on the outskirts of town. We crossed the Foss Way. The landscape appeared to empty. A northbound Virgin express hurtled by behind a Class 47. Its days are numbered. Richard Branson's stainless steel designs for twenty-first century rail travel are taking shape, though I cannot look forward to them with enthusiasm. I just wish he'd learn the basic lesson that trains aren't planes.

Within sight of the Civil War-haunted slopes of Edge Hill, Lionel voiced fond memories of a pub in the vicinity. A pattern was beginning to emerge of Lionel's affinity with ale. Beyond Harbury Tunnel we passed the hundred mile marker from Paddington, measured by way of the original Oxford route rather than the 1910 'cut off' via Bicester, which reduced the railway distance between London and Birmingham by almost twenty miles. Once there was a cement works at Harbury. Lionel had worked in and out of its sidings many a time. "We used to go up to Derby with a Forty-five, and sometimes on to Earle's sidings in the Hope Valley."

"A pretty line that," remarked Jim, who had not exactly been so much taciturn, as simply prevented from getting a word in between Lionel's flow of reminiscences. Jim can trace his family's involvement with the railways back to 1880, his great grandfather being a driver in the Ilkeston district. Jim himself had joined the railway in 1985, surviving a baptism of fire as a carriage cleaner at Etches Park, Derby. "I was in the heavy cleaning gang for six months on diesel multiple units." Judging by the state the 'great unwashed' leave trains in these days, this was one aspect of railway work I didn't envy anyone doing. Later he applied to the traction department to become a secondman, but was rebuffed because he wore glasses. Eventually he crept in by the back door, becoming a goods guard then, as their numbers dwindled, successfully reaching driver status at Saltley in 1989. "Even that recently we

"Momentarily, I glimpsed the soup course being partaken in gracious Pullman cars, but I wouldn't have traded places for the world."

> "The Stratford-on-Avon & Midland Junction Railway was typically parochial, impecunious and geographically short-changed, running on an east-west axis between Blisworth, Broom and oblivion."

had three hundred drivers, a hundred and twenty guards and thirty or forty maintenance staff." A sobering thought, then, that Saltley has shed eighty per cent of its staff; though, of course a decade ago, it would have been providing drivers and guards for a good proportion of Birmingham's passenger services as well.

One of those old cross-country lines, which you know by now that I'm so enamoured of, was fast approaching. The Stratford-on-Avon & Midland Junction Railway was typically parochial, impecunious and geographically short-changed, running on an east-west axis between Blisworth, Broom and oblivion. The last passenger train ran in 1952, with my friend, the transport artist, Brian Collings, aboard the footplate of 4F 0-6-0, 44525 bearing an inscription on its smokebox door 'Blisworth or Bust!' "I remember a Hall raced past us at Fenny Compton, blowing its whistle and the driver waving," Brian told me. "There were four of us on the engine; the driver, the fireman, me - I was only a kid - and the Mayor of Stratford." In 1960 the track at Fenny Compton was relaid to allow iron ore trains from Banbury to run via Stratford-on-Avon to the steelworks of South Wales. In those days, hard as it is to credit now, Britain's heavy industry was largely self-fuelled. Incredibly, a mile or two of the S&MJR survives to provide access to a military establishment at Kineton. "It's Top Secret down there,' said Lionel in suitably hushed tones. Yes, so secret I thought, that it's where they choose to 'hide' all the off-lease rolling stock which, on a less accountancy-led more public-service-orientated passenger network, could be used to prevent the overcrowding prevalent on many routes today.

We had plenty of time to mull over such matters because we'd come to an abrupt halt at a red signal half a mile north of Fenny. Lionel went to telephone the signalman and came back shaking his head. "They've stopped a train at Cropredy with its tail lamp missing." Ah Cropredy!, home to Fairport Convention's annual folk music reunion and location of that most charmingly timeless of pubs, the Red Lion. I was just about to ask Lionel if he knew it when the signal changed aspect and we got under way again. Luckily we were too long for the Fenny Compton loop, so even if he had wanted to let some of the backed-up passenger trains overtake us in the wake of the delay, the signalman couldn't. We waved cheekily at the box and passed the loops with their strange mix of colour light and semaphore signals, the latter featuring both upper and lower quadrant arms.

Claydon is Oxfordshire's most northerly outpost. In canal circles it is known for its flight of locks. Amongst professional railwaymen , I was about to learn, it is known as the location of 'Big Tits Crossing', so named, apparently, because of the regular appearance there of a well-endowed lady whose habit it was to wave enthusiastically - both with her hands and her other natural attributes - at passing enginemen. The printed page cannot do justice to the enthusiasm with which Lionel and Jim related this story, but you can gauge something of their appreciation for the woman in question by Lionel's reply to my query as to her age. "Can't say as I'd know - I never looked at her face."

I wrote a song once - *Diesel & Asphalt* - about the stresses and strains of growing up. It contained the immortal lines:

"I was standing on Banbury station, it was 1963
And the local to Woodford was simmering,
like the man inside of me."

And I *did* stand on Banbury station, several times in the early Sixties, trainspotting and trying not to grow up too quickly. Back then the station seemed ultra-modern, now it looks sadly ersatz, and I couldn't tell if the scaffolding was in place to facilitate refurbishment or to prevent the whole lot falling down. The eleven year old version of me saw big maroon coloured engines called *Western Buccaneer* or *Western Cavalier* or *Western Gauntlet* growl by with Paddington expresses. They were modelled on a German hydraulic design and were, as such, non-standard and confined to the Western Region of British Railways which had an enviable knack of going about its business as if nationalisation had never occurred. They were powerful and pretty reliable, and arguably the best looking large diesel ever to run in this country, but their very individuality was their downfall. Most of them ran for little more than a dozen years and one shudders to think of the cost to the taxpayer of their short, un-thought-out lives.

But my favourite train at Banbury was the Bournemouth-York cross country express, which would come in from the south, with green carriages, behind a steam engine - usually a Hall at that time, but later a Bulleid Pacific - and leave over the spur to Woodford Halse and the Great Central route to the north, hauled by a brand new English Electric Type 3 - the ubiquitous, big-nosed design which would become known, post computerisation, as Class 37. Banbury then still had a busy engine shed, home to long lines of for the most part filthy steam engines, slumbering between their dwindling duties. It was the first shed I was unceremoniously ejected from, another rite of passage, another small step in the process of growing up.

Back in my adult self, I felt like George Bowling in Orwell's *Coming Up for Air* who revisits the scenes of his youth and finds them built upon, both literally and metaphorically. Likewise, Banbury marshalling yard has become a housing zone, the station is crumbling, and the site of the engine shed a wasteland of willowherb. Jim and Lionel had fully expected to be 'put by' by Banbury's lady signallers and we were amazed to find ourselves floating through on a succession of greens. Then we saw that the up slow was in possession of the engineers so that, once again, Railtrack had no alternative but to send us on our way. How we laughed!

South of Banbury we were in the Cherwell Valley, tracing the river's course by banks of pollarded willows. At Kings Sutton we admired the parish church and its soaring spire, and pointed out to ourselves the old egress of the line to Cheltenham. At Anyho, Railtrack got its revenge, for we were signalled into the grass-grown loop, drawing to a halt tantalisingly close to the cool bar of the Great Western pub, a stone's throw from the long-closed but still intact Brunellian station building. Lionel, a keen gardener, told us that he had successfully taken sweet pea cuttings from the trackside here, though, in his experience, plants which thrive by railway lines seldom flourish in domestic cirumstances. Perhaps they miss the rhythm of the rail joints and the slipstream fragrance of oil and steam.

In early editions of my *Canal Companion* guides to the Oxford Canal, I would warn boaters not to moor overnight in the vicinity of Upper Heyford, because in doing so they risked being rudely awakened by planes taking off from the neighbouring American air base. That, however,was before the Berlin Wall came down, before the Cold War thaw set in. The Americans have gone home, Heyford's shops have shut, and its pubs emptied; nuclear fall out, you might say, in North Oxfordshire. Lionel remembered the

aircraft, the F111s which would use the trains he drove for simulated target practice. He recalled particularly the Libyian Crisis when the line was shut for several hours to let squadrons of planes take off.

We proceeded through the most delicious of landscapes, past Heyford station and its attendant canal wharf, past Tackley where trailing and facing crossovers facilitate bi-directional working when engineering work is taking place. We crossed the course of the Roman's Akeman Street, played hopscotch with the Cherwell, passed another redundant cement works, and saw the isolated church at Hampton Gay. In the graveyard here a headstone commemorates a victim of a railway crash on Christmas Eve 1874, thirty-four people died when a train became derailed and plunged irrevocably down the embankment into the icy waters of the Oxford Canal.

Oxford has never really had the railway station it deserves. In the 1840s the University was hostile to the notion of something as vulgar as a railway arriving on its cultured doorstep. Apathy apparently characterised the railway's architectural response. Where something mock-medieval - another Shrewsbury, another Lancaster - might have been more in harmony with the adjoining groves of Academe, a single-storey nonentity was erected, albeit with a timber train shed in place until 1890. Recent attempts to do justice to burgeoning passenger figures have been well meant but uninspired. The little, timber, London & North Western Railway station, closer to the centre on Rewley Road, was much prettier and featured a circular booking-hall acquired secondhand from the Great Exhibition of 1851. For many years, subsequent to its closure in 1951, its siding space was used for storing cattle cake, and access was effected by way of a swing-bridge spanning a navigable backwater between the Thames and the canal. Surrounded by new housing, the bridge is still in situ - though permanently open for boat passages - whilst Rewley Road itself has been transferred, plank by plank, to a new home at the Quainton Road Railway Centre in Buckinghamshire.

A Class 37 was waiting to back three freshly-loaded double deckers of Rover 75s on to our rear after we had shed the

The loop at Aynho

five empties. It had collected them from Morris Cowley and crossed the Thames at Kennington, on the remaining spur of what had once been an alternative railway route to London by way of Thame and Princes Risborough. Trainspotters watched our manoeuvres from a footbridge, well choreographed by the resident shunting team known to Jim and Lionel as 'Hall & Taggart'. Taggart was an exiled Scot from Dunfermline. I chatted briefly to him after effecting a personal facility break in bushes modestly beyond the view of passing commuters. Trundling through Oxford and held at signals before we could cross into Hinksey Yard, Lionel had shown me the cemetery, a resort of "lags and dossers", familiar to generations of undergraduates whose incoming trains would be held overlooking the gravestones until Oxford's 'at a premium' platform space could be reached.

Waiting for an up Freightliner and a down Thames Turbo to clear the main line, we ran to the throat of the yard with Jim at the controls, and stood for a moment of peaceful contemplation beside a backwater rich in lily pads and water iris. If we'd had longer, I expect Lionel would have been after a few cuttings for his garden, but we were signalled smartly away, quickly accelerating up to sixty, no longer compromised by lightweights on our tail. We ran through Radley where Didcot's cooling towers were revealed "resplendent on the horizon" as Jim poetically put it . He showed me the course of the Abingdon branch, which trip engines would run down

to collect MGs in the heady days when the marque was built in that most charming of Thameside towns. Lionel pointed out the "Railway Inn" at Culham; Jim, the authentic Great Western 'pagoda' waiting rooms at Appleford. At Didcot we swayed over pointwork onto the east curve and gave chase to a Prairie tank and an autocoach on the Great Western Society's short demonstration line. Jim entered into the spirit of the race with a cheeky fanfare on 66108's cacophonous horn. The steam engine's crew glanced over their shoulder and redoubled their efforts, whistling wildly back to us. A gang of Boy Scouts cheered. The diesel won the race but the steamer won their hearts.

Didcot is a busy centre for freight. There seemed to be trains everywhere. A Freightliner powered north, an EWS Class 58 on a train of box wagons waited in the loop. A regular flow of coal goes into the power station from Avonmouth and various sources 'up north'. There's also a good deal of Ministry of Defence traffic, whilst the Swindon-Longbridge automotive component carrying trains use the west curve. Beyond the station precincts Lionel drew my attention to the earthworks of the Didcot Newbury & Southampton Railway. "Drivers called it the Gold Coast line, because it took you so long to get there you'd make a fortune."

Now we were on Brunel's original Bristol-London Broad Gauge route. It has been quadrupled since his day, with relief lines laid to the north of the original tracks. Jim

66108 shunts in Hinksey Yard, Oxford

pointed out the tell-tale difference in adjoining arches at each road bridge. We were riding well on track passed - for passenger trains - for speeds of up to a hundred miles an hour. I was reminded of the opening page of John Buchan's *Mr Standfast* as Richard Hannay "slipped up the Thames valley on the smooth Great Western line". I should add, for the sake of accuracy, that the fast lines are passed for 125mph and that, fast as we seemed to be travelling, Paddington-bound First Great Western HSTs - in their rather harsh-on-the-eye revised livery - were overtaking us at double our speed. My companions felt that - given the right rolling stock - there was no reason at all why we couldn't have been travelling at up to seventy-five miles an hour, and I know that EWS management is keen to see their trains both faster and heavier to give them more edge in competition with road transport.

At Cholsey we saw the preserved track of the Wallingford branch make an entrance. Lionel had recently encountered a man and a woman emerging from the cutting, pumping away on a platelayer's trolley; at least that's what I took him to mean. Twice the railway crosses the Thames, on whose broad reaches narrow boats and cabin cruisers chugged along, speed not being of their essence. The Thames Valley station names evoke images of generations of commuter traffic: Goring, Pangbourne, Tilehurst. Before the Turbo revolution, I used to go out of my way to travel back from business appointments in London by this route, in order to savour a run in compartment stock. Behind a throaty Fifty, I would imagine myself as 'something in the city', on my way home to a waterside retreat, where a gin and tonic fizzed as expectantly as my beautiful and adoring wife.

We ran through a chalk cutting at Pangbourne. The line was very busy. A Sixty came by on the down relief, returning from Theale with empty tanks for Milford Haven. Then, close in its wake but on the fast line, a northbound Virgin express hauled by 47488, hired in from Fragonset and sporting the original two-tone green livery of the Brush Type 4s. An elderly enthusiast took a snapshot of us at Tilehurst, but I was more taken with the "Station Syren", as Betjeman might have classed her; though nowadays the book on her graceful lap was far more likely to have been Sebastian Faulks than Warwick Deeping.

There were lines of temporarily redundant automotive wagons stored in the yard at Reading West. A small, oddly old-fashioned looking boy took our photograph as we traversed the up goods road along the redbrick back of Reading station. It was quarter past three. We were still over an hour late. Jim accelerated away as a Thirty-seven in EWS red and gold went through on the down relief with a short train of MEA box wagons. We were on the last lap to Acton now, as far as Jim and Lionel were concerned, and they were discussing travel arrangements for their respective journeys home 'on the cushions'. Lionel was for Marylebone, and a direct train home to Dorridge. Jim had to make for St Pancras to get to his home in Long Eaton. They were making me feel tired. I'd been travelling for almost twelve hours, the normal extremity of an EWS working shift, and the breeze blowing through the window was a welcome antidote to incipient sleep.

Remember how John McBurney and Des Gringell showed me Terry Wogan's house at Maidenhead? This time it was Diana Dors' former residence which was brought to my attention. We all wondered aloud why Burnham was the only station with no platforms facing the fast tracks, coming to the logical, though unsubstantiated conclusion that it had only been opened *after* quadrupling had taken place. I won't bore you with a reprise of the journey to Acton. We got there just before four. The relief crew were kicking their collective heels at the far end of the yard, anxious to get away before the rush hour began to bite south of the Thames. They were Dollands Moor men, savvy guys with 'attitude' compared to the mild Midlanders I'd spent the greater part of the day with. In fact there were three of them, because I had a new minder too, in the shape of Dave Carder, a Wembley-based Driving Instructor, and he was accompanied by the booked driver, Robert 'Bob' Harris and his colleague, Geoff Holmes, who was route learning following a road accident which had kept him off work for some time.

I was inescapably shattered, and can only hope that I do the next stage of the journey justice. First up, we had to negotiate a complicated itinerary of cross-London routes; the equivalent, I guess, of motorists' 'rat runs', in the hope that we could find a way through the rush hour. Bob seemed particularly pessimistic

"The relief crew were kicking their collective heels at the far end of the yard, anxious to get away before the rush hour began to bite south of the Thames. They were Dollands Moor men, savvy guys with 'attitude'..."

> "Bob didn't hang about. The platform starting signal turned green, he gave a joyous blast on the horn, several commuters jumped in the air, and we made our way across Wandsworth Common."

of our chances, and frustrated by our late arrival. A red signal at Acton Wells Junction appeared to confirm his worst case scenario. "We won't be in Dollands Moor by ten at this rate," he sighed, eyeing me as if I was somehow responsible for the train's late-running. "This is what happens," I could hear him thinking: "when the company gives joy rides to journalists." Dave took up a politically neutral position with his back to the cab's inner door, while Bob and Geoff commenced a comical double-act. And I would have been amused if I hadn't been so world-weary.

Miraculously, as far as Bob was concerned, that Acton Wells aspect turned green and we looped down beneath the North London line and past Willesden's West Coast Traction Maintenance Depot to gain the West London line at Mitre Bridge Junction. So far so good, we were getting green lights and I'd still got a semblance of a grasp on the geographic 'plot' of our route. Through Kensington Olympia I was grilling the guys on the outlines of their respective careers. Bob's West Country burr gave his Exeter roots away. He's a third or fourth generation railwayman who, after a spell on the Western Region from 1974, 'emigrated' to the Southern, driving diesel-electric multiple units from Tunbridge Wells. Later on he made an even greater leap into the unknown, working coal trains out of Blyth Cambois depot in Northumberland. "How did you cope with the culture shock?" I wondered.

"I'm a pretty cosmopolitan guy," he responded, which brought a fit of laughter out of Geoff.

Geoff was a 'Southern' man, through and through, having begun work as a guard at Streatham Hill, working electric trains into and out of Victoria, in 1982. Eventually, by way of Norwood, Hither Green and Slade Green, with a change from guard's duties to traction secondman, then driver, on the way, he was washed up on the shores of Dollands Moor Railfreight Distribution depot. Both he and Bob wore Channel Tunnel accredited swipe cards on their chests, indicative of the high security associated with traffic *sous La Manche*.

Finally I came to Dave, a 'veteran' of 1966, whose first railway work was at Norwood. Following an interlude at King's Cross, he returned to the Southern Region at Victoria East, went to Selhurst, then moved north of the river to jobs at Stonebridge Park and Wembley. These brief summaries scarcely do the men justice, but

a sense of desperation had gripped us, and we were all concentrating on getting across the Thames and into the dense suburban network beyond Clapham where we'd feel safe in the knowledge that we'd got 'a foot in the door'. We passed the upmarket purlieus of Chelsea Harbour, which Dave remembered more prosaically as a coal basin, crossed the river and ground to a halt in Clapham Junction's southernmost platform. Dave went to telephone the signalman. "Tell him your wife's having a baby," urged Geoff. Bemused commuters regarded us quizzically, as if they had suddenly noticed a monster in their midst. Geoff and Bob leered back at the prettier ones. "All railwaymen are lecherous," explained Bob, somewhat unnecessarily, "especially in the London area."

With four of us in the cab, it was growing hotter and hotter. The Dollands Moor lads were missing the air-conditioned Class 92 electrics which they work, both through the tunnel to Frethun, Calais, and up as far as Wembley. Dave had returned from the signal smiling. "We're going through in the postal's path!" Bob didn't hang about. The platform starting signal turned green, he gave a joyous blast on the horn, several commuters jumped in the air and we made our way across Wandsworth Common. A weight had transparently lifted from Bob's shoulders. He became distinctly more chatty, talking me through his suburban driving technique: "Set your speed at twenty-five and sit back, there's no point pushing it, no point stressing-out."

I was beginning to enjoy these mazy runs along the veins and arteries of the capital's railway network. Too late in the day, for this was my third and last. My long held, and entirely irrational dislike of London was being replaced by stirrings of affection. It was like being won over by a woman you'd hitherto held in contempt. Seeing for the first time the subtleties of her beauty. I was growing addicted to place names: Balham, Tooting Bec, Streatham Park, Thornton Heath. At Selhurst they tried to make some sense for me of the galaxy of lines - they might just as well of explained the intricacies of the National Grid. And so we came to Croydon. Bob blew the horn again. A woman clapped her hands to her ears. It occurred to me that General Motors may have fitted the Sixty-sixes with a job lot of war surplus klaxons from the American Army, previously earmarked for use as air raid sirens in the event of a nuclear war.

Eurostar and TPO, Tonbridge

Taking the Brighton line, we headed for Stoats Lane Junction and Redhill. Geoff pointed out the old London Brighton & South Coast Railway engine shed at Purley, latterly a welding school, and the egress of the branch to Tattenham Corner - of Epsom Races fame. A line from Betjeman ran tantalisingly through my mind at Coulsdon; something about the 'living rail'. I tracked it down at home to a poem called *Love in a Valley*, the one which begins: "Take me, Lieutenant, to that Surrey homestead!" We went through Merstham Tunnel and out over the M25, putting London and its tentacles behind us. "They might have widened it," said Dave laconically, pointing to the motorway, "but at this time of night it's still just a big car park!"

It was half past five when we took the Tonbridge line out of Redhill, veering east along the foot of the North Downs. I was asking Geoff about his route-learning, and how many trips he would have to make over any given line before he was passed to drive over it solo. "The onus is on me, we're not rushed. I have to feel comfortable before they'll sign me."

There was a Maidstone local in front of us, and Bob was taking his time, letting the gap widen between us, so that we wouldn't be forever catching up with it and being forced to brake as it called at wayside stations. His approach made good sense, avoided wear and tear - to both train *and* driver - and, as a motorist, I could empathise, not being the sort to tailgate tractors on country lanes, preferring to hang back until they had turned off into some field of sugar beet or other, or until a long straight stretch safe for overtaking presented itself. So much for theory! Past Bletchingly Tunnel we were still palpably on its trail. "It's amazing," grimaced Bob. "We've wasted all that time and it's still not clear."

To relieve the tedium I asked Bob and Geoff if they enjoyed driving trains through the Channel Tunnel, what sort of reception they got on the other side, and what they thought of the SNCF. Geoff was enthusiastic: "Their railways are like ours were thirty years ago. Everyone is so friendly. You get down off the engine and they come up and shake hands with you. Sometimes we're over there for a few hours at a time, so we clubbed together and bought a push-bike to take us into Calais." It all sounded very idyllic, and having just returned from a wonderful French holiday, I felt a pang of envy that these guys could make the trip so regularly, even if it was 'all part of the job'.

It was pretty much downhill all the way to Tonbridge, and soon the local was far enough ahead for us to freewheel from one green aspect to the next. Bob showed me where we crossed the East Grinstead and Uckfield lines, but for the most part views beyond the lineside were obscured by trees which would have been frowned upon in the days of steam. There was a bit of a kerfuffle at Tonbridge. A red signal brought us to a halt beyond the station, though we could see that the following signal was green. To add to the mystery the down Dover mail was in the adjoining Post Office Terminal, topped and tailed by two Class

> "It was pretty much downhill all the way to Tonbridge, and soon the local was far enough ahead for us to freewheel from one green aspect to the next."

73s - prerequisites on this service on account of their noiselessness - which we could only assume would be let out on to the main line in front of us. Matters took a bizarre turn when a loaded Connex passenger unit drew up inside us on the slow line. Dave was sent to try and charm the signalman again, Bob and Geoff firmly believing by now that he held some sort of sway over Railtrack. "Take my orange vest," offered Bob.

"You'd better have mine," Geoff interrupted. "His'll look like a bell tent on you."

A few minutes elapsed, none of the three trains, marooned for that moment in Tonbridge, moved. Dave returned with a confident look on his face. "It's our road."

Bob shook his head. "Five minutes that's cost us - for nothing!"

Geoff drew our attention to the Connex driver. "I don't think that 'juicer drive's' well pleased."

From Redhill to Ashford the railway runs like a well struck cover drive across the orchards of Kent. "The Luftwaffe used to follow this line to Tonbridge then turn right for London," said Geoff. We passed plum orchards, oast houses and hopyards. Geoff watched me scribbling. "Do you have to write about all this stuff too?" he asked.

"Yeah! This is where I get seriously lyrical," I laughed.

"Well you can tell them that this is *Darling Buds of May* country," he added.

"Perrfick!" I replied.

At Headcorn we saw where Colonel Stephens's archaic Kent & East Sussex trains once went puffing off on their vagrant, time-consuming journeys to Tenterden and Robertsbridge. I was reminded of an old neighbour in Burton-on-Trent who was in the habit of coming down to Headcorn to buy hops for Bass. A Eurostar zoomed past us on its way to Waterloo. It was sevenish, the sun was coming in to land directly behind us, flinging a foreshortened shadow in front of 66108's cab. As we threaded our way through Ashford International, Bob and Geoff were delighted to see that a Eurostar had been held back for us to pass before being allowed to cross into the platform. I was shown Willesborough Crossing, the only one between Paris and Waterloo,

Dave Rogers, Longbridge

then, as were neared the end of our journey, we saw plenty of evidence of the Channel Tunnel Rail Link taking shape.

Geoff had a personal interest in the scheme. The six-hundred-years old, tile-hung Tudor farmhouse he had until recently rented was being carefully demolished and taken to a new location. Though railwaymen, both Bob and Geoff were concerned at the amount of land being gobbled up by Phase 1 of the £5 billion pound plus scheme. "It's cut a swathe across the countryside like the bison in *Silence of the Lambs*," Bob told me. I hadn't seen the film but I got the gist of what he was saying. Geoff just kept shaking his head and saying. "All these lovely houses," over and over again. Personally, I wondered what the ramifications for freight would be, and if the longer, faster, heavier trains which EWS Managing Director, Ian Braybrook, is campaigning for would be given sufficient paths on the new line.

Dollands Moor is the antithesis of Bordesley. No weeds here. Hi-tech and hygienic, the sidings fan out in neat rows behind high security fencing. Not so much a different world as a different planet. The shunting crews were already waiting for us, accompanied by a security guard.

Geoff went to sign off, Bob drove our Sixty-six away to be stabled. A Class 92 called *George Eliot* pulled silently out of a siding to hook up to our train. One of a pool owned jointly by EWS, EPS and SNCF, it would take the cars through the tunnel as far as Frethun where a French locomotive would take over for the next part of the journey. Had it not been late in the day, had I not have being travelling for over thirteen hours already, I might have enjoyed going through the tunnel with the train. But I was due to stay with Angela in Clapham and Dave was going to journey back with me from Ashford on a passenger train as far as Orpington. We went into the office to book a taxi. It was more like a hospital than a railway depot. If this was a glimpse of the future of rail freight, then we are definitely heading in the right direction. Why, even the taxi driver confessed that he'd like to be an engine driver!

jarrow or bust!

"**Y**OUR last trip, then," said Keith. "Mixed emotions?"

"You've got to be joking, I'm gutted," I replied. Seven months since my nervous start in Middlesbrough, I'd become so used to early starts, long days, and great feats of bladder control, that I didn't know how I was going to cope at the end of my last goods train ride. There was, however, a certain symmetry about its nature and its destination. I'd begun with a service from the Petrochemical portfolio, and here I was ending with one. I'd started my travels in the North-east, and I would be finishing them there - in Jarrow in fact, on the banks of the Tyne, with a train of petroleum from Immingham in Lincolnshire.

"Will you be able to find your way to the depot?" Paul Copperwheat had asked over the phone.

"Paul," I said, with as much irony as I could muster: "After what I've been through, I could take you straight to Lord Lucan."

Dawn had been dull, but it was brightening up. Paul, a Traincrew Standards Inspector based at Immingham, introduced me to the duty Trainsmaster, John Sleight. I made some fatuous comment about a Trainsmaster needing all the sleight-of-hand he could muster, but John was equal to it. "My Dad *is* a magician. He's nearly eighty now, and still does shows in old people's homes, but he was on the club circuit when he was younger."

"And has he passed any of his tricks on to you?" I asked.

"Well, there are times here when you need to be a magician to keep the trains moving!"

Immingham depot currently employs about a hundred drivers,

Main picture:
Humber Oil Refinery.
Inset: **Stuart Watt,**
Paul Copperwheat
and *Eastern* at
Immingham

the docks keep it busy, despite the remoteness of its setting on low-lying land beside the Humber Estuary. Before the Great Central Railway developed Immingham as a port, in the early years of the 20th century to take pressure off Grimsby, Immingham was a tiny village on a muddy creek - the last exciting event had been the embarkation of the Pilgrim Fathers in 1608. King George V and Queen Mary came to the opening on 22nd July 1912, touring the vast new deepwater dock in the railway company's own paddle steamer *Killingholme*. A network of lines spread out into the hinterland, none more bizarre than the Grimsby & Immingham Electric Railway, a passenger carrying tramway which coped manfully with generations of dockworkers and factory hands until its lamentable demise in 1961. Its single deck vehicles had more in common with American street cars than the average sturdy British tram, though none of them was ever called *Desire*. Immingham Dock also enjoyed a service of conventional passenger trains, linking it with New Holland until 1963 and Ulceby until 1969. Nowadays the emphasis is solely on freight, there no longer being even a passenger ferry service to Scandinavia, though I once, miserably, sailed from here to a printer's seminar in Sweden.

I spoke to Mike Hogg, EWS Regional Operations Manager for Humberside and Yorkshire, about the current traffic flows into and out of Immingham. He painted a vivid picture of a thriving port where rail holds the whip hand in a number of commodities. Vast tonnages of imported iron ore and coal run to British Steel's Scunthorpe plant. EWS and Railtrack are discussing the practicalities of operating a fleet of massive 200 tonne box wagons to carry the ore; a project nicknamed 'Elephant' for obvious reasons. Immingham has close links with Sheffield's stainless steel heartland too. Molten slabs cast by Avesta in Sheffield are exported to Sweden for conversion into hot rolled coil then returned to Sheffield for finishing. "Three-quarters of a million tonnes per annum," enthused Mike. There are other metals traffics as well, from Polish and Russian zinc, imported through the docks and railed to Bloxwich in the Black Country, to occasional loads of Workington-made rails exported to various parts of the world, most recently and spectacularly to India.

British mined coal was once one of Immingham's largest

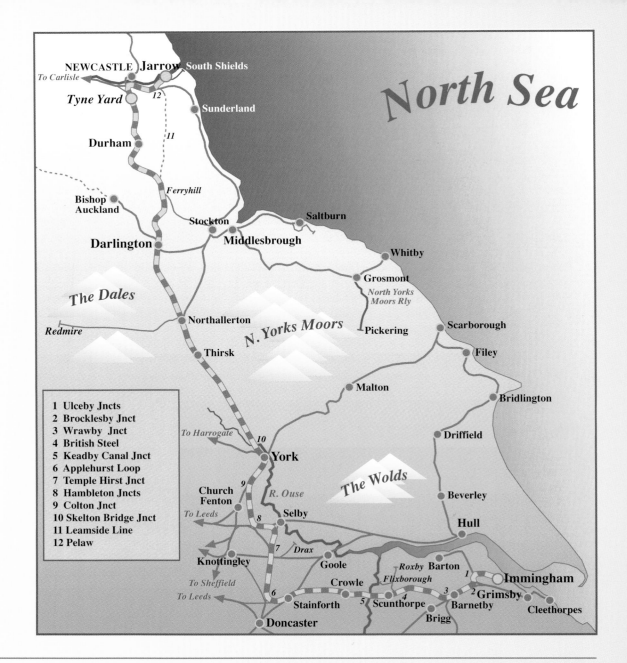

1 Ulceby Jncts
2 Brocklesby Jnct
3 Wrawby Jnct
4 British Steel
5 Keadby Canal Jnct
6 Applehurst Loop
7 Temple Hirst Jnct
8 Hambleton Jncts
9 Colton Jnct
10 Skelton Bridge Jnct
11 Leamside Line
12 Pelaw

exports, now the flow is entirely in the opposite direction, for steel-making, power generation and industrial use. CPL, a company based at Immingham, receive a daily train load of anthracite from South Wales which it converts into briquettes. Other significant commodities coming in through the docks include newsprint, which goes out to both Wapping and Glasgow and fertilizer. In the case of the latter, activity is centred on the Hydro Agri plant which imports compound fertilizers from Scandinavia. Following various stages of manufacture bagged fertilizer is currently transported by rail to eight destinations nationwide.

But it is on intermodal traffic that future growth will rely. Mike was upbeat. "I've eighty-four containers on the dock today, waiting to go out by Enterprise to South Wales, Widnes, Doncaster and Teeside of all places. We struggled with a lack of suitable wagons to start with, but it's developing nicely. Soon we'll need full train loads operating to key locations."

Echoing Henry Ford's immortal words, I'd previously told Paul that I didn't mind what sort of locomotive we had as long as it was *red!* I don't know how much influence we had, but sure enough, as we wandered over towards the depot to find 'Number 48', we came upon 60048 *Eastern* gleaming in EWS house colours in the brightening sunlight. Two or three hours were to pass before we began to regret this choice; whilst, incidentally, its name is derived from one of English Welsh & Scottish's power generating customers rather than any geographical reference. The Immingham-Jarrow run usually commands a Class 60, but, because we were hauling a shorter train than normal on this occasion, we hadn't been certain until the last moment what form the motive power would take.

Driver Stuart Watt was rostered to take us on the first leg of the journey as far as Barnetby, where another Immingham man would be taking over, for reasons I will explain later. Stuart had only been with the company a few months, having transferred from Eurotunnel of all places. "I wanted to test the antiques," he said cheekily, though I suppose being hitherto used to the massively powerful, Brush built Bo-Bo-Bo Shuttle fleet, the usual contents of Immingham depot *must* have had a certain timeless charm. Nevertheless, his training with both companies had been intense. A native of North Lincolnshire, Stuart had been involved in the

construction of the Channel Tunnel, driving heavy plant, yet half-heartedly putting in application forms to become a driver for Eurotunnel. A year and a half later he got 'the call', but still had to go through six months of interviews and tests before he was taken on. A full year's training followed. "Though it's shorter now, back then even the trainers were training." I didn't pry, but guessed that family roots brought Stuart back to Immingham. Again, the best part of a year passed in training with EWS before he passed out as a driver. "But it was training I needed," he frankly admitted. "A freight train is harder to drive."

All this had been aired while we worked our way, light engine, between the depot and the refinery. Immingham's railway infrastructure is endearingly antiquated; endearingly, that is, to an amateur like me. Quaint mechanical signal boxes of Great Central provenance abounded. I would have liked more time to familiarise myself with the surroundings, certainly they seemed to present a number of photographic challenges, but we were working to a tight schedule and the Jarrow service had a reputation as a 'good runner' to live up to. EWS featured Immingham in the autumn 1999 edition of its business magazine *Focus*. From it I gleaned that twenty million tonnes of oil enter the port annually, being piped to a pair of refineries which, between them, account for a fifth of the UK's refining capacity. We were bound for Conoco's Humber Oil Refinery. Opened in 1967 it produces a wide range of products: diesel, petrol, kerosene, aviation fuel and various liquid petroleum gases. It stands to the south of the main line. Across the track lies Total and Fina's Lindsey Oil Refinery, another heavy user of rail transport.

A refinery employee welcomed us into the yard. "Hello mate, back on to five please."

"Is the road all set," asked Stuart, and getting an affirmative thumbs up added: "OK - cheers." We were due out at nine on the dot and we were pretty much bang-on time. While the 'tapper' looked over the train we'd watched another Class 60 pull out of Lindsey Refinery with a train of tankers for Leeds. We were train 6N05. Usually it loads to twenty-seven bogie tankers, totalling an impressive 2666 tonnes, but on this occasion there were only sixteen wagons, weighing 1578 tonnes and measuring 969 feet in length. For safety reasons I was denied the opportunity of any

"we came upon 60048 *Eastern* gleaming in EWS house colours in the brightening sunlight. Two or three hours were to pass before we began to regret this choice;"

photography in the refinery. Wagons checked and brake test complete, we moved forward to the head of the loop and Stuart got down to walk to the signal governing exit from the yard. Formalities over, we left at 09.04, being scheduled to arrive, 155 miles later, in Jarrow at 15.27.

Sunlight poetically dappled the wooded cuttings and the engine left echoes reverberating beneath blue brick bridges as we ran through Killingholme to Ulceby. "The line speed here is thirty," Paul explained. At Ulceby we crossed the Barton-on-Humber to Grimsby line and curved in a south-westerly direction to the Dutch-gabled, high-chimneyed station at Brocklesby, given added ornamentation on account of its links with the altruistic Earl of Yarborough, owner of nearby Brocklesby Hall, once one of the most magnificent country seats in England. A train of empty coal hoppers, returning to the docks from Scunthorpe, passed in the opposite direction behind 66036.

Between Brocklesby and Wrawby Junction the Great Central had quadrupled the track in the days when traffic to and from Grimsby and Immingham was at its zenith. British Rail, predictably, ripped out the slow lines in the Eighties, but was soon forced to re-lay the down, eastbound slow because just two tracks were creating a bottleneck, particularly after British Steel began to rely more and more on imported raw materials and fuel.

Stuart's short journey was about to end. The next leg of his diagram necessitated catching a passenger train to Leicester from where he would return with the empty Langley-Lindsey petroleum tankers. Braking for Barnetby, he showed me some old maltings which had enjoyed a moment of local notoriety when thieves hired unsuspecting villagers to strip the roof of its valuable lead in broad daylight. Stuart's replacement - waiting on Barnetby platform amongst a gaggle of trainspotters - was Dave Doherty, Mayor designate of Immingham.

Barnetby is the archetypal country junction, existing more out of railway necessity than public need. I've always liked to think - albeit without a shred of evidence - that J.B.Priestley had Barnetby in mind when he created 'Dullingham Junction' as a meeting place for Inigo Jollifant and Morton Mitcham, the banjo player, in *The Good Companions*. Inigo had fled from life as a prep school master in the Fens and been given a lift through the night by a lorry driver as far as Dullingham. Asking where Dullingham Junction's trains ran to, he received the reply: "Up Lincoln and Grimsby way or Doncaster way." Not that it matters one iota, not that it has any bearing on this journey, simply that I have a sad tendency to scour literature for railway references, admiring Aldous Huxley's *Crome Yellow* and C.S.Lewis's *That Hideous Strength* and James Hilton's *Random Harvest* as much for the branchline journeys described within as any amount of literary merit.

There was none of your mayoral pomposity about Dave, no chain of office around his neck; metaphorical or otherwise. He was having to come to terms with public speaking. "I did my first speech last week. I was quaking, and kept having to look at my notes, but I think it went OK." He had come over from Immingham by taxi, the reason for his delayed start being that, if he had started with the engine and gone to the refinery, he would have amassed more than twelve hours on duty by the time he got back from Newcastle-on-Tyne with the empties that evening. In fact, Dave was booked to work our train as far as Tyne Yard, on the southern outskirts of Newcastle, from where a local man would drive it on to Jarrow. Paul and I planned to complete the whole journey, then return by passenger train. It was a toss up who'd get back to Immingham first, Dave or us.

Beneath splendid gantries of semaphore signals - on one of which a lampman was busily either oiling up, or trying to summon his genie - we came to Wrawby Junction, taking the northernmost of the three lines towards Scunthorpe. The middle line goes via Brigg and Kirton Lindsey to Gainsborough. Once considered the 'main' line, now it infamously supports a skeleton service of passenger trains which only run on Saturdays. Early each Saturday morning an EWS engine is despatched from Immingham to 'prove' the route, as Paul put it, checking that the line is safe before the first passenger train of the day is allowed to run. The southernmost line heads for Lincoln and Newark, the route used by the Lindsey-Langley (Slough) petroleum trains which carry aviation fuel to Heathrow.

The route we took - known to generations of railwaymen as 't' Yorkshire' - climbed steeply away to the north-west and up onto Wrawby Moor, passing beneath the A18 and the M180 in

"Beneath splendid gantries of semaphore signals - on one of which a lampman was busily either oiling up, or trying to summon his genie ..."

**North Lincolnshire - *Top left:* Iron ore empties thread their way through Barnetby. *Top right:* Petroleum empties at Ulceby.
Lower left: Semaphore signals at Wrawby. *Centre lower:* Melton Ross. *Lower right:* Appleby's signalman, Russell Bean.**

the process. The line speed limit here is fifty-five. We ran through deeply-drained fields of corn and sugar beet to Worlaby Crossing, scene, my companions were keen to tell me, of regular nude cavortings by a couple, apparently bereft of sexual inhibitions, but otherwise repressed enough to drive a Reliant Robin. There was a moment of excitement when we spotted a three-wheeler parked beside the River Ancholme, but it was apparently the property of an angler; a race seldom given to exhibitionism in any form.

Another train of coal empties came past us, emphasising the sheer volume of black stuff consumed by British Steel at its Scunthorpe plant. We ran over Appleby Crossing which carries a Roman Road called Ermine Street across the line. The crossing is presided over by a fine old signal box with 'proper' wheel-operated gates, something of a rarity in these automated days. I went back a week or two later for photographs, meeting its affable, bird-watching signalman, Russell Bean, and discovering that the wheel sits in a solid cast iron frame of LNER origin dated 1942. Mr Bean was modestly disposed towards it: "You should see the one at Ulceby, it's much bigger!" In years gone by there had been a station by Appleby crossing whose nameboards carried the suffix 'Lincs', presumably in case any passengers had become so wildly disorientated as to think they were alighting at Appleby in *Westmorland*.

On full power we breasted Appleby bank at thirty-three miles an hour, somewhat over par for the course. At Santon we saw the line which goes into British Steel's iron ore terminal. Dave told us that there had been a signal box here, and that his brother had been the last incumbent before it was demolished. Half a mile or so further on, on the opposite side of the line, we passed the coal terminal, its sidings accessed inconveniently from the west because that's where all the coal traditionally came from. Suddenly I was in familiar territory, having - you'll remember - travelled as far as Scunthorpe with a train of Manchester rubbish earlier in this book. Paul was due to go to Roxby Gullet himself with a Health & Safety Inspector, and was wondering what the official would make of the track. We passed the mouldering shell of a motive power depot at Frodingham. Both Dave and Paul had worked there in the Seventies. "It must have been a very different place

Keadby Canal Crossing

then," I ventured.

"We had a hundred and twenty drivers here in those days," Paul replied, and for the next few miles we weren't so much travelling through Scunthorpe as down Memory Lane. They talked about 'The Drummer' - a pick-up goods train which idled from country goodsyard to country goodyard; Cuckoo sidings; the Gunness Banker; iron ore trains from High Dyke near Grantham in the days before it was all imported; and the bringing in of Yorkshire coal to Keadby power station. Oddly enough, neither Paul nor Dave had joined the railway straight from school. Dave, in fact, who'd grown up in South Yorkshire after being adopted, had gone 'down the pit', at Manvers Main near Wath-on-Dearne.

Nowadays Keadby power station is gas fired. We saw it as we crossed the Trent and curved round to Keadby Canal Crossing. Although I was covering familiar ground, there was no sense of anti-climax. Paul was busy telling me about the organisation of a 'Q Train' he was involved in. The natives can be restless on

Scunthorpe's periphery - fulfilment comes from hurling masonry at passing railwaymen. The plan is to run a light locomotive up and down the line with a couple of burly policemen hidden aboard - mobile hooligan bait. In radio contact with a back-up car, they have every hope of a sizeable catch.

The fishermen strung out along the reed-fringed banks of the Stainforth & Keadby Canal had hopes of a sizeable catch as well. They looked a happy bunch. Say what you like about anglers, they know how to have a good time. Goodknow Bridge signal box had been rebuilt since my visit six months earlier. Not, as you might imagine in these godless days, replaced by a portacabin, but an authentic parody, all brick and bargeboards. Full marks Railtrack! At Medge Hall the Doncaster-Immingham Enterprise passed us with no less than four locomotives (2 x 56, 2 x 37) 'up front.' Not that, Dave reckoned, they'd all be under power. "Three of them are probably being worked back from weekend infrastructure duties," was his educated guess.

As we curved past Thorne to join the Goole line, Paul slid back the one side window which was working to check that the train was alright: no telltale wisps of smoke denoting a hot axle for example. Subconsciously, perhaps, he was showing the first signs of a gnawing unease. As we took the Skellow line at Stainforth Junction he said to Dave. "She's not exactly strong, this one. It's a good job we're not going to Leeds," going on to explain, for my benefit, that the Lindsey-Leeds petroleum trains face a particularly stiff climb on the outskirts of the city. I remembered how Roger and Ivor, on the steel run from Port Talbot, had told me that no two diesels were alike. Yet most railway enthusiasts would tell you that only steam engines display individual character. Paul warmed to his theme. "Everything's variable: the rolling stock, the track, wheels, brakes, weather."

At ten thirty we were traversing the Applehurst Loop, about to join the East Coast Main Line at Joan Croft Junction. A girl on a horse waited at the first of numerous level crossings over the next few miles, all of them innocent of automatic barriers, and operated instead by mechanical means from signal cabins or simple ground frames. At Barcroft Crossing I caught a glimpse of its keeper enveloped in an armchair with a book on his lap. Moss Crossing was operated by a more substantial cabin, beyond

it a road ran in solitary confinement into an infinity of flat farmland. A Class 66 hauled coal train thrummed throatily southbound past us, but Paul was more concerned with our own lacklustre performance. "We're only getting a thousand amps with sixteen on, we're not doing well at all," he thought aloud.

"They're all like this - it's the heat," suggested Dave. Another coal train came by and a pretty girl waved from her garden at Fenwick Crossing.

Girls and coal trains - what more can one ask of life? What Paul and Dave wanted was a healthier locomotive. Paul called John Spreckley, Immingham's maintenance maestro, on his mobile to see if anyone had spotted anything unusual about 60048 when it had been looked over the previous night. Dave and I listened intently, trying to interpret the other, inaudible half of the ensuing conversation. I imagined Dave was glad of our presence. It must be unnerving to cope with a recalcitrant locomotive on one's own. Picture being on a motorway with a malfunctioning car, all manner of uncertainties would crowd your mind. Paul completed his call. "John thinks it may be the hot weather. Atmospheric conditions can affect the governor, which is a bit like a carburettor in a car," he added, seeing the mystified look on my face. "John says they were all like it yesterday. I'm going back to check the internal doors."

We limped along a bit further, over the Aire & Calder Navigation and under the M62. A GNER express rocketed by, confirming our vulnerability on the East Coast artery. If we carried on at this rate we'd be causing a tailback. Paul returned in a rush, looking serious. "There's a leak in the engine room. I can't tell if it's fuel or water. I'm going to call Railtrack and get them to put us in at Temple Hirst." My last trip, my first 'failure'. For a silly moment I wondered if head office had set this emergency up for my benefit. But that was preposterous. We had a real train in tow, with an important customer's deadline to meet.

Temple Hirst is one of the newest junctions on the railway network. It dates from the opening of a new section of the ECML to by-pass subsidence in the new Selby Coalfield. Paul was proposing that we detour onto the original line, still intact as far as Selby, though reduced to the status of a public footpath and cycleway between there and York. Paul had phoned Railtrack,

> "We limped along a bit further, over the Aire & Calder Navigation and under the M62. A GNER express rocketed by, confirming our vulnerability on the East Coast artery."

Temple Hirst: 170 miles from Kings Cross; Paul and Dave consider their next move!

now he was on to EWS Control at Doncaster CSDC. "It's Paul Copperwheat here on 6N05. We've got a problem with the loco. We've asked Railtrack to be diverted off at Temple Hirst to clear the East Coast Main Line. I think the loco will shut itself down soon, or if it's a fuel leak we'll have to shut ourselves down. Whatever, I'm going to stop when we get clear of the main line and we'll look at it."

Temple Hirst is a quiet hamlet on the flood plain of the extravagantly meandering River Aire, but this was no time for me to dwell on its scenic qualities. We lumbered across a facing crossover and lurched on to the Selby line. Paul had gone to the cab door to look if he could see any better. "Something's spraying out of the engine room," he yelled. "I suspect it's fuel. Dave, stop at the first signal and I'll go and look."

Dave brought the train to a steady halt at signal S873 - S being for Selby. Paul leapt out and went along the locomotive. Dave went to talk to the signalman from the phone on the signal post. I hung nervously about the doorway, anxious not to interfere. "It's definitely a fuel leak," Paul called back to me. Then, raising his voice so that Dave could hear said. "Shut her down, Dave, shut her down!"

It was ten fifty, just twenty minutes since we'd joined the main line at Joan Croft Junction. As with all emergencies, it seemed as though time had stood still. I didn't know how far my experienced colleagues had allowed their thoughts to go. Paul had spoken calmly of potential fire hazards. Most diesel locomotive fires - and they are thankfully few - are caused by electrical faults, not fuel. Diesel doesn't ignite easily. But a fire on board a locomotive hauling a train of petroleum tankers has potential for catastrophic results. If Paul or Dave harboured such worries, however, they were keeping them to themselves, being calmness personified. Dave shut off the batteries and applied handbrakes to three of the tanker wagons while Paul got on to Doncaster again. "Hello its Paul Copperwheat again. Yes, we've made a snap decision to clear the main line. We're at signal S873 on the Selby line, can you get us a replacement loco?"

Control rang off to see what they could do. There was nothing for us to do but wait. We found what shade we could beside milepost 170 from London. A tractor was collecting bales from the neighbouring cornfield, a glider hung on friendly thermals overhead. We were surrounded by power stations: Eggborough and Ferrybridge on our left, Drax to our right. A procession of trains passed on the main line - at least we were spared the ignominy of blocking it. The mobile rang. Paul listened to what they had to say before turning to Dave. "Do you know Knottingley, are you passed for that route?" Dave shook his head. "It's not on our link." Knottingley is an important EWS depot close to Pontefract. It lay only half a dozen miles away as the crow flies, but if they had a spare locomotive it would have to come round in a wide northern arc via Milford and Selby. Nevertheless, it represented our best option. Trouble was, Knottingley didn't have a spare driver, and with Dave not being passed for that route, this particular solution to our problem lay tantalisingly out of reach.

Control went to have a rethink. We sat down on the ballast and watched some black and yellow, caterpillar-like insects going about their daily routine. "Are they glow-worms?" I asked.

"Couldn't tell you," said Paul, perhaps thinking that I was beginning to crack. "Don't rightly know," Dave chimed in.

After a pause I said. "We'll be able to tell when it gets dark."

Partly out of curiosity, partly to kill time, we went to inspect the engine room. The floor was wet with diesel. Paul took a torch to the machinery, examining each of the Mirrlees' eight cylinders individually. "It looks to me as if it's coming out of here, can you see?" he said, and Dave and I took turns to peer intently down the ray of light illuminating the glistening cylinder head, patently wet with spilt fuel. "Wouldn't Dave have got some sort of early warning on the control panel," I asked.

"Not necessarily," Paul replied. "The computer would have been clever enough to think that we were still getting power. But it would certainly have shut the engine down if things had gone on like that much longer."

It was too hot to linger in the engine room. Three-quarters of an hour had passed. We were pacing ourselves, mentally. "What'll be happening now," said Paul - partly by way of explanation, partly to keep up morale - "is they'll being using their computer to try and match a spare engine to a spare man. Trouble is, we don't have many spares of either. All our 'spare' engines are ready for scrap, and if there is a spare man at any of the nearby depots, the chances are he'll already be filling in on another job."

"How long can these delays take, Paul?" I asked, diffidently.

"A couple of hours, perhaps, sometimes longer," he answered. "The worst I've known is four or five hours." There wasn't much I could add to that.

The mobile went again. It was John Sleight this time. I called to Paul: "Ask him to get his Dad to *magic* us an engine." Paul treated this fatuous remark with the contempt it deserved and finished the call. "Change of plan," he announced: "They're sending a fitter out instead."

Two fitters actually. They arrived quarter of an hour later, having driven over from Knottingley, walking up the track with the gait of workmen everywhere. You know what I mean; weighed down by destiny. We were having our lunch, eking out meagre rations in case it was a long day. The men from Knottingley were Tim Cope and Phil Bullock and they didn't waste any time. They isolated the fuel pump to the offending cylinder. We wouldn't be able to operate on full power, but we'd get a lot more out of No. 48 than we'd got so far. Paul, Dave and I held a confab at track

level while the fitters went about their work. Paul thought aloud: "Can we get back on the main line at Hambleton, or have we got to go round by Sherburn?" Dave was pretty sure there was a linking loop to the East Coast Main Line at Hambleton and my ostensibly up-to-date Ordnance Survey map, not always trustworthy where railways are concerned, suggested, nevertheless, that he was right. Paul called John and asked him to pass a message on to Control: "Tell them 'N05's on the move again at 12.23."

So we had lost about an hour and three-quarters. It could easily have been worse. The worry now was that we'd missed our path. But basically we were just glad to be on the move again. Selby Abbey loomed ahead. We passed what looked like a World War II aerodrome, saw the earthworks and abandoned bridge abutments of the old Selby-Goole line - opened as recently as 1910 to cope with the sheer volume of goods traffic between Leeds and Hull - and crossed the Selby Canal, making its sluggish, duckweed-covered way between the Ouse and the Aire. In my barging days I had voyaged up-river from Hull to York on a vessel called *Selby Elizabeth* loaded with shea nuts from Africa for Rowntree's chocolate factory. Coastal shipping still trades to the animal feeds mills at Selby I believe, but barge traffic has all but vanished from the Ouse; even newsprint, traditionally carried to the *Yorkshire Evening Press* by water, has defected to road haulage. Throughout the Eighties, transport by inland waterway evaporated even more rapidly than that by rail. From time to time politicians utter sound bites concerning the transfer of freight to the waterways, but too little infrastructure remains extant, and insufficient suitable craft available for such a renaissance to be feasible. I recently hitched a ride with one of the few barge owners still operating in the North-east. He was weighed down by the bureaucratic tape involved in funding a new loading installation on the South Yorkshire Canal for an otherwise feasible traffic flow. English Welsh & Scottish have been there, done that, got the hackneyed T-shirt.

We took the Canal Goods curve to Selby West Junction, skimming the town in the process. Dave had to lean well over to locate the signals through an encroaching corridor of silver birch. The bogie tanker wheels squealed in protest at the tight radius. Conditions in the cab had begun to resemble a sauna - though, so far, we'd kept our clothes on. Thunder flies crawled across our flesh. "They're like greenhouses these Sixties," muttered Dave. Being a keen gardener, he should know. Earlier he'd admitted: "I pinch ideas from lineside gardens." We ran along the boundary of Selby Cricket Club where, I have it on good authority, a distant relative of mine once equalled Gary Sobers' exploits by whacking half a dozen sixes in an over.

Paul was checking the timing sheet. "We should be in Darlington by now!" We were surrounded by fields of sugar beet, approaching Hambleton East Junction. In the distance we could see Gascoigne Wood Colliery, the only mine that ever opened in what, in the Eighties, was going to be Selby's big new all-singing, all-dancing coalfield. We got lucky, amazingly being signalled straight onto the East Coast Main Line without delay.

You wouldn't need to be an expert to tell that this is a relatively new stretch of railway. There's an indefinable feel about its relationship with the landscape quite different from its nineteenth century brethren. An absence of level crossings, for example. All the way from Doncaster the original route is littered with them, and Railtrack probably regards them with the same distaste most of us display towards litter. At best, when automated, they hold up road traffic - though that seems an acceptable tactic to me. At worst, mechanically controlled, they need shifts of operators and the retention of signal boxes which pure technology could have eliminated years ago.

60048 was producing an acceptable 2000 amps now. Though not exactly eating up the miles, we were politely nibbling at them. Dave and Paul were discussing strong rumours that Immingham's sphere of operation would soon be extended and that lodging turns would be introduced. Dave had no problem with this, recognising that flexibility is vital if freight is to be won from the roads. A low but lengthy concrete bridge carried us over the River Wharfe and Ozendyke Ings. I was suddenly reminded of a journey along this line with my son, Eden, when he was five or six. We'd been passing yellow fields of oil seed rape when an American in the seat behind us tapped me on the shoulder and asked : "Say mister, what's this yellow crop?" I winked at Eden, turned round, smiled broadly and whispered: "Custard!"

At Colton Junction we met the quadruple track coming in from Leeds and Sheffield. I spent seven elongated years at a boarding school in York and, as I told Paul and Dave, it would be somewhere along this stretch of line that my sinking heart would finally be submerged under saltwater waves of despair on the journey up by train at the start of another interminable term. Correspondingly though, the journey back, holidays stretching beguilingly ahead, was pure exhilaration. Another happy memory of the line concerns surreptitious early morning rides out to Church Fenton for the express purpose of riding back on the Manchester newspaper train; by 1967, the last regularly steam-hauled passenger service into York. It was a

Jarrow-bound, approaching Colton Junction on the East Coast Main Line

Tea time with Dave

journey riddled with uncertainties: could I escape from the dormitory without waking the prefect; would I been seen leaving school; would the outgoing diesel multiple unit be late and leave me stranded? The schedule left only minutes to spare at Church Fenton. One morning the trains arrived simultaneously. I dashed across the island platform. The porter held a door on the newspaper train open for me. "I thought I just saw you come *from* York lad!"

"I did," I grinned sheepishly: "I'm only here for the steamer!"

In all those years I spent at York, much of the time, I confess, in the environs of the station and the engine shed, I never, of course, travelled along the goods loop, which ran cryptically and mysteriously beyond the cognisance of the trainspotters who thronged the massive station's platform ends in those days. Here stood the great carriage works, one-time employer of a good proportion of the city's male population, whilst their wives and sweethearts worked on chocolate production lines. The hiatus in rolling stock orders, brought about by the uncertainties of privatisation, precipitated an end to over a hundred years of carriage building in York. The last man out switched off the lights and the site would presumably, in time, have become a retail park had not Thrall, an American company, with the encouragement of some sizeable orders from the fledgling EWS, stepped in and re-opened the works as a wagon building plant. We could see some of the fruits of that association waiting to carry their first loads in sidings alongside the goods loop. Freshly painted, a line of massive MBA box wagons caught our eye. Multi-purpose, these monsters have a 72 tonne payload and EWS has ordered three hundred of them. Bufferless, they look very American to the eye. In another siding we saw some FAA low loader wagons, characterised by huge brake reservoir cylinders mounted at one end. Thirdly, there was a handful of the kind of hooded coil carriers I'd encountered on my steel train travels in Wales. It was all heartening stuff - like watching tanks roll off a production line in time of war, in the knowledge that they will help you eventually to win. Need I be more specific?

We reached Skelton Junction at 13.18, as opposed to 11.42 on the schedule. The sugar beet factory was at its least noisome. I had lived for years with the vagaries of its aromatic output. A coke train came by, southbound. That's the Redcar-Scunthorpe,"

said Paul. Overlooked by Nether Poppleton church we came to Skelton Bridge Junction and crossed the River Ouse. I'd sculled upstream this far many times. Luckily without a mail train dropping on top of me, as had been the case recently when, according to Paul, a driver had taken the S curve a bit too quickly and sadly lost an arm in the process.

Now we were on the North Eastern Railway's famous 'racetrack' where generations of traction have 'stretched their legs', how appropriate that so many of them should have been named after racehorses. We were racing a Yorkie chocolate bar lorry on the A19 - and winning! - Dave having urged 60048 more or less up to its 60mph limit. "It's years since I've eaten a Yorkie bar," said Dave. I was thinking more deeply about that 'innocent' lorry's function and how it's load might be carried logistically by rail. Later that evening, returning by passenger train, Paul and I discussed the merits of piggyback operation, agreeing with each other that a timetabled sequence of trains, made up of low loader wagons which lorries could be driven straight on and off, should be tried between the main centres of distribution. There is nothing new about such thinking, but to our knowledge, it had never been instigated. If the Government is serious about transferring traffic from road to rail, then such schemes should be implemented, the sooner the better. That Britain's railways suffer from restricted loading gauges is received but flawed wisdom. Piggyback trials have been carried out successfully. The Government should underwrite such services for as long as it takes for them to become popular. Road operators know that the future spells 'gridlock'. Use of the road system is, to all intents and purposes, 'free'. An equally 'free' piggyback service for long and even medium hauls, with 'mess' facilities for accompanying lorry drivers, could, should and *would* work, given an even chance. Or does, I wondered, the Government derive too much revenue from road licences for it to take alternative transport modes seriously?

I was nearing the end of my goods train travels, but rail freight, I firmly believe, is only beginning its. A miserly six or seven per cent of the UK freight market is just not enough. On the Hambledon Hills the White Horse gleamed in the afternoon light. We passed The Sidings restaurant and hotel complex, a rare case of a restaurant actually *relishing* its proximity to a railway.

But then this is not surprising when one learns that it is the brainchild of a former railway manager, and that old railway carriages form an integral part of the eating area. Understandably, a good proportion of The Siding's patronage comes from people with a railway bent.

In the 1920s the London & North Eastern Railway public-spiritedly erected a series of metal signposts at significant points between London King's Cross and Edinburgh Waverley. The halfway point between the two capital cities is at Tollerton, eight miles north of York and here, on each side of the line, these impressive structures remain intact to this day. We might have talked of these, but for the fact that the next signal was at red, probably to let one of Northern Spirit's Middlesbrough-bound services call at Thirsk, which nowadays only has platform faces on the outer, slow lines. We didn't lose much more time. A Class 158 sprinter in Northern Spirit's attractive plum-red and gold livery whizzed past us, and barely had it disappeared from sight before we got a green and recommenced our journey.

A good deal of traditional railway infrastructure remains in place: distinctive cast iron mileposts erected by the North Eastern Railway; concrete platelayer huts and quaint brick signalboxes (disused) from the Thirties; whilst, here and there, a former goods shed still finds use for storage. At Thirsk, trainspotters were picnicking on the old loading bank, knowledgeable enough, I suspect, to be wondering why we were running late. The novelist J.L.Carr's father was a railwayman at Thirsk. The family lived nearby at Carlton Miniott, and Carr's best known book, *A Month in the Country*, is steeped in this North Riding landscape. We were seeing it at its best, the wide fields bare from harvesting, the Dales on one side and the North York Moors on the other, lying like low clouds on the horizon.

Paul had never travelled beyond Northallerton before, leastways not on the footplate. It was seven minutes after two when we reached Longlands Junction where a loop line skews off to go burrowing under the main line on its way to Yarm and Middlesbrough. At the same point, the melancholy earthworks of the line which once ran up from Ripon, Harrogate and Leeds, betray the course of yet another unnecessarily ripped-up railway which could usefully have survived Beeching's flawed ecomomies.

We ran through Northallerton station, and the Wensleydale line, which the army still uses occasionally to move armoury to and from Catterick Camp, trailed off to the west. Sane, albeit ambitious, proposals exist to relink it to the Settle & Carlisle beyond Hawes to take the pressures of tourism off the local roads, but we work at such things so slowly and pedantically in this country that such a sensible project is probably light years away from inception.

"Where are we now?" Paul asked.

"East Cowton I'd say," replied Dave. And, according to my map he was bang on. "We were given two weeks to learn this route last year," he continued. "We had the choice of doing it from Immingham, one out and back trip a day, or lodging and doing two trips a day. I lodged. We used Thirty-ones with a light load. It felt like going abroad! The funny thing is you always seem to pick a route up faster one way than the other."

We knew we were making progress when we crossed the River Tees. The sun, which had been sulking for a while in the wake of a heat haze, shone brightly again, adding lustre to purple cuttings of rosebay willowherb. At Croft Junction we were put in the loop to let an express overtake. Dave kept a nervous eye on the high security lineside fencing. It looked formidable to me, but apparently the local vandals have a method of scaling it, and have been known to uncouple wagons from waiting trains. The express clattered past us, a GNER High Speed Train. We must have been holding it up on the double track section since Northallerton. "I'm surprised he didn't whistle 'arseholes' as he went by," Paul remarked.

And so we came to the cradle of railways, Darlington. My mother is from Tyneside and, throughout my Fifties childhood, there would be long railway journeys, up from Leicestershire, to visit relatives. Sometimes, for reasons difficult at this distance to fathom, we would have to change at Darlington, and I remember being shown *Locomotion* on its pedestal by the south facing bays and being told, in tones of hushed reverence, that 'this was the first steam engine'. Of course, I know better now, and can put that well meant claim of my mother's in historical perspective. Darlington 'Bank Top' remains a magnificent station with a typically massive North Eastern train shed, triple-arched and an extravagant thousand feet long. It was the work of William Bell,

"A good deal of traditional railway infrastructure remains in place: distinctive cast iron mileposts erected by the North Eastern Railway; concrete platelayer huts and quaint brick signalboxes (disused) from the Thirties; whilst, here and there, a former goods shed still finds use for storage."

DARLINGTON - *Upper:* Exterior with passing coal train. *Lower:* Interior of William Bell's magnificent station

successor to William Peachey, whose work I encountered on that first evening of my travels at Middlesbrough. Bell worked for the North Eastern Railway for an astonishing forty-six years and was also responsible for the imposing stations at Hull (Paragon) and Alnwick. Darlington is an early example of the use of an 'island' platform to avoid duplication of passenger facilities. Non-stop trains bypass the station, which stands to the west of the main line. Amazingly, sadly, typically, Darlington is currently without freight facilities. And of too many similarly large British towns can the same be said.

By quarter to three we'd reached Newton Aycliffe. The Low Fell-Plymouth main came past us, topped and tailed by Forty-sevens, pending delivery of the new Spanish-built Class 67 design. At Ferryhill we saw the Stillington line come in from Stockton, the route I had followed with the Hoyer containers on my first trip. Terrace-houses with cobbled alleys descended the hillside. "I wonder if there was a mine here," said Dave. "They look like pit houses." A former miner himself, he should know, and of course he was right. I found it clearly marked on the Ordnance Survey one inch Sheet No. 85, along with a cat's cradle of lines no longer with us, criss-crossing the County Durham coalfield. One route which has survived, albeit in a mothballed state, is the Leamside line; potentially a parallel route to Tyneside, earmarked in Railtrack's 1999 Network Management Statement as a feasible case for upgrading as a high capacity freight alternative to the East Coast Main Line. Significantly, though, a footnote suggests that passenger services might also be introduced - with local authority funding - to serve a new necklace of stations in and around Washington, which all sounds a tad counterproductive.

Croxdale Viaduct carried us across the River Wear. How pretty these North Pennine-born watercourses look on the western side of County Durham, before they reach old age in the post-industrially blighted, former dockland settings of Middlesbrough and Sunderland. You get one of the great railway views of the world from Durham Viaduct. Trying to get a photograph of the viaduct in juxtaposition with the cathedral and castle, I wandered into a nearby hospital and asked if I could borrow their roof. "This is a secure psychiatric establishment sir," blinked the porter,

The Jarrow petroleum train crosses Durham Viaduct

obviously under the impression that I was a potential patient. No one would describe our bird's-eye view of Chester-le-Street as breathtaking, but we could tell it was market day, and it made me remember that my mother always seemed to rouse herself at this point, look across the compartment to me and say: "Chester-le-Street, time to get the cases off the rack."

Subconsciously, we were getting our 'cases off the rack', as the *Angel of the North* came into view, but like footballers, railwaymen have to concentrate even into 'injury time'. "It's worse than I thought it would be," was Paul's reaction to Gormley's sculpture: "It looks like a crashed aeroplane. What a waste of public money!" Diplomatically, I kept mum. Dave checked his watch. He was due out of Tyne Yard at four o'clock with a returning set of empty tankers from the overnight Immingham-Jarrow service. So, apart from the loss of an hour's break, his working day was unaffected by all our adventures. It raised the subject of tiredness, though, and made us wonder why radios were banned from locomotive cabs. Road drivers and motorists have access to them, and in most cases they are looked upon as beneficial aids to concentration. Since the demise of double-manning, a driver's greatest enemy is tiredness, hence, one imagines, the increased occurrence of SPADs - signals passed at danger.

We dropped down into Tyne Yard at 15.25, just over an hour late. Pretty good by any standards, but fate wasn't finished with us yet. We expected to see the relieving driver waiting to leap aboard at the far end of the yard, but there was no one in sight. We drew up to the head of the loop and waited, and waited. If there was life in Tyne Yard as we know it, as a scientific theory it had yet to be proven. I got out to make use of the time by taking photographs and Dave went off to catch his return working which we'd seen waiting for him at the other end of the yard. Paul got on the phone to Control. By the time he'd finished he looked distinctly miffed. "They're replacing the loco. I can't believe it, we've only got a mile or two to go!"

A shunter called Frank emerged from behind a long line of wagons and uncoupled us. Simultaneously a Class 56 appeared from the distant fuelling point and trundled towards the northern end of the yard. Paul was gently fuming. "It just seems like more wasted time." The Fifty-six ran to the throat of the yard then reversed towards us, stopping short of the pointwork leading to our loop. Its driver disembarked and walked along the ballast towards us. "I hear you've had some bother," he laughed, in Geordie tones the page can't replicate. His good humour broke the ice and defused our frustration. Besides, as he explained, Control had decided to change the locomotives now, as opposed to later, because, as there were only sixteen wagons instead of the usual twenty-seven, there was no need for the usual tactic of splitting the train at Tyne and working it in two portions to Jarrow. So John Carlyle, as we learnt he was called, would wait with the locomotive at Jarrow until the train had been discharged, precluding

an early examination of the fault if 60048 had been retained. Paul and I accepted the logic of this arrangement and bowed to Control's better judgement. Perhaps we were just getting tired.

How can I describe that last lap to Jarrow without descending into pathos? It took less than half an hour, but it seemed like five minutes. My goods train travels had boxed the compass. I'd been to Penzance, Inverness, Port Talbot and King's Lynn. I'd carried chemicals and coal and rubbish and rocks. I'd met dozens and dozens of brilliant people making an unsung living. I wanted this book to be their sounding-board. I wanted it to land on the desks of movers and shakers, make them smile a bit, then make them take their freight off the roads.

In the old days, when my mother and I reached Newcastle, we'd bundle out into the South Shields train, a third rail electric which would glide down the south bank of the smoky, soot-encrusted Tyne, pausing at lamplit stations with names like distant planets: Felling, Pelaw, Hebburn, Jarrow. "In the war," my mother told me, "a Canadian, hearing a porter call 'Heb'n, Heb'n', had stuck his head out of the window and shouted back: 'If this is Heaven, I sure as never want to go to Hell.'

John's thick blond head of hair belied his thirty years on the railway. He'd started as a goods guard, then done a spell at Blyth, before moving to Tyne in 1979. A third generation railwayman, his dad had been a guard at Blaydon, his uncle a guard at Tyne and his grandfather a Scammell driver, delivering local consignments by road in the now undreamt of days when ninety per cent of the country's goods made the bulk of its journey by rail. "My son's no interest at all," John added. "So it looks like the railway's going to finish with me."

Approaching Gateshead, class doyen 66001 went by with a southbound coal train. "What do you think of them?" I asked John.

"I'm the wrong man to ask," he winced. "I had my hand trapped in the bodyside door on one of them at Carlisle. It didn't feel like much until I took my glove off and the blood spurted out. I had to go to the infirmary and have five stitches put in. I was off work for weeks." In seven months Class 66 had increased in size from a handful to over a hundred and thirty in use. Waiting on Newcastle station for our passenger train home, Paul and I saw 66136. "That's one reason why EWS shopped abroad," Paul told me. "No British firm could have delivered them so quickly."

Our Fifty-six, No. 127, looked positively antiquated compared with its new Canadian cousins. Nevertheless, it rekindled fond remembrance of my Scottish coal travels. It was pure R&B compared to synthesised soul; simple but deadly. We rocked and rolled past Gateshead Stadium, filled, on this occasion, with wrinklies taking part in the Veteran Games. In place of the electric trains of my boyhood, Newcastle's Metro trams had taken over the service to South Shields, and John told us that they would soon be running to Sunderland as well. Another huge change, it almost goes without

Main picture: 56127 shunts Jarrow oil terminal
Top inset: 'Metroland', Pelaw
Lower inset: John Carlyle and Paul at Tyne Yard

saying, was that a forest of masts and funnels no longer showed above the rooftops of riverside buildings. Tyneside's rail freight has contracted almost as dramatically as its shipping; and no wonder, for the two invariably went arm in arm. I told John how I could remember the National Coal Board's overhead electric line, which carried coal from Westhoe down to the staithes, from where it would be taken by classically proportioned steam ships to power stations on the Thames. It didn't take him long to list current traffics. "There's this, coal from Wardley Opencast Disposal Point, and Nissan cars from Tyne Dock, and that's about it." We came to the inescapable conclusion that we were forty years too late to see Tyneside in its pomp.

At Pelaw the line trifurcates, the southernmost route being the aforementioned Leamside line, the central route heading for Sunderland and Hartlepool, and the route which we were about to take making for South Shields. Although apparently double track to Hebburn, the parallel running lines are bi-directional and unconnected, the one on our right being used by Metro trams. Half a mile beyond Hebburn station

we curved suddenly away to the north, crossed the apparently gridlocked entrance to the Tyne Tunnel, and trundled into the petroleum terminal. It was five o'clock. Tommy Anderson the shunter came to let us in. There are two discharge sidings, each capable of holding eight bogie tankers. Tommy handed John a short wave and proceeded to uncouple the train. John ran round and propelled the wagons into their respective sidings. The sun had gone in but I went up to the end of the yard, away from any danger of making sparks, and took a few photographs. Paul telephoned for a taxi to take us to Newcastle station. I telephoned timetable enquiries. As far as I could make out we'd have an hour's wait for a connection at Doncaster.

"Paul," I said, "you can't drink on duty can you?"

"No Michael I can't."

"I was just thinking, when we get back to Doncaster we could have a pint to celebrate."

"Nice idea, but no."

"Tell you what, I'll have a pint and you watch me!"